MYSORE AND COORG

FROM THE INSCRIPTIONS

D1830511

MYSORE AND COORG

FROM THE INSCRIPTIONS

BY

B. LEWIS RICE, C.I.E.

GYAN

Published by

Gyan Publishing House
5, Ansari Road
Daryaganj, New Delhi-110002
Phone: 011-47034999, 9811692060
E-mail: books@gyanbooks.com

Distribution Network
gyanbooks.com
India, USA, Canada, UK, Australia

© Publisher

All rights reserved. No part of this work may be reproduced, stored, adapted, or transmitted in any form or by any means, electronic, mechanical, photocopying, micro-filming, recording or otherwise, or translated in any language, without the prior written permission of the copyright owner and the publisher.

ISBN: 978-81-212-5969-9 (PB)
First Published, 1909

2nd Impression 2024

Printed at: Gyan Press, Delhi.

The book is sold subject to the condition that it shall not, by way of trade or otherwise, be lent, resold, hired out, or otherwise circulated without the prior publisher's written consent.

MYSORE AND COORG FROM THE INSCRIPTIONS
Author: B. LEWIS RICE

MYSORE AND COORG

FROM THE INSCRIPTIONS

MYSORE AND COORG

FROM THE INSCRIPTIONS

Published for Government

BY

B. LEWIS RICE, C.I.E.

M.R.A.S., M.R.S.A.

LATE DIRECTOR OF ARCHÆOLOGICAL RESEARCHES

FORMER DIRECTOR OF PUBLIC INSTRUCTION IN MYSORE AND COORG

EDITOR OF THE GAZETTEERS OF MYSORE AND COORG FOR THE

NEW IMPERIAL GAZETTEER OF INDIA

LONDON

ARCHIBALD CONSTABLE & CO. LTD

1909

The Inscriptions of Mysore and Coorg have been published in the *Epigraphia Carnatica* as follows :—

VOL.			CONTAINING	PUBLISHED
I.	Coorg Inscriptions .	.	23	1886
II.	Inscriptions at Sravaṇa-Beḷgoḷa .	.	144	1889
III.	Inscriptions in the Mysore District.	Part I.	803	1894
IV.	Inscriptions in the Mysore District.	Part II.	964	1898
V.	Inscriptions in the Hassan District .	.	941	1902
VI.	Inscriptions in the Kadūr District .	.	626	1901
VII.	Inscriptions in the Shimoga District.	Part I.	658	1902
VIII.	Inscriptions in the Shimoga District.	Part II.	938	1902
IX.	Inscriptions in the Bangalore District [1]	.	1069	1905
X.	Inscriptions in the Kolar District	.	1347	1905
XI.	Inscriptions in the Chitaldroog District	.	623	1902
XII.	Inscriptions in the Tumkūr District [2]	.	733	1904

Containing numerous Facsimiles, and the Original Text of all the Inscriptions, in the Vernacular Characters, with Transliteration into Roman Characters, and English Translations.

An Index volume to the whole is in preparation.

Published by the Mysore Archæological Department, and printed at the Mysore Government Press, Bangalore, except Volumes V and X, printed at the Basel Mission Press, Mangalore.

On sale by the Curator, Mysore Government Central Book Depôt, Bangalore.

[1] Including 46 belonging to Coorg.
[2] Including 2 belonging to Coorg.

PREFACE

THE present volume is the outcome of researches extending over a number of years. All who have had to do with Mysore and Coorg know the attraction of their grand and varied natural features, their agreeable climate, and their interesting racial characteristics. Indeed, a Kannaḍa poet describes the Hoysala country, that is Mysore, especially the west, as a hand-mīrror (or reflection) of Kashmir. Regions so inviting could never have been entirely secluded from the general current of public affairs, but stirring events of recent times had brought them more prominently to notice. Curiosity was thus awakened as to their past. For though their chronicles could perhaps be fairly retraced for about five centuries, earlier periods were more or less a blank. To supply this want it was recognised that an examination was imperative of the inscriptions to be met with in all parts, which furnish almost the only contemporary records for the various periods to which they relate.

These inscriptions are mostly on either stone or metal. Their primary object is, in general, to record the erection of temples or other public structures, the endowment of gods or Brāhmans with lands and gifts, or to commemorate acts of heroism or self-sacrifice. But occasion is taken to give at the same time details as to the ruling powers of the day, their ancestry and past achievements, and other information invaluable for historical purposes. Those on stone are engraved on natural rocks, on prepared pillars or slabs set up at the spots dedicated, and on the walls of temples and the gateways of forts and other buildings. Those on metal are generally on copper plates of a convenient size, strung together on a metal ring, which is secured with an impression in metal of the royal seal. Being portable, these can be secreted, and thus have often survived when inscriptions on stone have been destroyed.

To arrive at a just conception of the past annals of the countries, therefore, no better or indeed other way existed than to collect copies of all the inscriptions wherever they could be discovered, and to combine their historical contents into a consecutive narrative. Such has been the task accomplished in the volumes of the *Epigraphia Carnatica* (see list above, p. v), of which the present volume forms a compendium—a convenience for consultation.

As regards previous efforts in this direction, it is related that the Mysore king, Chikka-Dēva-Rājā, who ruled from 1672 to 1704, had lists and copies made of the inscriptions throughout his country, but this was for the purpose of checking the endowments. The register so compiled was unfortunately one of those in the royal library which, during the usurpation of the throne in the latter part of the eighteenth century, was ordered by Tipu Sultān to be taken for boiling the gram or *kulti* for the horses. On the restoration of the Hindū Rāj in 1799, during the Survey operations conducted at the beginning of the nineteenth century by Colonel Colin Mackenzie, copies were taken of inscriptions to the number of several thousands. But neither would the former of these collections, had it survived, nor the latter, the examination of which would be but labour lost on account of its unreliable character, satisfy the critical demands of the present day. Numberless errors have been unwittingly propagated in past times by copies that were not trustworthy of inscriptions and other records.

The means of obtaining mechanical facsimiles, and the use of the photographic lens, together with a juster appreciation of the absolute necessity of exact and veracious counterparts, have raised the processes of epigraphy to those of a fine art. Scholars seated in their own libraries are thus now placed in possession of the texts in a form that cannot be surpassed for exactitude, and even easier to study than the originals.

It was in 1865, when Mr. L. Bowring, C.S.I., was Chief Commissioner of Mysore and Coorg, that the services of Major Dixon, an officer skilled in the new art of photography, were engaged to obtain copies by that process of inscriptions in various places easily accessible, where they were known to be numerous, such as Chitaldroog, Harihar, Belgāmi, and the north-west. These, numbering 150, were, in the then imperfect state of the art, taken on a scale so reduced that they could only be read with a magnifying glass, and even so, owing to insufficient cleansing and preparation of the originals, with difficulty. The photographs, however, were eventually, after other efforts to deal with them, placed in my hands for decipherment of the ancient characters and for translation in such leisure time as could be found from my regular duties. My only qualifications for the work were a knowledge of the language and the country. Otherwise it was new to me, and the task was not an easy one, as I was already engaged on extra duty in compiling the first edition of the *Gazetteers of Mysore and Coorg*, published in 1877. But by 1879 I contrived to bring out, in a volume called *Mysore Inscriptions*, translations of all those photographed as above, and of some other inscriptions collected by myself. Archæology had now become a hobby.

After the Rendition of Mysore in 1881 to the Native Government, on return from serving as Secretary to the Education Commission under Sir W. W. Hunter in Calcutta, I was appointed in 1884, in addition to my office of Education Secretary to Government, as Director of Archæological Researches, being relieved for that purpose of the Police Department, of which I also had charge. In 1886 was published the volume of *Coorg Inscriptions*, and in 1889 the volume of *Inscriptions in Śravaṇa-Beḷgoḷa*.

So much interest was excited by this work [1] that in 1890, at the instance of the Dewan, Sir K. Sheshadri Iyer, a regular Archæological Department was formed under me. The exploration and copying of all the inscriptions throughout the country on a regular system, District by District, were now entered upon. The work was much interrupted by the outbreak of plague in 1898, and I was otherwise also greatly occupied with bringing out a new edition of the *Gazetteer of Mysore*, published in 1897. But several months each year were spent in the arduous work in camp, and the results of the Archæologicaw Survey continued to appear in successive volumes of the *Epigraphia Carnatica*, according to the list on page v. The last (IX) bears date 1905, but was really issued in 1906. The total number of inscriptions and the magnitude of the whole undertaking far exceeded what had been anticipated either by myself or by the Government, and I am thankful to have been allowed to complete it.

Of the results obtained by the Survey, the details of which are contained in the volumes above referred to, the present volume is a summary. Their importance has been abundantly

[1] As it has long been out of print, a new edition is in preparation.

acknowledged by competent authorities. The history has been traced back, with scarcely a break, to the third century B.C., and former conceptions in regard to it have been considerably modified. A few of the principal items, before unknown, which have been brought to our knowledge may here be briefly mentioned. The earliest in order of time, and among the first in novelty and interest, are the account of the migration of Jains from the North under their great leader Bhadrabāhu, and the statement that he was accompanied by the celebrated Chandra Gupta as his disciple, and that both ended their lives at Śravaṇa-Beḷgoḷa in the Hassan District. These cannot be said to be proved as undeniably true, for they are perhaps now incapable alike of proof or disproof. But there are probabilities in favour of the occurrences as narrated, while they are not discredited by any anachronism. And the crowning discovery by me of Edicts of Aśōka, which placed beyond all doubt the fact that the north of Mysore in his time formed part of the Maurya empire, may also be held to lend support to the alleged connection with this country of Chandra Gupta, whose grandson Aśōka was. A local seat of the Maurya Government had evidently existed for some time at Isila, which is probably indicated by the Sidda of Siddapura in the Molakālmuru tāluq, where the edicts were found.

The rule of the Āndhras or Śātavāhanas, in succession to the Mauryas, has moreover been established. So also that of the line of Mahāvali or Bāṇa kings, hitherto unknown, has been made clear, together with details of the origin and rise to power of the Kadambas, who sprang from the Mysore country. The Gangas, who ruled over Mysore and Coorg for several centuries down to the end of the first millennium of the Christian era, but whose very name had been lost in oblivion, have been restored to their place in history. The Pallavas, equally unknown before, have now been recognised as a great ruling power in the South, whose dominion was perpetuated in Mysore by the Noṇambas or Noḷambas. The influence of the Chalukyas, especially their western branch, and the important part played by the Rāshṭrakūṭas or Raṭṭas, who for two centuries supplanted them, have been amply elucidated. The first clue to the chronology of the Chōlas was obtained from Mysore, and the range of their conquests here has been made manifest. In regard to the indigenous royal dynasty of the Poysalas or Hoysalas, who made a name in the South, their place of origin has been identified, and the building up of their power shown in detail. Not to mention the Śāntaras and others, the Changālvas and Kongālvas, lines of kings quite unknown, have been brought to light, and a large blank in the history of Coorg thus filled up.

For the more modern period, from the establishment of the Vijayanagar empire in the fourteenth century, less ignorance prevailed, but abundance of material has been obtained for adding to our knowledge and correcting previous misconceptions. Most important information has also been acquired regarding Karṇāṭaka literature and other matters which it is difficult to specify in a few words. The volumes of which this is a compendium can vouch for themselves, and I would bespeak for it as favourable a reception as has already been accorded to them.

HARROW-ON-THE-HILL,
Christmas 1908.

CONTENTS

LIST OF ILLUSTRATIONS

KEY TO ABBREVIATIONS FOR THE NAMES OF TĀLUQS

Sign.	Tāluq.	District.	Vol.	Sign.	Tāluq.	District.	Vol.
Ar.	Anekal	Bn	IX.	Kp	Koppa	Kd	VI.
Ag	Arkalgūd	Hn	V.	Kr[1]	Krishnarājpet	My	IV.
Ak	Arsikere	Hn	V.	Kg	Kunigal	Tm	XII.
Bg	Bāgepalli	Kl	X.	Mi	Maddagiri	Tm	XII.
Bn	Bangalore	Bn	IX.	Ma	Māgaḍi	Bn	IX.
Bl	Bēlūr	Hn	V.	Ml	Malavalli	My	III.
Bp	Bowringpet	Kl	X.	Mr	Mālūr	Kl	X.
Cl	Challakere	Cd	XI.	Md	Maṇḍya	My	III.
Ch	Chāmrājnagar	My	IV.	Mj	Manjarābād	Hn	V.
Ci	Channagiri	Sh	VII.	Mk	Molakālmuru	Cd	XI.
Cp	Channapatna	Bn	IX.	Mg	Mudgere	Kd	VI.
Cn	Channarayapatna	Hn	V.	Mb	Mulbāgal	Kl	X.
CB	Chik-Ballāpur	Kl	X.	My	Mysore	My	III.
Cm	Chikmagalūr	Kd	VI.	Ng	Nāgamangala	My	IV.
Ck	Chiknāyakanhalli	Tm	XII.	Nr	Nagar	Sh	VIII.
Ct	Chintāmani	Kl	X.	Nj	Nanjangūd	My	III.
Cd	Chitaldroog	Cd	XI.	Nl	Nelamangala	Bn	IX.
Cg	Coorg	Cg	I.	Pg	Pāvugaḍa	Tm	XII.
Dg	Dāvangere	Cd	XI.	Sa	Sāgar	Sh	VIII.
Dv	Dēvanhalli	Bn	IX.	Sr	Seringapatam	My	III.
DB	Doḍ-Ballāpur	Bn	IX.	Sk	Shikārpur	Sh	VII.
Gd	Gōribidnūr	Kl	X.	Sh	Shīmoga	Sh	VII.
Gb	Gubbi	Tm	XII.	Sd	Sidlaghatta	Kl	X.
Gu	Gundalpet	My	IV.	Si	Sīra	Tm	XII.
Hn	Hassan	Hn	V.	Sb	Sorab	Sh	VIII.
Hg	Heggaḍadevankōte	My	IV.	SB	Sravaṇa-Belgoḷa	Hn	II.
Hr	Hiriyūr	Cd	XI.	Sg	Śringēri	Kd	VI.
Hk	Holalkere	Cd	XI.	Sp	Śrīnivāspur	Kl	X.
HN	Hole-Narsipur	Hn	V.	Tk	Tarikere	Kd	VI.
Hl	Honnāli	Sh	VII.	Tp	Tiptūr	Tm	XII.
Ht	Hoskōte	Bn	IX.	Tl	Tīrthahalli	Sh	VIII.
Hs	Hunsūr	My	IV.	TN	Tirumakūḍal-Narsipur	My	III.
Jl	Jagalūr	Cd	XI.				
Kd	Kadūr	Kd	VI.	Tm	Tumkūr	Tm	XII.
Kn	Kānkānhalli	Bn	IX.	Yd	Yedatore	My	IV.
Kl	Kolar	Kl	X.	Yl	Yelandūr	My	IV.

1 By mistake Kp has been used for this in a few places.

WORKS REFERRED TO

ASI. — *Archæological Survey of India.*
ASWI. — *Archæological Survey of Western India.*
EC. — *Epigraphia Carnatica.*
EHD. — *Early History of the Dekkan.* By Dr. R. G. Bhandarkar.
EHI. — *Early History of India.* By Vincent A. Smith.
EI. — *Epigraphia Indica.*
GI. — *Gupta Inscriptions.* By Dr. J. F. Fleet.
IA. — *Indian Antiquary.*
JRAS. — *Journal of the Royal Asiatic Society.*
KD. — *Dynasties of the Kanarese Districts of the Bombay Presidency.* By Dr. Fleet.
SII. — *South Indian Inscriptions.* By Dr. E. Hultzsch.
VOJ. — *Vienna Oriental Journal.*
ZDMG. — *Zeitschrift der Deutschen Morgenländischen Gesellschaft.*

Volumes referred to without any name are those of the *Epigraphia Carnatica.*

GUIDE TO PRONUNCIATION OF INDIAN WORDS AND NAMES

VOWELS

a ā as the first and second *a* respectively in "afar."
e ē as *e* in "pen" and "prey" respectively.
i ī as *e* and *ee* respectively in "redeem."
o ō as the first and second *o* respectively in "morose."
u ū as *u* in "full" and "rule" respectively.
ai as *i* in "mine."
au as *ou* in "mouse."

CONSONANTS

g is always hard, as in "get"; never like *j*.
ṭ ḍ like *t* in "tat" and *d* in "dot" respectively.
t d like *th* in "thin" and *th* in "that" respectively.
ph like *ph* in "haphazard"; never like *f*.

For other under-dotted letters the English sounds may be used, as their correct pronunciation is not easy to explain.

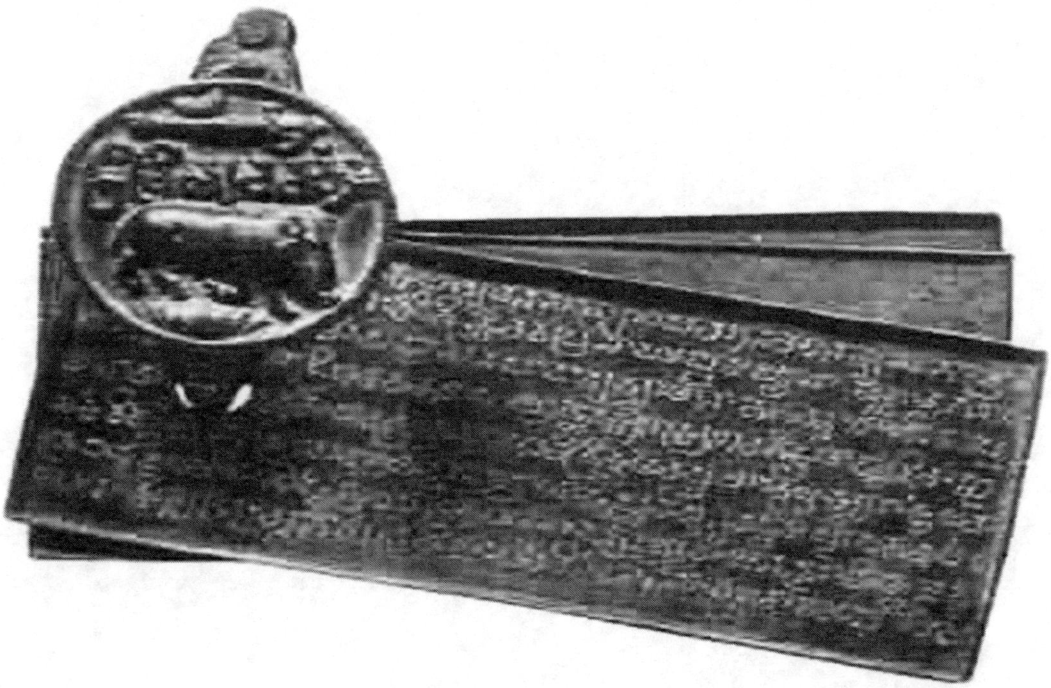

Specimen of Chalukya grant on copper plates (reduced) *To face*
From the British Museum.

MYSORE AND COORG
FROM THE INSCRIPTIONS

THESE eloquent records of bygone ages are not, as might be expected, altogether silent in regard to the epic period. As preliminary, therefore, to the authenticated history, a brief reference may be made to notices in our inscriptions of incidents in the Rāmāyaṇa and the Māhābhārata.

Rāma, on his expedition to Ceylon for the recovery of his wife Sītā, who had been carried off by Rāvaṇa, is generally admitted to have passed through the Mysore country. On the abduction of Sītā, as she was borne along by her captor in his air-car, her rescue was attempted by Jaṭāyu, king of the vultures, who was slain by Rāvaṇa. According to an inscription at the place (Mk 27), it was on the Jaṭinga Rāmēśvara hill in the Molakālmuru tāluq that Jaṭāyu fell when mortally wounded. But before he died he was able to impart the information as to who the despoiler was. This led to the despatch of Hanumān, the monkey chief, as a spy to Lankā or Ceylon to obtain confirmation of the report. Meanwhile Rāma made an alliance with Sugrīva, the king of Kishkindha, on the Pampā or Tungabhadrā river (near the site of the mediæval Vijayanagar), with the aid of whose forces he marched against Rāvaṇa in Ceylon. On his way through the Mysore region Rāma seems to have crossed the Kāvērī river at Rāmanāthpura in the Arkalgūd tāluq (Ag 53, Yd 25, 26). The tributary Lakshmantīrtha river, close by, is named after his brother Lakshmaṇa. The return journey, after his triumph, seems to have been by way of Āvani in the Mulbāgal tāluq—where there is a group of temples dedicated severally to Rāma, Lakshmaṇa, Bharata, Śatrughna, Vāli, and Sugrīva—through Nandi in the Chik-Ballāpur tāluq (CB 29), and perhaps Mulukuṇṭe in the Tumkūr tāluq (Tm 14).

With regard to the Māhābhārata stories, Kaivāra in the Chintāmani tāluq is said to be Ēkachakrapura (Ct 86, 87). Kunti-dēvī, the mother of the Pāṇḍavas, is said to have rebuilt a temple in the Chik-Ballāpur tāluq (CB 29). An inscription at Belgāmi in the Shikarpur tāluq (Sk 126) says that, after the performance of the Rājasūya sacrifice, the Five Pāṇḍava brothers came there, and set up the Five Lingas of the Panchá Linga temple. King Virāṭa's capital, Matsya, where the Pāṇḍavas spent the last year of their exile in disguise, is identified with Pānungal or Hānugal in Dharwar, just over the north-west border of Mysore.

I. RULING DYNASTIES

I. MAURYAS

THE earliest undoubted inscriptions in Mysore are the Edicts of Aśōka in the Molakālmuru tāluq (Mk 21, 14, 34), discovered by me in 1892. They belong to the first half of the third century B.C., and are unquestionable evidence that the north of the Mysore State was included in the Maurya empire. But there are inscriptions relating to a period still farther back. For the Mauryas had as their predecessors the Nandas, and one inscription (Sk 225) states that Kuntala, a province which included the western Dekhan and the north of Mysore, was ruled by the Nandas. Another (Sk 236) derives the descent of the Kadambas, the early rulers of the north-west of the country, from Nanda. But these are of comparatively modern date, the twelfth century, and need not be further noticed.

Much more ancient and definite are the Jain inscriptions relating to Bhadrabāhu and Chandra Gupta. The first discovery of those at Sravaṇa-Beḷgoḷa was made by me in 1874. The oldest are incised on the natural and irregular horizontal surface of the rock on the summit of the lower hill, called Chandragiri. One (SB 17), of (?) about 600, which almost runs into the big one (SB 1), to be mentioned farther on, couples together "the pair (*yugma*), Bhadrabāhu along with Chandra Gupta munīndra," and says that theirs was the safe (or auspicious) faith (*dharmma*). Two inscriptions on the north bank of the Kāvērī near Seringapatam (Sr 147, 148), of about 900, describe the summit of the Kalbappu hill, that is,

Chandragiri, as marked by the footprints of Bhadrabāhu and Chandra Gupta munipati. At Śravaṇa-Beḷgoḷa, one of 1129 (SB 54) mentions Bhadrabāhu—the śrutakēvali—and Chandra Gupta, who by being his disciple acquired such merit that he was for a long time served by the forest deities. Another there, of 1163 (SB 40), speaks of Bhadrabāhu, the last of the śrutakēvalis, and his disciple Chandra Gupta, whose glory was such that his *gaṇa* of munis was worshipped by the forest deities. A third in the same place, of 1432 (SB 108), after extolling the yatīndra Bhadrabāhu, the last of the śrutakēvalis, says that his disciple was Chandra Gupta, the greatness of whose penance caused his exalted fame to be spread into other worlds (or lands).

In literature, the *Bṛihatkathākōśa*, a work by Harishēna, dated in 931, says that Bhadrabāhu, the last of the śruta-kēvalis, had the king Chandra Gupta as his disciple. A similar account is contained in the *Bhadrabāhu-charita* by Ratnanandi of about 1450; and is repeated in the *Rājāvali-kathe* by Dēva-chandra, which is a modern compilation, of about 1800.

The tradition—thus ancient in origin, and referred to in subsequent ages down to the present as well known—is that Bhadrabāhu died at Śravaṇa-Beḷgoḷa, on the Kaṭavapra or Kalbappu hill, that is Chandragiri, while leading a migration of Jains from the north, and that Chandra Gupta, who had accompanied him as his chief disciple, was the only attendant on him in his last moments. The latter survived his teacher for twelve years, which were spent in penance on the hill, and then died there himself.[1]

For further local testimony to the truth of this, we have Chandra-giri, the name of the hill, given to it after Chandra Gupta. On it is pointed out the cave in which Bhadrabāhu expired (SB 71). In the centre of the group of temples there, and the most ancient among them, is the Chandra Gupta basti.

[1] "The story would be very interesting if it could be believed," says Mr. Vincent A. Smith (*EHI.* 137). Unfortunately he has been entirely misled as to its being a modern invention.

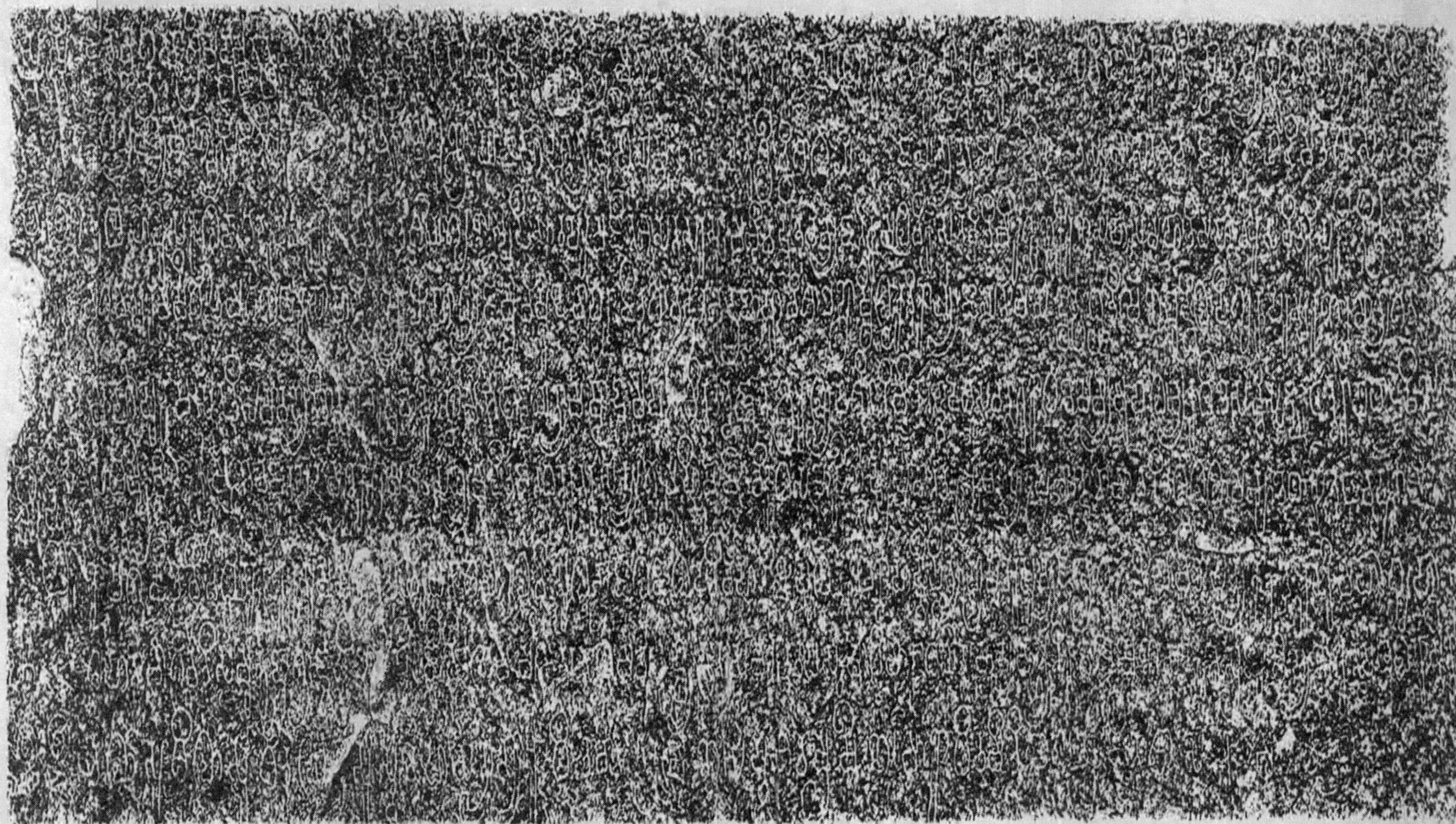

Bhadrabāhu rock inscription at Śravaṇa.

facing which, as being then the sole object of adoration on the hill, must be read the semicircle of rock inscriptions (SB 1-35) recording the death, by *sallēkhana* or fasting, of various distinguished Jains. The façade of this basti is a perforated stone screen containing ninety sculptured scenes of events in the lives of Bhadrabāhu and Chandra Gupta. This, however, from the name of the sculptor, may be a work of the twelfth century, and made for its protection.

But of the rock inscriptions at Śravaṇa-Beḷgoḷa, which mostly consist of only two or three lines, the longest and most important is SB 1, in Sanskrit, not dated, but, from the characters, belonging to not later than the fifth century.[1] For they closely correspond with those of the Kavaḍi stone (Sb 523), recording the death of the Kadamba king Ravivarmma and his queen; and phrases are grouped in a similar way in both, leaving a space between. Comparison may also be made with the characters of the Siragunda stone (Cm 50), which is of the time of the Ganga king Nirvvinīta or Durvvinīta, who came to the throne in 482.

After verses in praise of Vardhamāna or Mahāvīra, whose doctrine (it says) is even to-day in favour in Viśāla (? Vaiśāli), a line of holy men is named who succeeded him. They were: Gautama gaṇadhara, his personal disciple Lōhārya, Jambu,[2] Vishnudēva, Aparājita, Gōvardhana, Bhadrabāhu,[3] Viśākha, Prōshṭhila, Kṛittikārya, Jayanāma, Siddhārtha, Dhṛitishēna, Buddhila,[4] and others. Bhadrabāhu-svāmi, of this illustrious succession of regularly descended great men, by his power of knowing the past, present, and future, having foretold in Ujjayini a period of twelve years of dire calamity (or famine), the whole of the *sàngha* (or Jaina community) went forth from the North to the South. By degrees they had arrived at a populous and prosperous country, when the Āchārya, Prabhā-

[1] The seventh, in the opinion of Drs. Leumann (*VOJ.* vii. 382) and Fleet (*EI.* iv. 25).

[2] These were the three Kēvalis. The second is generally called Sudharma.

[3] These were four of the five Śrutakēvalis.

[4] These seven were Daśapūrvis, out of eleven.

chandra by name (or (?) with Prabhāchandra also), on this mountain named Kaṭavapra, perceiving that but little time remained for him to live, in order that he might perform the penance before death, bidding farewell to them, sent away the entire *sangha*, and with one single disciple, worshipping on the cold rocks covered with grass, gained emancipation from his body.

Now here we have the prediction by Bhadrabāhu of twelve years of famine in the North, and the migration in consequence of the Jains to the South. As Dr. Leumann says,[1] the migration to the South is "the initial fact of the Digambara tradition." After a critical examination of Jain *paṭṭāvalis* or succession lists of gurus, Dr. Hoernle says:[2] "Before Bhadrabāhu the Jain community was undivided; with him the Digambaras separated from the Śvētāmbaras. . . . The question is who this Bhadrabāhu was. The Śvētāmbara paṭṭāvalis know only one Bhadrabāhu, who, from the dates assigned to him by the Śvētāmbaras and Digambaras alike, must be identical with the Bhadrabāhu I of the Digambaras. Considering the varying and contradictory character of the Digambara traditions, the probability is that the inception of the great separation took place under Bhadrabāhu I, who died 162 A.V. according to the Digambaras, or 170 A.V. according to the Śvētāmbaras." Dr. Jacobi says:[3] "The date of Bhadrabāhu's death is placed identically by all Jaina authors, from Hēmachandra down to the most modern scholiast, in the year 170 A.V." This is 297 B.C.

The inscription records the death of a certain Āchārya, who was evidently a leader of the migration to the South, for he bade farewell to the entire sangha—that is, the sangha previously mentioned as migrating with him to the South—and sent them on their way, in order that he might remain on the hill and perform the penance before death. During this final period he was ministered to by one single disciple (out of those who had accompanied him). The name of the

[1] *loc. cit.* [2] *IA.* xxi. 59, 60. [3] *Kalpasūtra*, Introd. 13.

Āchārya is apparently given as Prabhāchandra, but if the other reading above noted, proposed by Jains on the spot, might stand, Prabhāchandra would indicate the disciple, and is explained as the clerical name adopted by Chandra Gupta. The Āchārya would therefore be Bhadrabāhu.[1] That this was the name of the last of the Śrutakēvalis there is no doubt whatever. And that the first Maurya emperor, Chandra Gupta, the Sandrakoptos of the Greek historians, who reigned from 321 to 297 B.C., was contemporary with him, and disappeared from public life in the same year that Bhadrabāhu, as above shown, died, is equally clear. The question then naturally arises, What evidence is there that they were in any way connected?

As to this, Mr. Thomas says:[2] "That Chandra Gupta was a member of the Jaina community is taken by their writers as a matter of course and treated as a known fact, which needed neither argument nor demonstration. . . . The testimony of Megasthenes would likewise seem to imply that

[1] He is described as *pūrna-chandra* in SB 104.—It has been attempted by Dr. Fleet (*EI.* iv. 24) to make out that the Bhadrabāhu of the inscription was a later one of that name, who is said to have lived in the first century B.C., and that Chandragupta means his disciple Guptigupta. But no necessity appears for assuming that a long period intervened between the Bhadrabāhu in the opening portion and the one with whom the narrative begins, and that they were different persons. For even in the *Kalpasūtra* of Bhadrabāhu the section headed *Sthavirāvali* extends to many generations beyond him, which is accounted for as being for the sake of auspiciousness (see Introd. 23). Guptigupta, again, is nowhere mentioned in any inscription. The solitary instance in which the name was supposed to occur has been shown by Dr. Lüders (*EI.* iv. 339) to have no such meaning. Moreover, this Guptigupta is said to have had other names, one of which, it is significant to note, was Viśākha, the name of the successor of Bhadrabāhu I. To imagine also, with Dr. Leumann (in his kindly critique), that Prabhāchandra belonged to some still more distant period, farther removed from both, is in direct contradiction to the inscription, which unmistakably shows that he accompanied the *sangha* on its migration. The name Prabhāchandra is not an uncommon one among the Jain gurus, and occurs at all periods. But the one honoured with this unique memorial was no ordinary man. In the effort to discover some one of the name of sufficient distinction to whom it can be fitted, a certain Digambara teacher is suggested, who cannot be shown to have lived till a later time than that of the inscription, and of course he would in no way be connected with the migration. To justify this proposed piecemeal and disjointed treatment of the inscription, it is represented that the first portion was a customary introduction to Jain inscriptions. But plausible as this may appear in theory, it is opposed to fact, for not a single inscription has been found with this introduction.

[2] *Jainism, or the Early Faith of Asoka*, 23.

Chandra Gupta submitted to the devotional teaching of the Sermanas as opposed to the doctrines of the Brāhmans." In treating of the Hindu religious sects, Professor Wilson says:[1] "It has been supposed that we have notices of the Jaina sect as far back as the period at which Megasthenes was sent ambassador to Sandracoptus, and that these notices are recorded by Strabo and Arrian." Colebrooke, who examined the passages referred to, says:[2] "The followers of Buddha are clearly distinguished from the Brachmanes and Sarmanes. The latter, called Germanes by Strabo and Samanæans by Porphyrius, are the ascetics of a different religion, and may have belonged to the sect of Jina or to another." Megasthenes, in his *Indika*, says[3] of the Sarmanes who live in the woods: "They communicate with the kings, who consult them by messengers regarding the causes of things, and who through them worship and supplicate the deity." The story of Chandra Gupta's accession to the throne of the Nandas is dramatised in the Sanskrit play named *Mudrā Rākshasa*, by Viśākhadatta, which has been translated by Professor Wilson.[4] In this we see that Jains held a prominent position at the time, and Chānakya—also called Vishnugupta and Kauṭilya—who was the prime agent in the revolution, employs a Jain as one of his chief emissaries.

We are therefore not without warrant for assuming that Chandra Gupta was a Jain by creed. At the period when he becomes associated with Bhadrabāhu, he was much troubled in mind on account of sixteen dreams with which he had been visited. These are mentioned in many narratives relating to him. Bhadrabāhu in the course of his travels having come to Pātaliputra, the capital, the king consulted him as to their

[1] *Works*, i. 324.

[2] *Essays*, ii. 203.

[3] McCrindle's *Indika of Megasthenes* (*I.A.* vi. 244).

[4] *Theatre of the Hindus*, ii. 125. The work is no doubt much older than he thought, owing to his erroneous opinion that the Jains were later than the Buddhists. It is now well established that they were more ancient. Professor Speyer (in his recent *Studies about the Kathāsaritsāgara*) also says: "Viśākhadatta and his admirable drama are to be placed many centuries earlier than is generally done" (*JRAS*, 1908, p. 910).

interpretation, and was dismayed at the coming troubles which they portended, including the twelve years of famine. He seems consequently, impressed by Bhadrabāhu's exhortations, to have resolved to retire from the throne, and to place himself under the guidance of this the most distinguished Jain teacher then living, for the right performance of penitential acts in view of the impending calamities. He was, as Mr. V. A. Smith has pointed out,[1] not fifty years of age at the time. He is not expressly stated to have died, and no special reason appears for his death at this early age. Had he fallen in battle, or his life been cut short by accident or disease, the circumstance could not fail to have been mentioned. But if he retired from the throne in order to devote himself, in accordance with the dictates of the Jain religion, to an ascetic life in the last stage of his existence,[2] and accompanied Bhadrabāhu to the South, this affords a reasonable explanation of his early disappearance from public notice and of the silence regarding his further career, for absolute renunciation of all earthly ties was of the essence of the vow he had taken. On the other hand, the southern accounts represent him as living an ascetic life at Śravaṇa-Beḷgoḷa for twelve years after the decease of Bhadrabāhu.[3] His death then occurred when he was about sixty-two years of age, which seems more natural and so far entitled to credence.

That the north of Mysore may even at that period have been a part of the Maurya empire is not beyond probability. For the Edicts of Aśōka are evidence that it was so two generations later ; and as the only conquest Aśōka is said to have made was that of Kalinga or Orissa, it follows that the rest of his empire was inherited from his predecessors. If it be true, moreover, as above stated, that the Nandas ruled over Kuntala, then the Mauryas naturally acquired it in succession

[1] *EHI.* 128.

[2] Aśōka, who was his grandson, did the same, as will be seen below.

[3] Twelve years of penance were always thought essential for obtaining perfection, and for every ascetic who endeavours to quit this life with the best claims to enter one of the highest heavens or even Nirvāna (Jacobi, *SBE.* xxii. Introd. 18).

to them. One inscription, indeed (Sb 263), says that Nāgakhanda (the Shikarpur tāluq) "was protected by the wise Chandra Gupta, an abode of the usages of eminent Kshattriyas"; but this is of the fourteenth century and too much cannot be built upon it. Of special interest, however, is the statement in the work by Harishēna before referred to, that when, as described in the Śravaṇa-Beḷgoḷa inscription, the *sangha* were sent on their way, "they went by the guru's direction to the Punnāta country, situated in the South."[1] This was a province in the south-west of the Mysore State. It is mentioned in the second century by Ptolemy as Pounnata, "where is beryl." It is also named in the fifth century in connection with the Ganga king Avinīta (Cg 1), whose son Durvvinīta married the Punnāḍ king's daughter, and united it to the Ganga territory. An inscription of the Punnāḍ Rājas[2] gives Kitthipura as their capital, which is identified (Hg 56) with Kittūr on the Kabbani river in the Heggaḍadēvankōṭe tāluq. One of the ancient rock inscriptions on Chandragiri (SB 7) records the death of a Jain guru from Kittūr.

To turn now to the Edicts of Aśōka. They are also engraved on the natural horizontal surface of the rock, in three places near to one another in the Molakālmuru tāluq. The most perfect is on a big boulder at the north-west foot of Brahmagiri (Mk 21). The other two, which are much effaced, are one to the north of Siddapura, which is about a mile to the west (Mk 14), and the remaining one on the Jaṭinga Rāmēśvara hill, about three miles to the north (Mk 34). They are all three virtually alike, but differ from three somewhat similar ones in the north of India,—those at Bairāṭ in Rājputāna, Rūpnāth in the Central Provinces, and Sahasrām in Bengal,—in containing two edicts and not one, of which the second is a brief summary of the precepts of *dhamma* or the moral law. Another peculiarity is that, although they are

[1] *Sanghō'pi samastō guru-vākyataḥ dakshinā-patha-dēśastha-Punnāṭa-vishayam yayau.*
[2] *Id.* xii. 13; xviii. 366.

Edicts of Aśōka on rock at Brahmagiri (Mk 21)

Brāhmī and Kharōshṭhī characters, Māgadhi language.

inscribed in the Brāhmī characters,[1] written from left to right, common to these edicts in other parts, the last word, in which the scribe states his profession, is in the Kharōshṭhī characters,[2] written from right to left, which are found only in the extreme north-west of the Punjab. The date of these edicts is believed to be expressed in the figures 256 which occur at the end of the first edict, and which are understood as referring to the number of years from the death of Buddha, though they have been also interpreted in many various and quite irreconcilable ways.[3] The edicts themselves would thus belong to the year 231 B.C. This was the last year of Aśōka's life, and thirty-eight years after his coronation-anointing. Dr. Fleet professes[4] to have discovered that "particular interest attaches to the Mysore versions, because the Brahmagiri text discloses the fact that it was framed on the anniversary of Aśōka's abdication, and when he was living in religious retirement on the hill Suvarnagiri, still known as Songir, which was one of the hills surrounding the ancient city of Girivraja in Magadha." Whether all this be so or not is by no means determined.[5]

The language of the edicts is what is known as Māgadhi, with some local peculiarities. All three in Mysore begin in the same way, with greeting from the Ayaputa (Āryaputra or Prince) and the Mahāmātas (high officials) of Suvannagiri (identified as above) to the Mahāmātas[6] of Isila (possibly Sidda in Siddapura). The edicts are introduced with the formula "Devānam Piye commands" or "Thus says Devānam Piye."[7]

[1] The source of the Devanāgarī and other alphabets of India. It is apparently of Semitic origin, and was introduced into India in about the ninth century B.C. But an indigenous origin has also been claimed for it (see *I.A.* xxxv. 253).

[2] A form of Aramaic script introduced by the Persians after the conquests of Darius in the sixth century B.C.

[3] For a summary of these, see *JRAS*, 1904, p. 4 ff.

[4] *JRAS*, 1905, p. 304.

[5] See *Aśōka Notes*, by V. A. Smith and F. W. Thomas, in *I.A.* xxxvii.; also *The Last Edict of Aśōka*, by Fleet, in *JRAS*, 1908, p. 811.

[6] It is interesting to find this term *mahāmātra* in use so late as the eleventh century (see Nl 1).

[7] This formula, with which most of the edicts are introduced, recalls the similar one in the famous trilingual inscription of Darius at Behistan, of 516 B.C., every section of which commences with, "Says Darius the king."

This name (Devānām priyaḥ), meaning "Beloved of the gods," was a royal title borne by the Maurya kings. It is sometimes used alone, but more often in conjunction with the king's name. It thus occurs as an epithet of Piyadasi (Priyadarśi) and of Dasaratha his grandson. The main object of the present edicts is to exhort all classes to greater effort in pious duties. In doing this the king adduces his own example, how while he was a lay disciple he did not exert himself strenuously, but after he entered the sacred Order he did so, and as the result the men who were (regarded as) true in Jambu-dvīpa (were shown to be) false, together with the gods. This was the fruit of effort or exertion, and in the same way the lowly, as well as the great, could by exertion attain to *svarga* (or heavenly bliss). A precept to this effect is quoted, said to have been delivered by the Vyūtha (or the Departed, that is Buddha) 256 (? years ago).

With regard to the various circumstances referred to in the above summary. The king, in the thirteenth Rock Edict, had proclaimed that remorse on account of the slaughter and devastation that attended his conquest of Kalinga, which was effected in the ninth year of his reign, had made him resolve for the future to maintain peace and devote himself to religion. At length he became a Buddhist—and he here says that during the time when he was an *upāsaka* (or lay disciple) he did not put forth much effort. But more than six years before our present inscriptions, he entered the *saṅgha* (or sacred order) and vigorously exerted himself. What ensued from these special efforts has been stated above, but the sentence is elliptic and not over clear. It is generally agreed, however, and there can be no question, that the reference is to the Brāhmans, who are designated throughout Hindu literature by several terms which mean "gods on earth." As M. Senart says: "After his conversion the king proceeded to deprive the Brāhmans of the almost divine prestige they enjoyed throughout the whole of India." Their authority being rejected, their gods were also deposed. That it was to Buddhism the king was converted there can be no doubt. Previous to this change of faith he was apparently a Jain. Akbar's minister Abul Fazl says in the *Ain-i-Akbari* that Aśōka introduced Jainism into Kashmir, and this is confirmed by the *Rāja-tarangini*, the Brahmanical history of Kashmir. That he was a Jain has also been deduced from his edicts.[1] But some are of opinion that he followed the Brāhman creed. His conversion at length to Buddhism was not signalised by persecution of his former co-religionists, but by inducing a revolution throughout India in the public estimation of them. In short, the members of the Order no doubt took advantage of the king's presence and adhesion to influence him to depose their rivals, whether Brāhmans or Jains, from their former pre-eminence. This action of his does not invalidate the express injunctions to toleration contained in so many of his edicts, wherein he inculcates more than once the duty of reverence to and the bestowal of alms upon both Brāhmanas and Śramanas. Toleration was denied only to their false claims. On the other hand, it would be strange if no trace whatever could be discovered of the resentment which would naturally be evoked by so powerful though silent and peaceful a revolution in time-honoured beliefs. And we may perhaps find a trace in the fact that Devānāmpriyaḥ, as one word, is explained by Kātyāyana in the Vārttikas to Pāṇini as synonymous with *mūrkha*, a fool! This was a very characteristic retaliation, if so meant, and the use of the word thus authorised has come down even to the present time, and is common, I am told, at all events among the Brāhmans.[2]

The second edict in our inscriptions is as follows: "Thus says the Beloved of the gods:—Obedience should be rendered to mother and father. So also regard for living creatures should be enforced. Truth should be spoken. These virtues

[1] Thomas, *Jainism, or the Early Faith of Asoka*; also by Professors Kern (*IA*. v. 275), Pischel, Minayeff, etc. Reasons have been given above for the belief that Chandra Gupta, the grandfather of Aśōka, was a Jain. His grandson Sampadi or Samprati was also a devoted Jain.

[2] See also the satirical verses on Aśōka quoted in vol. v., Introd. 30, 31, from the *Bhōja Prabandha*.

of the sacred law should be practised. So also the teacher should be honoured by the pupil, and towards relations due respect indeed should be shown. This is the ancient standard (of piety),—this conduces to long life, and this should thus be done." There is a striking resemblance here to the fifth commandment of the Mosaic code. The whole tone indeed of the Edicts of Aśōka is both higher than and quite different from that of any other inscriptions found in India. Solicitude for the welfare here and hereafter of all his subjects, high and low, is manifest throughout, and it extended even to peoples beyond his boundaries in an all-embracing humanity. His concern for the latter was shown practically by the despatch of missionaries to bordering lands. Among other places, it is of special interest to note that he sent a *thēra* named Mahadeva to Mahisa-maṇḍala, the country round Mysore [1]—which must therefore have been a place of importance even at that period—and a *thēra* named Rakkhita to Vanavāsi, known as Banavāsi, on the north-west of the State.

2. ŚĀTAVĀHANAS

Next to our Edicts of Aśōka, whose discovery formed—as has been said by the eminent French authority—an epoch in Indian archæology, the oldest inscriptions that have been found in Mysore are those in Prākrit on a pillar at Malavalli in Shikarpur tāluq. The first of these (Sk 263) is a grant by Hāritīputta-Sātakanni, of the Mānavya-gotra and Vinhukaḍḍa-chuṭu family, king of Vaijayanti, that is Banavāsi, engraved in what are called Cave characters. He commands the *mahā-valabham rajjukam* [2] that the village Sahalāṭavi has been given

[1] Mysore, properly Maisūru, derives its name from *mahisha*, Sanskrit for buffalo, reduced in Prākrit to *mahisa* and in Kannaḍa to *maisa*, and *ūru*, Kannaḍa for town or country; which commemorates the destruction of Mahishāsura, a minotaur or buffalo-headed monster, by Chāmuṇḍi or Mahishāsura-mardani, the form under which the consort of Śiva is worshipped as the tutelary goddess of the reigning family. Mahisa-maṇḍala appears in the Tamil form Erumai-nāḍu in Mānūlanār's *Aganānūru*, which is of the second century.

[2] The *rajjukas* were first appointed in the time of Aśōka, but perhaps for other purposes. They were, however, properly Revenue and Settlement officers. For, as

for the enjoyment of the Maṭṭapaṭṭi (that is Malavalli) god, as a Brāhman endowment, to Koṇḍamāna, a Hāritiputta of the Koḍinya-gōtra. It is dated in the second fortnight of the hot season, the first day of the first year. In Banavāsi is also an inscription (*IA*. xiv. 333) of apparently the same king, dated in the twelfth regnal year, in the seventh fortnight of the winter, the first day. In this the Mahārāja's daughter, the Mahābhōji Sivakhada-Nāgasiri (Sivaskanda-Nāgaśrī) makes the grant of a *nāga* (the cobra in the middle of the slab on the margin of which the inscription is engraved), a tank, and a *vihāra*. Moreover, in the Tālgunda pillar inscription (Sk 176) Sātakarṇṇi is named as one of the great kings who had worshipped at the temple there. Again, to the west of Chitaldroog, on the site of an ancient city whose name is said to have been Chandrāvali, were found[1] in 1888 a number of leaden coins, among which were some bearing the legend "Sadakana-Kaḷalāya-Mahārathisa,"—that is, Sātakarṇṇi-Kaḷa-lāya-Mahārathi—surrounding a humped bull, and having on the reverse the Buddhist symbols of a *bōdhi* tree and a *chaitya*.

These are all evidence that the north-west of Mysore was at that period in possession of the kings who bore the general name of Sātakarṇṇi. They are often spoken of as the Āndhras, and identified with the Andaræ described by Ptolemy as a powerful nation, and also mentioned by Pliny. The Purānas, however, seem to call them Āndhrabhṛityas, or servants of the Āndhras. But from inscriptions in the western caves it appears more correct to call them Śātavāhanas,[2] a name from which has arisen the form Śālīvāhana. The Indian era named after Śālīvāhana, reckoned from A.D. 78, is in general use. For many centuries it was called the Śaka-kāla

Dr. Bühler has pointed out (*ZDMG*. xlvii. 466), the name literally means "holder of the rope," that is, their duty was concerned with the survey of the land. In name they are represented by the modern *sheristadār*, a corruption of the Persian *sar-i rishta dār*, he who holds the end of the rope.

[1] See *EI*. vii. 51. Others have since been found there of the same series, together with Roman coins of Augustus; and a clay seal, bearing the figures of an elephant and what looks like a sentry standing facing it. Some letters at top, said to be Brāhmī, have not been deciphered.

[2] Bhāndārkar's *EHD*. 24.

or Śaka-nṛipa-kāla—the time of the Śakas or of the Śaka kings. But eventually the word *śaka* came to be misunderstood as itself meaning era, and to distinguish it, was then called the Śālīvāhana-śaka. A reminiscence of its origin is, however, contained in Sk 281, of 1368, which is dated in the Śātavāhana-śaka instead of the Śālīvāhana-śaka. So far as I have observed, the decided use of the latter term came in with the foundation of the Vijayanagar empire in the fourteenth century. The Mysore State is spoken of in 1717 as in the Śālīvāhana country (Cm 109).

The territory of the Śātavāhanas extended over the whole of the Dekhan, and Sātakarṇṇi is called the lord of Dakshiṇā-patha in the Kshatrapa Rudradāman's inscription. Their chief capital appears to have been at Dhanakaṭaka in the east (Dhāranikoṭṭa on the Krishnā), but their chief city in the west was Paithan on the Gōdāvari. The Hathigumpha inscription of Kharavela in Kalinga tells us of a Sātakani in the second century B.C., but the Sātakarṇṇi of our inscriptions may be referred to the first or second century A.D. A peculiarity of these kings is that the name of his mother always appears with that of the king. Thus we have Gautamīputra Sātakarṇṇi, Vasishṭhīputra Pulumāyi, and here, Hāritīputra Sātakarṇṇi. This is a Rajput custom due to polygamy. The actual names of the mothers are not given, but they are called after the *gōtra* of their family priest.[1] The two branches of the Gōdāvari which form the Delta are still named after the two great queens—the northern is the Gautamī, and the southern the Vasishṭhī.[2] With regard to the Kaḷalāya of the coins, he was doubtless a viceroy under Sātakarṇṇi.

In the early centuries of the Christian era we find the Mahāvalis or Bāṇas occupying the east of Mysore, the Kadambas the north-west (where they succeeded the Śāta-vāhanas), and the Gangas the centre and south. To take these up in order.

[1] See Dr. Bühler, in Cunningham's *Stūpa of Bharhut*, 129.
[2] Sir Walter Elliot, *S. I. Coins*, 21.

3. MAHAVALIS OR BANAS

The Mahāvalis held the country east from the Pālār river and north into the Madras districts. According to one inscription (*IA.* xiii. 6) their territory lay to the west of the Āndhra or Telugu country, and Mb 157 describes them as ruling a Seven-and-a-half Lakh country, having twelve thousand villages, in the Āndhra-maṇḍala. This seems to have been known as the Vaḍugavaḷi Twelve Thousand (*SII.* iii. 90), in Sanskrit the Āndhrāt-pathaḥ (*EI.* iii. 76). They claim descent from Mahāvali or Mahā Bali (Bali the Great) and his son Bāṇa, whence they are also called Bāṇas. They may have been connected with Mahābalipura, known as the Seven Pagodas, on the coast south of Madras. Their flag displayed a black buck, and their crest was a bull (Mb 126).

Bali was a Daitya or Dānava (or, as we should say, Titan) king, who by the power of his penance defeated Indra, humbled the gods, and dominated the three worlds. The gods appealed for help to Vishnu, who assumed the Vāmana or Dwarf incarnation, and appearing before Bali as a Brāhman dwarf, begged for only three paces of ground. This being granted, he assumed his godlike dimensions, and with two strides having covered heaven and earth, there being no place for the third, planted his foot on Bali's head, and forced him down to Pātāla (the nether world and abode of the Nāgas or serpents), which on account of certain virtues was left in his possession. The germ of this legend is found in the Ṛig-vēda, where Vishnu is represented as taking three strides over heaven, earth, and the lower regions—typifying perhaps the rising, culmination, and setting of the sun.

Bāṇa was Bali's eldest son, a giant with a thousand arms. He propitiated Śiva, who agreed to live in his capital,[1] and Bāṇa appointed him guardian of the gates, or doorkeeper, as the inscriptions put it. Bāṇa's daughter Ushā became

[1] According to the Vishnu Purāṇa (Bk. V. chap. xxxiii.) this was Śōṇitapura, said to be Dēvikōṭa, near the mouth of the Coleroon, on the Madras coast.

enamoured of a prince she saw in a dream, whom, on being shown a number of portraits, she identified with Krishna's grandson Aniruddha. Him her female friend Chitralēkhā then contrived to introduce clandestinely into the princess's apartments. When discovered, he was seized and imprisoned by Bāṇa, and a war ensued. Krishna came in person from Dvāraka to besiege the capital. Śiva guarded the gates and fought for Bāṇa, who worshipped him with his thousand hands. But Krishna found means to overthrow Śiva, and having taken the city, cut off Bāṇa's thousand hands, except two, with which he obliged him to do homage.

This line of kings was first brought to notice by my discovery of the two big stone inscriptions, Sp 5 and 6 (vol. x), originally published by me in 1881 (*IA.* x. 36). The plates published in 1884 by the Rev. T. Foulkes (*IA.* xiii. 6)[1] added to the information regarding them. Many inscriptions were later found in the Kolar District (vol. x), and some further details were contributed by inscriptions at Tiruvallam, north of Vellore in North Arcot (*SII.* iii. 88), a place described as Vāṇapuram (Bāṇapuram), situated in Perum-Bāṇappāḍi, the great Bāṇa country, or country of the Great Bāṇa (see Bṛihad Bāṇa, farther on). The records in Mysore supply only three dates—338,[2] 909, and 961. Those at Tiruvallam add one—888—but do not specify the name of the Bāṇa king whose time it was.

A table of the Mahāvali or Bāṇa kings so far as known is appended, with dates where given :—

[1] Published again by Dr. Kielhorn in 1894 (*EI.* iii. 74).

[2] This date has been examined by Dr. Kielhorn (*IA.* xxiv. 10) and Dr. Fleet (xvii. 239), who find only the week day disagrees.

Bali, Mahābali,
lord of the Dānavas, regent of the Asuras,
|
Bāṇa,
who made Paramēśvara (worshipped by all the three worlds, the lord of gods and demons) his doorkeeper.

In his line was born
Bāṇādhirāja.

After many Bāṇa kings had passed away, there were
Nandivarmma
|
Vijayāditya
|
Vadhūvallabha Malladēva Nandivarmma, 338
⋮
Jaya-Nandivarmma
|
Vijayāditya
|
Malladēva Jagadēkamalla
|
Bāṇa Vidyādhara, Vikramāditya Jayamēru,
married Kundavvai, daughter of Pratipati (Prithuvipati I), the son of Kongunivarmma-dharmma-mahārāja Śivamahārāja-Permmānaḍigal (the Ganga king Śivamāra II)
|
Prabhumēru
|
Vikramāditya, (?) 888
|
Vijayāditya, Bejeyitta, Pugalvippavar-gaṇḍa, 909
|
Vijayabāhu Vikramāditya,
the friend of Krishna Rāja (? Rāshṭrakūṭa king, 884-913)
⋮
Sambayya, 961
ruling under the Pallava king Iriva-Nolamba or Dilīpa (943-966).

The first Ganga king, Kongunivarmma, who is assigned to the second century, is said (*SII.* ii. 187) to have been consecrated to conquer the Bāṇa country, and in DB 67 to be a wild-fire in consuming the stubble of the forest Bāṇa. Mayūraśarmma, the progenitor of the Kadambas, at about the same time is said (Sk 176), when an outlaw in the forests of Śrīparvata (Karnūl District), to have levied tribute from Bṛihad Bāṇa (the great Bāṇa[1]) and other kings. The Chōla king Killi-Valavan, who reigned about 105 to 120, married the princess Sithathakai, claiming descent from Mahābali. She was probably the daughter of a king in the Mysore country[2] (no doubt a Bāṇa). The Kolar volume gives an account of such details as the various inscriptions there supply regarding

[1] If this indicates the first Bāṇa, it furnishes a clue to his period.
[2] Kanakasabhai's *The Tamils Eighteen Hundred Years Ago*, 77.

the Bāṇas. The first Nandivarmma is said to have promoted the fortunes of his family, and obtained the crown and the throne amid the blessings of Brāhmans. He was possessed of mighty elephant and other forces, which secured him against conquest by the most powerful kings. Malladēva Nandivarmma is said to have been like a sun in waking up the lotus lake of the Bāṇa family, and in compassion for all living things in the three worlds was like Bōdhisattva or Buddha.

For other references—the Chalukya king Vikramāditya (655-680) is said (*IA.* vi. 75; *Seven Pagodas*, 127) to have conquered Rājamalla of the Mahāmalla family, that is the kings of Māmallaipura, the common name for Mahābalipura—in other words the Mahāvalis. Under the Gangas in 776 the Nirgunda Yuvarāja, Duṇḍu, is said (Ng 85) to have put the Bāṇa family to confusion. The Ganga king Nītimārgga, in about 850, is said (Mb 228) to have captured Bāṇarasa's Mahārājara-nāḍ, which was chiefly in the Kadapa District. The Chōla king Vīra-Nārāyaṇa or Parāntaka in 921 claims (*SII.* ii. 387) to have uprooted by force two Bāṇa kings, and conferred the title of Bāṇādhirāja on the Ganga prince Prithuvīpati II, great-grandson of Śivamāra I. The Bāṇas, therefore, though claiming friendship with Krishna Rāja, no doubt a Rāshṭrakūṭa king and an enemy of the Chōlas, seem to have lost their independence in the first half of the tenth century. Hence we find (Mb 126) Śambayya in 961 ruling a district under the Pallava king Iriva-Nolamba or Dilīpa.

But they by no means disappear from history. The Bāṇa kingdom is mentioned along with others in southern India of the twelfth century in Vaidyanātha's *Pratāpa-Rudriya.* Trivikrama-dēva, the author of the Prākrit grammar *Trivikrama-vṛitti*, of probably the fifteenth century, claims to be a descendant of the Bāṇa family (*IA.* xiii. 13). Moreover, inscriptions at Śrīvilliputtūr in the Tinnivelly District show that two kings, named Sundara Tol and Muttarasa Tirumala, who obtained possession of the Pāṇḍya throne in 1453 and 1476, call themselves Mahāvali Vāṇādhirāja (*ib.* xv. 173).

Sātakarnni inscription on stone

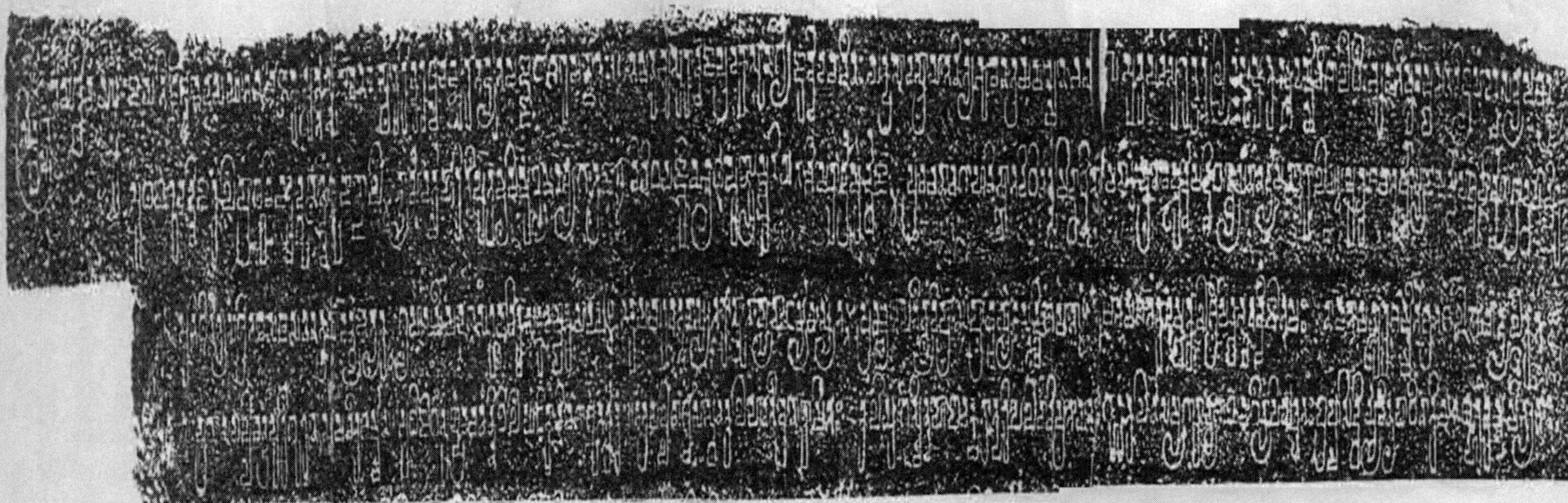

Kadamba inscription on stone

4. KADAMBAS

The Kadambas were independent rulers of the west of Mysore from the third to the sixth century, together with Haiga (North Kanara) and Tuluva (South Kanara). They were of Mysorean origin, and are identified with Banavāsi as their capital, which is on the west frontier of the Sorab tāluq, an ancient city mentioned as one of the places to which Aśōka sent a mission in the third century B.C., and also by Ptolemy in the second century A.D. Its Brahmanical name was Jayanti or Vaijayanti. In later times Banavāsi, or Banavase, as it is often spelt, was a Twelve Thousand province, corresponding more or less with the Shimoga District.

The origin of the Kadamba family is mixed up with various legendary stories (see my *Mysore Gazetteer*, i. 295) centering in a Mukkaṇṇa or Trinētra and a Mayūravarmma. The former, also called Jayanta Trilōchana, is described as their progenitor, and as a son of Śiva and Pārvatī. The country being at the time without a king, he is said to have obtained the throne on being spontaneously wreathed by the State elephant, an indication of his royal destiny. Mayūravarmma,[1] apparently of the fourth generation after him, seems to have established the family in power, and is hence also at times regarded as their founder. According to Sb 179, he had seventy-seven successors on the throne.

A fine pillar inscription at Tālgunda (Sk 176) gives a realistic account of the family, beginning with him. But here he is named Mayūraśarmma, the latter affix indicating a Brāhman. According to this record he was of a devout Brāhman family of Sthānakundūr (Tālgunda), an agrahāra founded by Mukkaṇṇa (see Sk 186) for Brāhmans whom he had induced to come from Ahichchhatra in the North and settle here (see also Nj 269), there being none at that time in the South. The family had growing near their house a *kadamba* tree, of which they took special care, and thus became

[1] Some Orientalists write this affix as *varman*, the only objection to which is that it is never met with in that form. And so with similar cases.

known as the Kadambas. Along with his teacher, Mayūraśarmma went to the Pallava capital (Kānchī—Conjeeveram, near Madras) in order to complete his vedic studies. There he had a fierce quarrel with the Pallava horse or stables,[1] by which he was so enraged at Kshattriyas lording it over Brāhmans that, in order to revenge himself, he resolved to adopt the life of a Kshattriya. Practising himself in the use of arms, he overcame the Pallava frontier guards, and escaped to the inaccessible forests near Śrīparvata (Karnūl District), where he became so powerful that he levied tribute from Bṛihad Bāṇa (the great Bāṇa) and other kings around. The Pallavas having led an army against him, he fell upon them like a hawk unawares in night attacks, and inflicted such loss upon them that they saw it was hopeless to put him down. Thus driven to take him as an ally, they recognised him as king of a territory stretching from the Western Ocean to Premāra. He was succeeded by his son Kangavarmma, whose son was Bhagīratha, whose son was Raghu, whose brother was Bhāgīrathi or Kākustha. The latter was a powerful ruler, and his daughters were given in marriage to the Gupta and other kings. He had a reservoir made for the temple (of Praṇaveśvara at Tālgunda, now in ruins) at which Sātakarṇṇi and other great kings had worshipped. His son was Śāntivarmma, who wore three crowns ; in whose time the inscription was composed and engraved.

This valuable and interesting record states that Mayūraśarmma was anointed to the throne by Shaḍānana, after meditating on Senāpati and the Mothers. In like manner other early grants describe the Kadambas as purified by meditation on Svāmi-Mahāsēna and the group of Mothers.[2] They are also said to be lords of Vaijayanti (Banavāsi), of the Mānavya-gōtra, Hāritīputras, and *pratikṛita-svādhyāya-charch-*

[1] All that the inscription says about this is : *tatra Pallavāśva-saṃsthēna kalahēna tīvrēna rōshitaḥ.*

[2] Shaḍānana, Senāpati, and Svāmi-Mahāsēna all refer to the god of war, Kārttikēya, son of Śiva. The Seven Mothers, Sapta Mātṛikā, were his nurses, and are identified with the Pleiades.

chāpārās.[1] As the grants are dated only by the ancient system of the seasons, or in regnal years (running from 2 to 11), they furnish no definite dates for the kings. But one (*IA.* vi. 23), issued when Kākusthavarmma was Yuvarāja, is ascribed to the eightieth year of his victory (*sva-vaijayika*), for which there is at present no explanation.

Certain allusions, however, occur which serve as a guide to the Kadamba period. It is known, for instance, from inscriptions that the Chalukya king Kīrttivarmma, who reigned from 566 to 597, subdued the Kadambas.[2] Their independence must therefore have been before this. On the Malavalli pillar (Sk 264) a Kadamba grant immediately follows one by Sātakarṇṇi, who, when he made his, was in possession of Banavāsi.[3] The Tālgunda pillar (Sk 176), again, names Sātakarṇṇi as one of the great kings who worshipped at the temple there. Between the time of the fall of the Śātavāhanas, the beginning of the third century, and that of the reign of the Chalukya king Kīrttivarmma, the latter part of the sixth century, seems thus marked out as the period of Kadamba independence; during which also they claim to have performed many horse-sacrifices—evidence of supreme power.

This estimate is confirmed by other considerations. For the statement that Kākustha gave his daughters in marriage to the Gupta and other kings most probably refers first to Samudra Gupta, the only one who is known to have made an expedition to the South, as recorded on the pillar at Allaha-

[1] This difficult phrase is rendered by Dr. Kielhorn (*EI.* vi. 17), "studying the requital (of good or evil) as their sacred text," and he adds: "If this interpretation be correct, I cannot help thinking that the epithet alludes to the history of the Kadambas as told in the Tālgund inscription. So long as the Kadambas were private Brāhmans it was one of their chief duties to study the sacred texts; in other words, they were *svādhyāya-charchāpārās.* When they had become kings, it was an equally sacred duty for them to requite good and evil; to do so was what the study of the Veda had been to them before; and thus, having been *svādhyāya-charchāpārās*, they then were *pratikṛita-svādhyāya-charchāpārās.*" Another translation proposed in *EI.* viii. 148 is: "well versed in repeating the sacred writings one by one."

[2] *Virugnam aśēshataḥ pṛithu-Kadamba-kadamba-kadambakaṃ* (*EI.* vi. 5).

[3] The translation should be: . . . Śiva[khada]varmma, having heard that they were formerly given by the Hāritīputra, of the Mānavya-gōtra, the lord of Vaijayanti, with great pleasure made the grant a second time to . . . (as pointed out by Dr. Fleet).

bad,[1] and this took place in the latter half of the fourth century. Then the Ganga king Taḍangāla Mādhava, for whom we have (Sk 52) the date 357, is said to have married a sister of the Kadamba king Krishnavarmma. She was thus a daughter of Kākustha, and the Gangas are another royal family to which one was given. But her son was an infant on his mother's lap when he was crowned in 430, and so here again we get the end of the fourth century for the time of Kākustha. The rare metre, too, which is employed in the main part of the Tālgunda inscription is one that has been found only in a few documents of the fourth or fifth century. The victory in the eightieth year of which Kākustha was Yuvarāja might (if it is correct) perhaps refer to the events by which Mayūravarmma (to give his name in the form of that of a king) gained his throne, which would thus be at the beginning of the fourth century. But if he had predecessors going back four or five generations, the rise of the Kadambas may safely be placed early in the third century, the time at which the Śātavāhana power came to an end.[2]

Our attention may now be directed to the old Anaji inscription (Dg 161). This informs us that Krishnavarmma-Rāja's army was totally defeated in a battle with Naṇakkāsa-Pallava-Rāja, and that the prince Śivanandavarmma, whose country was thereby ruined, retired in consequence from the world and gave himself up to a life of penance. That Krishnavarmma was a Kadamba king there can be little doubt, and Śivanandavarmma was probably his son. The latter was perhaps responsible for the disaster, and may have been the governor of a province in the east of the Kadamba dominions. But he is described as devoted to the feet of his mother and father, and to be born also in the family of the Kēkayas, who made intermarriages with the Ikshvākus (perhaps the Gangas, who claim to be descended from Ikshvāku). Now the Kadamba king Krishnavarmma is said (Bl 121) to have

[1] *GI.* No. 1.

[2] The latest date assigned to the Śātavāhanas is about 218 A.D. (see Bhandarkar, *EHI.* 45).

married a daughter of Kaikeya, and this identifies him with Śivanandavarmma's father. Vishnuvarmma was the eldest son born of the union, and Śivanandavarmma would thus appear to have been a younger brother of his. That bitter hostility existed at this period between the Kadambas and the Pallavas we have evidence in the statements (*IA.* vi. 24) that Mṛigēśavarmma was a destroying fire to the Pallavas, and that Ravivarmma uprooted Chaṇḍadaṇḍa, the lord of Kānchī, and therefore a Pallava.

By collocating the various items regarding them the following table[1] may be constructed of the Kadambas :—

- **Mukkaṇṇa, Trinētra, Trilōchana**
  - **Madhukēśvara**
    - **Mallinātha**
      - **Chandravarmma I**
        - **Chandravarmma II**
          - **Mayūraśarmma, Mayūravarmma**
            - **Kangavarmma**
              - **Bhagīratha**
                - **Raghu**
                - **Bhāgīrathi, Kākustha, Kākusthavarmma (end of fourth century)**
                  - **Śāntivarmma, Śāntivaravarmma**
                    - **Mṛigēśavarmma, Mṛigēśvaravarmma**
                      - **Ravivarmma**
                        - **Harivarmma**
                      - **Bhānuvarmma**
                      - **Śivaratha**
                    - **Māndhātṛivarmma**
                  - **Krishnavarmma I, m. the daughter of Kaikeya**
                    - **Vishnuvarmma, Vishnudāsa**
                      - **Simhavarmma**
                        - **Krishṇavarmma II**
                          - **Dēvavarmma**
                    - **Śivanandavarmma, was also of the Kēkaya family**
        - **Purandara**

---

[1] The one in vol. viii. Introd. p. 2, contains obvious mistakes, for which I am unable to account. In the above, the exact position and relationship of Māndhātṛivarmma are not known, but in 486 (Mi 110) the Ganga king Durvvinīta is, by a singular mistake, called the Māndhātṛivarmma of the age, instead of the Māndhātṛi, and the substitution may be intended as a flattering allusion to this king. Śivanandavarmma and Dēvavarmma have been placed conjecturally, but the latter it is known was the son of a Krishnavarmma.

Of the predecessors of Mayūravarmma we have no inscriptions, unless Śivakhadavarmma (Śivaskandavarmma) of the Malavalli pillar represents one. But Mukkaṇṇa is often mentioned, and seems to be an historical person. In Sk 186 he is said to have founded the Sthānakundūr agrahāra, the existence of which before the time of Mayūravarmma is clear from the Tālgunda inscription. In fact, the Brāhmans settled there from the north are said to have made an effort later to leave the province. But they were brought back again, and in order to prevent a repetition of the attempt, were compelled to leave unshorn a lock of hair on the forehead, as a distinguishing mark. From these are descended the present Haiga or Havika Brāhmans of the north-west of Mysore, who wear their hair in that fashion. Ethnologically, their colour and features support the tradition of a northern origin. Of the other kings, the first Chandravarmma appears to be the Chandrahāsa who is the hero of a popular romantic tale ; the second one is perhaps the progenitor of the Coorg race.

The Kadamba dominions seem to have been at times divided, and ruled by more than one king, while at others they embraced an extensive united empire. Hence the statements that Bhagīratha was the sole ruler, and that Śāntivarmma had three crowns. The latter is said to have been master of the entire Karṇṇāṭa region, while Krishnavarmma I is described as the sovereign of Dakshināpatha or the South. Though the proper capital was always Banavāsi, there were other royal seats,—at Palāsikā (Halsi in Belgaum District), at Uchchāśṛingi (which I am inclined to think may have been Uchchangidurga near Molakālmuru, and not the well-known one south of Bellary), and at Triparvata (not identified). The royal insignia, either at this period or later, were the lion crest and the monkey flag, and a musical instrument called *permatti*. The kings are styled dharmma-mahārājādhirāja, and their family god was Jayanti Madhukēśvara of Banavāsi.

For some time from the seventh century the Kadambas are not prominent, though names occasionally appear, which, owing to the absence of dates, are not easy to place. Such are those of Madhuvarmma (Sk 66), who must belong to the earlier period, Kundavarmma (Kp 38), and Mādivarmma (Cm 128). On the other hand we know from Mb 38 and 50 that the Kadamba princess Dīvāmbikā or Dīvalabbarasi was married to the Pallava Nolamba king Vīra-Mahēndra, who reigned from about 878 to 890.

But from the end of the tenth century the Kadambas emerge as rulers of various provinces. This was a period of general subversion of old dynasties in the South. The Rāshṭrakūṭas were brought to an end, and the Western Chālukyas regained ascendancy. The Pallavas and Eastern Chālukyas were subdued by the Chōlas, who also overthrew the Ganga sovereignty in Mysore. The Hoysalas were there rising to power, and the Nolambas, who were Pallavas, having subjected the Mahāvalis or Bāṇas, whom the Chōlas finally absorbed, were forming the Nolambavāḍi province of Mysore. Following upon this period of general commotion and transition, we find Kadambas ruling Bayal-nāḍ (the Wynaad) from the tenth to the twelfth century, Manjarābād in the eleventh century, Hāngal (in Dharwar) and Goa from the tenth to the thirteenth century, Lunke (near Molakālmuru) in the eleventh and twelfth century, Nāgarakhaṇḍa (the Shikārpur tāluq) in the twelfth century, and the Banavāsi Twelve Thousand (the Shimoga District) from the tenth to the fourteenth century.

Inscriptions of the twelfth century give us different versions of their origin and genealogy. Sk 117, at Belgāmi, derives them from a person named Kadamba, who had four arms and an eye in his forehead, and who was born from a drop of sweat that fell from the forehead of Hara or Śiva. From him were descended Mayūravarmma, Ravivarmma, Nṛigavarmma, and Kīrttivarmma, in whose line arose Vikrama Tailapa or Tailama, whose son was Kāma-Dēva, whose son was Malla, whose son was Sōma, ruling the Banavāsi country in 1118.[1]

[1] An inscription of 1108 at Kargudari in the Hāngal tāluq gives much more detail (*IA.* x. 249).

Dg 35, at Harihar, derives the family from Mayūravarmma, also called Mukkaṇṇa, who was born to Rudra or Śiva under a *kadamba* tree. On account of the eye in his forehead, the crown could not be bound there, as it would cover up the eye. The crown or diadem was therefore bound near his knee, where it would show well. Growing up in the shade of the *kadamba* tree, his family became known as the Kadambas. In course of time Barmma-Dēva was born in the line, whose son was Boppa-Dēva, whose son was Sōyi-Dēva or Sōma, ruling in the Nāgarakhaṇḍa Seventy in about 1160. Sk 236, at Bandalikke, says that a king Sōma, when Paraśurāma destroyed all the Kshattriyas, was saved by his guru Aśvatthāma or Īśvarāmśa. They went to the Kailāsa mountain to worship Pārvatī, and there saw the king Nanda, who had been supplicating Śiva for a long time for a son without result. Suddenly some *kadamba* flowers fell there, and on offering these the god appeared, granting Nanda the boon that he should have two sons called Kadambas, at the same time introducing him to Iśvarāmśa. The two sons thus born were Kīrttivarmma and Maylavarmma. To the latter was born Tayla, whose son was Śānta, whose son was Maila. After many others, there was born in his line Boppa, whose son was Sōma or Nigalanka-malla, ruling in Nāgarakhaṇḍa in 1174. Of these three accounts, which add little to our knowledge of the Kadambas, the first may be of some value. The other two were evidently invented for the purpose of glorifying Sōma-Dēva, and the last one to flatter the Kalachurya king Rāyamurāri-Sōma as well. But in the later stages they probably give the correct names of the kings who preceded.

The Kadambas do not disappear from history till the rise of Vijayanagar in the fourteenth century, and the founders of that empire may have been connected with them. Actually the last Kadamba inscription is Sa 32, the date of which is 1307. The royal line sprung from the simple Brāhman student whose outraged feelings in so singular a manner transformed him into a Kshattriya thus held the field for a thousand years.

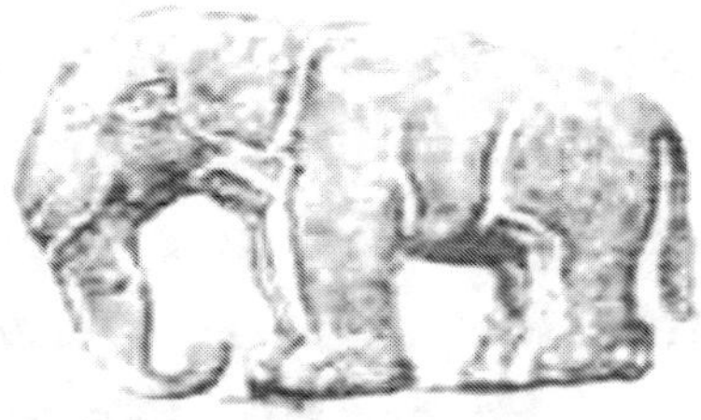

5. GANGAS

The Gangas ruled over the greater part of Mysore from the second to the eleventh century. Their grants have been found in all parts, from Coorg in the west to North Arcot and Tanjore in the east, and from the extreme south of the Mysore State in the south to the Belgaum District of Bombay in the north. To the time of Śivamāra I (680) these are mostly on copper plates, though a few, such as Mb 263 and Cm 50, are on stone. From his time stone inscriptions are the most numerous. The Ganga territory was known as Gangavāḍi, a Ninety-six Thousand province, and the existing Gangaḍikāras, who form the largest section of the agricultural population of Mysore, represent its former subjects, their name being a contraction from Gangavāḍikāra. At the time of the foundation of the Ganga kingdom its chief city was Kuvalāla (Kolar), but the capital was removed in the third century to Talakāḍ on the Kāvēri, in the south-east of the Mysore District. This remained the permanent capital, although the royal residence was fixed at Mankunda (west of Channapatna) in the seventh century, and at Mānya-pura (Maṇṇe, north of Nelamangala) in the eighth century.

The name, Ganga, of the dynasty is not an ordinary one, and the only other occurrence of such a name in history is in the Greek and Roman accounts relating to the times of Alexander the Great and Seleucus. Chandra Gupta, and the Nandas before him, are described as ruling over the Prasii and the Gangaridæ. The latter, the people of the Ganges valley, are mentioned by Ptolemy; and the Latin authors Virgil, Valerius Flaccus, and Curtius also make reference to them. Pliny writes of the Gangaridæ Calingæ, or Gangas of Kalinga, who, as he terms them *gens novissima*, were not so ancient. We know from inscriptions that there was an important line of Ganga kings in Kalinga in the seventh and eighth centuries, and Ganga kings continued there down to as late a period as the sixteenth century. But the Gangas in Mysore were the main line, as the Kalinga Gangas admit. Both branches trace their name to the river Gangā or Ganges.

Although Ganga inscriptions professing to be of the third century have been found, the earliest which contain a detailed account of the origin of the family are stone inscriptions of the eleventh and twelfth centuries in the Nagar and Shimoga tāluqs (the chief being Nr 35, Sh 10, 4, 64). If any such of older date existed, which is not improbable, they have been lost or destroyed. According to the above records—which were inscribed in the time of the great Chalukya king Vikramāditya or Vikramānka, the son of a Ganga princess—the Gangas were of the Ikshvāku and therefore Solar race. They were descended from Dhananjaya, whose son was Hariśchandra, of whom the first two say Daḍiga and Mādhava were the sons. The other two make them the sons of Padmanābha descended from Hariśchandra, and interpose a number of steps. Thus Hariśchandra's son was Bharata, whose wife was Vijayamahādēvi. At the time of conception she bathed in the Gangā or Ganges to remove her languor, and the son born in consequence was named Gangādatta, whence his descendants were called the Gangas.[1] After a time there was Vishnugupta, who, by performing a certain sacrifice, pleased the god Indra and received from him an elephant. Vishnugupta had two sons, Bhagadatta and Śrīdatta, between whom he divided his dominions. To Bhagadatta was given Kalinga, and he ruled as Kalinga Ganga. Śrīdatta had the ancestral kingdom, together with the elephant, which thus became the Ganga crest. Later on there was Priyabandhu, to whom the god Indra gave

[1] The Kalinga account (*IA.* xiii. 275) is that Turvasu, the son of Yayāti, being without sons, practised self-restraint and propitiated the river Gangā, the bestower of boons, by which means he obtained a son, the unconquerable Gāngēya, whose descendants were victorious in the world as the Ganga line.

five tokens, with a warning that they would disappear if the kings adopted any other faith. At length arose Padmanābha, who by his penance obtained two sons. When, some time after, Mahīpāla, the ruler of Ujjayini, suddenly attacked him, demanding the five tokens, Padmanābha refused to surrender them and prepared for war. But first sent them away, along with his two sons, to the South, accompanied by their sister and attendant Brāhmans. At the time of their departure he gave his sons the names Daḍiga and Mādhava, and the history continues only in connection with them. Their line was the Ganga line—*tad anvayō Gangānvayaḥ* (Nr 35).

When they arrived at Perūr, which is still distinguished from other Perūrs as Ganga-Perūr (in Kadapa District), they met there the Jain āchārya Simhanandi. He was interested in the story of these Ganga princes, and taking them by the hand, gave them instruction and training, and eventually procured for them a kingdom.[1]

This was obtained as a boon from the goddess Padmāvatī, who confirmed it with the gift of a sword. Mādhava, who is said to have been but a boy at the time,[2] seizing the sword with a shout, struck with it a stone pillar, which broke in two. So favourable as an omen, this feat is mentioned in nearly all the inscriptions that refer to him. What the pillar was it is difficult to say, but one account describes it as an obstacle in the way of his gaining the throne (SB 54). The kingdom thus founded was named Gangavāḍi, a Ninety-six Thousand country. Its boundaries were—north, Marandale (not identified); east, Toṇḍa-nāḍ (the Madras country east from Mysore); west, the ocean in the direction of Chēra (Cochin and Travancore); south, Kongu (Coimbatore and Salem

[1] He is named as a great poet by Indrabhūti, in his *Samayabhūshana*, along with Ēlāchārya (Padmanandi, the guru of Śākaṭāyana) and Pūjyapāda (*IA.* xii. 20). In SB 54 he is mentioned next to Samantabhadra, who belongs to the second century; and the Bāṇa plates (*SII.* ii. 387) say the Ganga dynasty obtained increase from the great Simhanandi (*yas Simhanandi-mahima-pratilabdha-vṛiddhir Gangānvayō*). In Nr 35 and 36 he is described as *Ganga-rājyamam māḍida Simhanandy-āchāryya*—the āchāryya Simhanandi who made the Ganga kingdom.

[2] A little boy playing at big boys' games (*prabala-śiśu-līlēna śiśunā*).

Districts). Its chief city was Kuvalāla[1] (Kolar), and its stronghold Nandagiri (Nandidroog).

The first king was Mādhava, who was called Konguṇivarmma,[2] a title used for all the subsequent kings of the line, and they are styled dharmma-mahādhirājah or dharmma-mahārājādhirājah. They are said to be of the Kānvāyana-gōtra, and some records trace them back to Kanva. A line of Kanva kings ruled immediately before the Śātavāhanas. Konguṇivarmma would naturally be brought into conflict with the Bāṇas, who were in power to the east and north of Kolar. He is accordingly said to have been consecrated to conquer the Bāṇa-maṇḍala, and to be a wild-fire in consuming the stubble of the forest called Bāṇa. Towards the west, Daḍiga and Mādhava are said to have erected a *chaityālaya* at Mandali near Shimoga, when on their way to subdue Konkaṇa. The date 103 is given for Konguṇivarmma in Nj 110, in which he is called the first Ganga, and is said to have made a grant then of Kuḍiyāla (in the Nanjangūḍ tāluq). If reliable, the date must have been very early in his reign. The Tamil chronicle called *Kongudēśa-rājākkal* gives 189 as a date in the first king's reign, and he is said to have reigned for fifty-one years. In either case the rise of the Gangas falls in the second century.

He was succeeded by Kiṛiya Mādhava, the son of Daḍiga, born in Kōlāla, who seems to have been not at all eager to fill a throne, as he is said to have assumed the honours of the kingdom only for the sake of the good government of his subjects. He was of a literary turn of mind, a touchstone for (testing) gold—the learned and poets, was proficient in the *nīti-śāstra* or science of politics, and wrote a treatise on the *dattaka-sūtra* or law of adoption.

Harivarmma, his son, next came to the throne, and he removed the capital to Taḷekkāḍ or Talakāḍ (Talavana-pura in Sanskrit), situated on the river Kāvērī in the south-east of the Mysore District. He is commonly described as having

[1] This name appears later as Kovalāla, and then Kōlāla.

[2] A common form is Konganivarmma, and in rare cases Konguḷivarmma, Kongoṇivarmma and Kongiṇivarmma.

employed elephants in war, and having gained great wealth by the use of the bow. Two grants of his time have been found. The first (*IA*. viii. 212), obtained in Tanjore, gives his name in the Tamil form Arivarmma. It records a gift by him, in 247, of the Oṛekōḍu village in the Maisu-nāḍ Seventy (now Varakōḍu in the east of Mysore tāluq[1]) under somewhat interesting circumstances. A Bauddha disputant named Vādimadagajēndra (a rutting elephant as an orator) in the pride of his learning affixed to the main door of the palace at Talavana-pura a *patra*[2] (as a challenge) in which he asserted the claim that he was the foremost scholar in logic, grammar, and all other branches of knowledge.[3] Whereupon a Brāhman named Mādhava-bhaṭṭa put his pretensions to the proof (before the Court), and when the opponent speaker denied the existence of the soul, established its existence, and with the elephant-goad his speech forced him to crouch down (like a vanquished elephant). The king being pleased, gave the Brāhman the title Vādībhasimha (a lion to the elephant disputant) and with it the Oṛekōḍu village. Whatever objection may be taken to this inscription on palæographical or other grounds, it must be confessed that the details related in it are singularly in keeping with its professed period. The other grant of this king is in the Tagaḍūr plates (Nj 122) of the date 266. In this, a Gāvuṇḍa or farmer who had made important captures in a battle at Henjeṛu (now Hemāvati, on the northern border of Sīra tāluq) received as a reward the Appogāl village. Yet another record may be mentioned. This is Mb 157, the Muḍiyanūr Bāṇa plates of 338. On the back of the first plate is an erased Ganga grant, which, as far as it is legible, goes down to the time of Harivarmma, but no fresh information regarding him is to be obtained from it.

[1] Hancha, one of the boundary villages, still exists. The inscriptions at Varakōḍu appear in My 46 to 49, one of which is in Tamil. Near to Varakōḍu is the ancient village of Varuṇa (for inscriptions there see My 34-45 and 55) connected with a Chālukyan family of the name of Goggi.

[2] The palmyra leaf commonly used for writing upon.

[3] One is reminded of Martin Luther affixing his theses to the door of the church at Wittenberg.

His son Vishṇugōpa next became king. He is said to have been devoted to the worship of gurus, cows, and Brāhmans, and seems to have set aside the Jain faith for that of Nārāyaṇa (Vishṇu), for the five tokens before mentioned now vanished. In one place (DB 67) his mental energy is said to have been unimpaired to the end of life, implying that he lived to a great age. In kingly policy he was the equal of Bṛihaspati, and in valour equal to Śakra (Indra).

His son, or grandson, Taḍangāla Mādhava, followed.[1] Of him it is said (DB 68) that his two arms were grown stout and hard with athletic exercises, and that he had purchased his kingdom by his personal strength and valour. He favoured the worship of Tryambaka (Śiva), and revived the donations for long-ceased festivals of the gods and Brāhman endowments, being daily eager to extricate the ox of merit from the thick mire of the Kali-yuga in which it had sunk. He married the sister of the Kadamba king Krishnavarmma, and she, as above shown, must have been a daughter of the famous Kākustha. There are two grants of this reign. One (Sh 52; *IA.* vii. 172), of apparently the date 357, is on plates engraved in a curious jumble of alphabets,[2] and records a grant of land to a Gavuḍa or farmer who forced his way into Henjeṛu (see above) and rescued Rājamalla's wife and guards. The other is Mr 73, of his 13th year, about 370. In this he makes a grant, on the advice of the āchārya Vīradēva, for the Arhad temple in the Perbbolal village of the Mudukottūr district. The fragmentary stone inscription Mb 263 also stops at this reign.

The son born to Mādhava by the Kadamba princess is known as Avinīta. Several inscriptions state that he was crowned when an infant on his mother's lap. He may therefore have been a posthumous son, and his father evidently had a very long reign. Avinīta was brought up

[1] According to Sh 4 he was the son of Pṛithivī-Ganga, who was the son of Vishṇugōpa, and his father cannot have come to the throne.

[2] Other instances of plates engraved in a similar mixed fashion are the Kalinga Ganga inscriptions in *IA.* xiv. 10 and *EI.* iii. 220.

as a Jain, the learned Vijayakīrtti being his preceptor (Mr 72). The king himself is described as being the first among the learned, of unstinted liberality, and devoted to protecting the South in the maintenance of castes and religious orders (DB 68). The grant of his first year (Mr 72), which from DB 67 we can assign to 430, was made to two Arhad or Jain temples, one at Uranūr and the other at Perūr. In the latter case the grant consisted of a fourth part of the *karshāpana*[1] levied as outside customs. In DB 67, which is of his 29th year, 459, a Brāhman of Tippūr (in Dod-Ballāpur tāluq) was given a village called Mēlūr (perhaps the one in Sidlaghaṭṭa tāluq), with freedom from all the eighteen castes. This is an interesting allusion, as evidence of the antiquity of these *paṇas*, composed of the agricultural, artisan, and trading classes, who form the Right-hand and Left-hand factions. The king, it says, at this time held Brāhmans as supreme, and was devoted to the worship of Hara (Śiva). Still, in 466 he made a grant to a Jain, as recorded in the Mercara plates (Cg 1). From DB 68 we arrive at 482 for the termination of his reign, and seeing that he was crowned at or soon after his birth, this is not allowing an unreasonable time for him.

Durvvinīta, his son, thus succeeded him in 482. His tutor is described (Tm 23) as "the divine who was the author of the *Śabdāvatāra*," that is, the celebrated Jain grammarian Pūjyapāda, and he is said (Mi 110) to have walked according to the example of his guru. He thereby acquired a taste for literature, and wrote a commentary on fifteen sargas of the *Kirātārjunīya*, a Sanskrit poem by Bhāravi. He is also no doubt the Durvvinīta named in Nṛipatunga's *Kavirājamārgga* as one of the distinguished early Kannaḍa authors. He married the daughter of Skandavarmma, the Rāja of Punnāḍ, who, as a royal princess, claimed the privilege of *svayamvara* by choosing

[1] Copper coins of 80 *ratis* weight, belonging to the earliest native coinage (Rapson, *Indian Coins*)

him for herself, though from her birth she had been intended by her father, on the advice of his own guru, for the son of another (DB 68). Punnāḍ is of course the Punnāṭa in the south-west of Mysore to which reference has been made before, in connection with the Jain migration under Bhadrabāhu. Many inscriptions state that Durvvinīta waged sanguinary wars for the possession of Andari, Ālattūr (in Coimbatore District), Porulare (? in Chingleput District), Pennagaram (in Salem District), and other places. He thus considerably extended the limits of the kingdom to the east and south. He seems also to have annexed the whole of Pānnāḍ and Punnāḍ (Tm 23). Another inscription (Nr 35) says that he captured Kāḍuveṭṭi on the field of battle, and placed his own daughter's son on the throne in Jayasimha's hereditary kingdom (that of the Pallavas). And this is confirmed by the interesting old Siragunda stone inscription (Cm 50), in which he is called Nirvvinīta. Nr 35 indulges in puns on the Vinīta names, and says that these kings were like *avi-nītar* (riders on the ram, that is, Agni or fire) to the forest the army of *avinīta* (wicked) hostile kings, and *a-vinītar* (unbending) in successful and severe battles,—such being their reputation in *avanī* (the world). The Vinītēśvara temple mentioned in Ch 63 may have been a memorial of them. The first grant we have of this king's time is Bn 141, of his 3rd year, 485, recording a donation to a Brāhman named Vasaśarmma, but the details are missing. Then, after those relating to him above referred to, we have DB 68, of his 35th year, 517, making a grant at Bempūr (Bēgūr in the Bangalore tāluq) to a Brāhman named Dēvaśarmma, who was called Mahadēva. This inscription attributes to the king, as in the case of his father, the maintenance of the castes and religious orders which prevailed in the South. He appears to have favoured the religion of Vishnu. How much longer he ruled we do not know.

But he was followed by his son Mushkara or Mokkara, of whom little is known. Savage kings are said to have rubbed against one another in paying homage at his feet. From the inscription published in *IA.* xiv. 229, we learn that he married the daughter of the Sindhu Rāja. The Mokkara-vasati mentioned in the Lakshmēśvara inscription in Dharwar (*IA.* vii. 101) must be a memorial of him, and points to an extension of the Ganga kingdom in that direction. From this time the State seems to have adhered to the Jain religion.

Of Śrīvikrama, son by the Sindhu princess, who came next, no particulars are recorded, except that he was the abode of fourteen branches of learning, and well versed in the science of politics in all its branches.

He had two sons, who in turn succeeded to the throne. The elder, Bhūvikrama, was a great warrior, whose chest was marked with the scars of wounds inflicted in battle by the tusks of elephants. He defeated the Pallava king (Narasimhapōtavarmma) in a great battle at Vilanda, and is said to have captured the whole of the Pallava dominions. Some other details are given in Md 113 and Tm 23. On account of his successes in war he received the title Śrīvallabha, and in Sr 160 is called Dugga. He made Mankunda (Channapaṭṇa tāluq) the royal residence. From Md 113 we obtain the date 670 for the end of his reign.

His younger brother Śivamāra followed, and ruled to at least 713. The Eṛeganga of *IA.* xiv. 229, who was governing the Toṛe-nāḍ Five Hundred, the Kongal-nāḍ Two Thousand, and the Male Thousand, and who made a grant to Vinadi and Keśadi, the chief temple priests of Panekoḍupāḍi, may have been his son (though not so stated) who is unnamed in the genealogical lists. Śivamāra was also known as Nava Kāma, and as Śishṭa-priyaḥ (beloved by the good), the name by which he describes and signs himself (Md 113). He is moreover styled Pṛithivī-Kongaṇi. He had two Pallava princes in his charge (Md 113), perhaps as hostages, or as their guardian, which goes to confirm the account of his elder brother's conquests. They were the sons of the Pallava yuvarāja, who is not named, and are called Pallavādhirājas. Beginning with

Nj 26 of this reign, which records a grant in the Punnāḍ Six Thousand, stone inscriptions become the general rule.

It was during the sixth and seventh centuries, while the Gangas were thus engaged in conquests to the east and south, that we hear of attacks on them in the north-west. The Kadamba king Mṛigēśavarmma claims (*IA.* vi. 24) to have overthrown (*utsādī*) the lofty (*tunga*) Gangas, which apparently indicates no more than some encroachment on their territory, as they were certainly not overthrown in the usual sense of that word. The more powerful Chalukyas, who were invading the South and subdued the Kadambas in the sixth century, naturally came into contact with the Gangas. Thus Kīrttivarmma, who reigned from 566 to 597, is said (*IA.* xix. 17) to have inflicted damage (*avamardda*) on them as well as on a number of other kings. And in about 608 the Ganga and Ālupa kings (the latter belonging to South Kanara) are said (*EI.* vi. 10) to have felt the highest pleasure in attending on Pulikēśi. In 694 they are said (Dg 66) to have been, along with the other principal kings of the South, brought into his service by Vinayāditya. But in this passage the Ālupas and Gangas are distinguished by the epithet *maula*, which means ancient, of long standing, of original unmixed descent,—unimpeachable testimony to their having been long established in their kingdoms, and that their ancestry could be traced back for a considerable period. It also seems to show that they were entitled to special consideration.

The Gangas may be said to have reached the height of prosperity during the long reign of Śrīpurusha, who came next, and in whose time the kingdom was called the Śrī-rājya or fortunate kingdom. He was the grandson of Śivamāra, whose son is not named and had therefore probably died before his father. This son may have been the prince Eṛeganga above noted, as the heir-apparent seems often to have been a governor of Kongal-nāḍ, along with other western provinces. Śrīpurusha's personal name was Muttarasa, and he is also called Pṛithivī-Kongaṇi. His date is fixed by Mg 36 of 750,

Ganga stone inscription at Talakāḍ (TN 1)

Now in the Victoria Institute, Mysore.
Pūrvada Haḷa-Kannaḍa characters and language.

his 25th year, Gd 47 of 762, and Ng 85 of 776, his 50th year. TN 1 is of his 1st year, Kl 78 of his 26th year, Mb 80 of his 42nd year. There are numerous other records of his time without dates. One has recently been found of his 7th year.

Bannūr seems to be called his town in TN 115, and his house was apparently situated there. Perhaps to the time before he came to the throne belong Ht 86, in which he appears as ruling the Kerekunda Three Hundred, and Bp 13, in which he is ruling the Elenagar-nāḍ Seventy, the Āvanya-nāḍ Thirty, and the Ponkunda Twelve. The latter calls him Mādhava Muttarasa, and speaks of the army marching against Mahāvali Bāṇarasa. Mi 99 says that while Śrīpurusha was ruling, the Raṭṭas rose up against Gangavāḍi. But the chief military exploit of his reign was a crushing defeat of the Pallavas in a battle at Vilarde. Nr 35 says that he slew the valiant Kāḍuveṭṭi of Kānchī, captured the Pallava state umbrella, and took away from him the title Permmānaḍi, which is always afterwards assumed by the Gangas, and is often used alone to designate them. He is said to have written a work on elephants, called *Gaja-śāstra.* He removed the royal residence to Mānyapura (Maṇṇe, Nelamangala tāluq), and this was before 733.

The details of the grant in Mg 36, of his 25th year, point to the east of the Bellary District as being within the limits of his kingdom northwards. Ng 85, of his 50th year, shows him making a grant for a Jain temple erected by Kandāchchi, granddaughter of Pallavādhirāja and wife of Parama Gula, the Nirggunda Rāja, whose father Duṇḍu is described as a confounder of the Bāṇa family. In Kl 6, of Śrīpurusha's 28th year, we have (his son) Śivamāra ruling Kadambūr. In Kd 145 we have his son Vijayāditya ruling Āsandi-nāḍ. In Sp 65 we have his son Duggamāra Eṛeyappa ruling Kovalāla-nāḍ; in Mb 80, of the king's 42nd year, the same prince was ruling the Kuvalāla-nāḍ Three Hundred and the Ganga Six Thousand, while his queen was ruling Āgali; in Mb 255 he was ruling the same provinces, and the army was sent against Kampili (on the Tungabhadrā in the north of the Bellary District); in Sp 57, besides the above two provinces, he was ruling Panne-nāḍ, Belattūr-nāḍ, the Pulvaki-nāḍ Thousand, the Mu..-nāḍ Sixty, and one or two others whose names are not clear.

Śrīpurusha's son Śivamāra Saigoṭṭa came to the throne in the latter part of the eighth century.[1] In his reign the prosperity of the Gangas underwent a reverse, and they became subject to calamities which threatened the extinction of the Ganga power altogether. These arose from the Rāshṭrakūṭas, who had recently, under their king Krishna I, ousted the Western Chālukyas and established their own supremacy. Krishna's son Dhōra, also called Dhruva, Nirupama, and Dhārāvarsha, who had superseded his elder brother (owing to the latter's addiction to pleasure and indifference to his royal duties, *EI.* iv. 287), seized and imprisoned the king of the Gangas, who are expressly said (Nl 61; *EI.* vi. 248) never to have been conquered by others. The motive for this harsh step may possibly have been that Dhārāvarsha, having determined to set aside his elder son Kambha or Stambha in favour of a younger son Gōvinda,—whom he appointed yuvarāja or heir-apparent, and to ensure whose succession to the throne he even offered to abdicate,—had it in his mind to compensate the former by giving him the Ganga kingdom. But another account (*EI.* iii. 104) states that Ganga was one of the hostile kings whom Gōvinda brought into the country as an aid to himself. Hence the resentment against Ganga. In any case, we find Kambharasa in Hg 93 governing the Ninety-six Thousand (a common designation of the Ganga territory) under his father. In SB 24, where he is called Raṇāvalōka Kambaiya, he is said to be ruling the kingdom of the world; and in 802 was still in power (Nl 61). After him, in 812, when his

[1] From Cl 8 it appears that Duggamāra attempted to dispute the succession, but was opposed by Singapōta, the Nolamba king.

younger brother Gōvinda Prabhūtavarsha was on the throne, we find (Gb 61) Chāki Rāja was chief ruler (*adhirāja*) of the entire (*aśēsha*) Ganga-maṇḍala. This is the latest date we have for the Rāshṭrakūṭa occupation.

Gōvinda, either, as seems likely, on the death of his elder brother, or moved by reasons of compassion or policy, released Ganga from his "long and painful confinement," but owing to his hostility had again to confine him (*EI.* vi. 249). During this period of release may have occurred the victorious attack he made at Mudugundūr (Maṇḍya tāluq) on the Vallabha (or Rāshṭrakūṭa) army encamped there, which may have been the cause of his being again consigned to prison. Eventually, however, Gōvinda not only reinstated him in his kingdom, but took part in his coronation, he and the Pallava (or Ganga-Pallava) king Nandivarmma binding the diadem on his brow with their own hands (Yd 60, Nl 60[1]). The actual ceremony may perhaps not have been performed before. Kl 231 and Gd 54 show that Śivamāra was ruling. According to *IA.* xviii. 309, his reign extended into that of the Rāshṭrakūṭa king Amōghavarsha, who came to the throne in 814. Śivamāra Saigotta is there presented as his feudatory (the solitary instance in which the Gangas acknowledge an over-lord); the crowning is mentioned; and Śivamāra is said to be ruling the Gangavāḍi Ninety-six Thousand up to Marandale as his boundary (see above, p. 31). He erected a Jain temple in Kummadavāḍa (now Kalbhāvi, in Belgaum District).

Of Śivamāra himself, besides what is said in other places, a lengthy account is given in Nl 60. He is said, here and in Kl 90, to have been brought into a world of mingled troubles, or placed in a world of endless calamities, like matted pairs of top-knots or twisted top-knots. But he seems to have been a learned and accomplished man, supporter of the fine arts, builder of an ornamental bridge (see Md 113), esteemed as a poet, proficient in logic and philosophy, skilled

[1] It was no doubt Nandivarmma's claim to Ganga descent which led to his being invited to join in the performance of this important act of State.

in all matters connected with the stage and drama, and a special authority on the treatment of elephants and horses. He wrote an important work on elephants, called *Gajāshṭakam*, expounding his system (Nr 35).

During his detention as a prisoner, his son Mārasimha claims to represent the Ganga rule. Sr 160 shows him as the Yuvarāja, under the name Mārasing-Eṛeyappa and with the title Lōka Trinētra. Two Pallava princes, father and son, obtained permission from him to make a grant. The father's name was Kolliyarasa, and from Sb 10 it would seem that the Rāshṭrakūṭa king Gōvinda Prabhūtavarsha took Kolli into his service. Nl 60, dated in 797, describes Mārasimha, though only Yuvarāja, as ruling the entire (*akhaṇḍa*) Gangamaṇḍala, and decorating all the feudatories. But he must have died while his father was still in captivity. For Nj 269 contains the important statement that Śivamāra gave charge of his kingdom to his own younger brother Vijayāditya, who, like Bharata, knowing the earth (or land) to be his elder brother's wife, refrained from enjoying her (as his own).

Śivamāra had a second son, who is called Pṛithivīpati (or Piḷduvipati). He gave shelter to refugees from Amōghavarsha, and defeated the Pāṇḍya king Varaguna at Śrī-Purambiyam (near Kumbhakōṇam [1]). But no more is heard of him, so both he and Vijayāditya probably died before Śivamāra. For the latter was succeeded on the throne by Vijayāditya's son, called Rājamalla (or Rāchamalla) Satyavākya, which are titles borne by all the Ganga kings who came after. Rājamalla is said (Yd 60) to have rescued from the Rāshṭrakūṭas his country, which they had held too long, as Vishnu in the form of a Boar rescued the Earth from the infernal regions. He thus established his independence. He also married Singapōta's granddaughter, Pallavādhirāja's daughter, the younger sister of Nolambādhirāja. But he was not suffered to remain unmolested. For the inscription at *EI.* vi. 25 informs us that a chief named Bankēśa was ordered by Amōghavarsha to uproot

[1] *Salem Manual*, ii. 387.

Bas-relief of the Death of Nītimārgga, on Doḍḍa Huṇḍi

the lofty forest of fig trees—Gangavāḍi, difficult to be cut down. He accordingly captured Kedala (Kaidala near Tumkur), which was strongly fortified and defended. Having occupied that part of the country, he drove away the hostile lord of Talavana-pura (the Ganga king of Talakāḍ). He then sprang like a lion across the Kāvērī, and shook the dominion of him who was even able to shake the world (meaning the Ganga). But at this point he was recalled by Amōghavarsha on account of some rebellion at home, which looks like an excuse for his having been forced to retire. But that he took Kaidala may be true, as Tm 9 and Nl 84 show us a line of chiefs established there and at Śivaganga who claimed to be lords of Mānyakhēta, the Rāshṭrakūṭa capital.

Rājamalla was succeeded by his son styled Nītimārgga, a title also used by the subsequent kings of this line. His real name was Eṟeyanga, but he is mentioned as Raṇa Vikramayya in Yd 60. He gained a great victory (Kl 90, Nj 269) over the Vallabha army at Rājāṟāmuḍu, which is to the north of the Kolar District. Besides this, he captured Bāṇarasa's Mahārājara-nāḍ (Mb 228). This is called in Ct 30 the Mārājavāḍi Seven Thousand, with Vallūr as its capital. It was chiefly in the Kadapa District. Kl 79 shows that under Nītimārgga the Pallava king Nolambādhirāja was ruling the Ganga Six Thousand, and sent against Bāṇarasa a chief named Pompalla, who was killed in a battle at Murggepāḍi. At the head of the Doḍḍahuṇḍi stone (TN 91) is a rude but interesting bas-relief depicting Nītimārgga's death, the exact date of which event is not known, but his eldest son Satyavākya was present. One of the king's followers evinced his fidelity by being buried under him. Nītimārgga's younger sister Jāyabbe was married to the Pallava king Nolambādhirāja (Si 24, 38), who was Pōlalchōra Nolamba.

Rājamalla Satyavākya (II), the eldest son of Nītimārgga, was his successor on the throne, and distinguished himself in a battle at Rēmiya (Nj 269). An inscription of his occurs in North Arcot District (*EI.* iv. 140). His younger brother named Būtugēndra or Būtarasa was Yuvarāja in 870 (Nj 75), and governing Kongal-nāḍ and Pūnāḍ. Būtarasa is said (Nj 269) to have defeated Rājarāja (which is a Chōla name), and in Hiriyūr (Chitaldroog District) and other places was victorious over Mahēndra, the Pallava Nolamba king. Five times he overcame in fight the Kongas (Tamil people of Coimbatore and Salem), who resisted his tying up elephants, and he captured many herds according to old custom. He married the daughter of the Rāshṭrakūṭa king Amōghavarsha I.

He must have died before his elder brother the king, as Ereganga, his son by the Rāshṭrakūṭa princess, became Yuvarāja (Sr 147). This prince his uncle Rājamalla Satyavākya associated with himself in the government, and crowned under the name of Ereyappa (Nj 269). The date of which act must have been about 886, as Ag 70 makes Satyavākya's 37th year correspond with Ereyappa's 21st year, and the former's 18th year was 887 (Cg 2). In Hg 103 Ereyappa appears governing Nugu-nāḍ and Navale-nāḍ. In Hs 92 he is ruling the Kongal-nāḍ Eight Thousand, and Būtuga's queen ruling Kūrgal. In Nj 130 we have Permmāḍi (the supreme king), the Queen, and Ereyappa acting together. In other cases we have Permmāḍi and Ereyappa acting together, as in Nj 139, which is of Satyavākya's 22nd year. Perhaps the queen was now dead. In Satyavākya's 29th year we have mention of Ereyappa's son (Kn 48).

Sh 96 shows Ereyappa reigning as supreme, and Būtuga under him governing the Manḍali-nāḍ. Bn 83 and Kn 52 are also of his reign; Cp 48 may be, and Cp 161, which is dated in 913. Ereyappa is often distinguished by a special set of epithets not used of any other kings of the Ganga line, as in Sr 134, Kr 38, Bn 83. He is called in some cases Nītimārgga (II), as in Ag 26, 61, and in others Satyavākya, as in Cn 251. But being engaged in hostilities with Mahēndra, whom he eventually slew in battle, perhaps at Penjeru, he obtained the distinctive title Mahēndrāntaka. From Md 13 of 895, Mi 52 of 897, Md 14 of 907, and Kd 6 it would appear as if Mahēndra and his son Ayyapa, both styled Nolambādhirāja, exercised some authority in the Ganga kingdom. But Cm 129 describes an attack upon the latter. At about this period the Chōlas having suddenly uprooted the Bāṇas, the Chōla king Parāntaka claims in 921 (*SII.* ii. 387) to have conferred the Bāṇa sovereignty on the Ganga prince Prithivīpati, grandson of the Prithivīpati before mentioned, giving him the name Hastimalla (see also *EI.* iv. 225).

Ag 5 and 27 record the death of a king who in the former is called Rāchamalla Permmānaḍi, and in the latter Nītimārgga Permmānaḍi, but they seem to refer to the same person. The second says that his death was caused by hiccough, owing to phlegm sticking in his throat; and the first says that it occurred at Kombāle. Both relate how certain men committed themselves to death in the fire through sorrow for his decease. The wording makes the identification difficult, but it seems probable that the king Satyavākya Rāchamalla II is intended in both, unless only the first refers to him and the second to Ereyappa, who is mentioned in the other in such a way as to exclude him.

Ereyappa left two sons, Rāchamalla and Būtuga. The former appears in Ag 61 making a grant in 920. HN 14 may possibly refer to his queen and Tp 10 of Kachcheya Ganga's 3rd year may also be of his time. But his reign must have been a short one. Hg 116 apparently refers to a proposed division of the kingdom between the brothers. But Md 41 informs us that Būtuga slew Rāchamalla and took possession of the whole. He was a close friend of the Rāshṭrakūṭa king Baddega or Amōghavarsha II, who gave him his daughter Rēvaka to wife (*EI.* iv. 350), with a dowry of the Beligere Three Hundred, the Belvola Three Hundred, the Kisukāḍ Seventy, and the Bagenāḍ Seventy (provinces in the Dharwar, Belgaum, and Bijāpur Districts). On the death of Baddega, Būtuga assisted his son Krishna or Kannara III in securing the throne from an usurper named Lalliya. And when Kannara was at war with the Chōla king Rājāditya,

Būtuga rendered him a great service by slaying the Chōla king at Takkolam (near Arkōnam), and was rewarded with the Banavase Twelve Thousand province (Md 41). This was in 949 (*EI.* vii. 194). He may have been assisted in gaining his own throne by Kannara, who (*EI.* iv. 249) claims to have planted in Gangapāṭi, as in a garden, the pure tree Bhūtārya, having uprooted the poisonous tree Rāchyamalla. Būtuga has the distinctive titles Nanniya Ganga and Ganga Gāngēya. Among other exploits, he is said (Nr 35) to have taken Chitrakūṭa by assault, and conquered the Seven Mālavas, the boundaries of which he marked out with stones, and gave the country the name Mālava Ganga.

His son by the Rāshṭrakūṭa princess was Marula Dēva, and a daughter, married to the son of Krishna III, became the mother of Indra Rāja, the last of the Rāshṭrakūṭas. Mj 67 may be a memorial of her. If so, her name was Kundana-Sōmidēvi. But Būtuga was succeeded on the Ganga throne by Mārasimha, his son by another wife. Of him a long account is contained in SB 38 of 973. He led an expedition against Gurjjara or Gujarat on behalf of Kannara or Akālavarsha III (who had made extensive conquests in the South as far as Tanjore, *EI.* iv. 280), fought against the Western Chālukya prince Rājāditya, put down a dangerous chief named Naraga (in the Chitaldroog District), and brought the Nolamba family to an end. On account of this last he has the special title Nolambakulāntaka. He is also styled Guttiya Ganga and Pallava-malla. He made grants in the Dharwar District in 968 (*IA.* vii. 101, 112). He appears to have promoted the coronation of Indra Rāja in an attempt to maintain the Rāshṭrakūṭa power. But this was shattered by the Chālukyas beyond recovery in 973, and Indra Rāja starved himself to death by the Jaina rite of *sallēkhana* at Śravaṇa-Beḷgoḷa in 982 (SB 57). Mārasimha had retired to Bankāpura in 973 to end his days in religious exercises at the feet of Ajitasēna, and died in 974. The kingdom in his reign extended as far as the great river, the

Face of Gomaṭa,
the colossal Jain image at Śravaṇa-

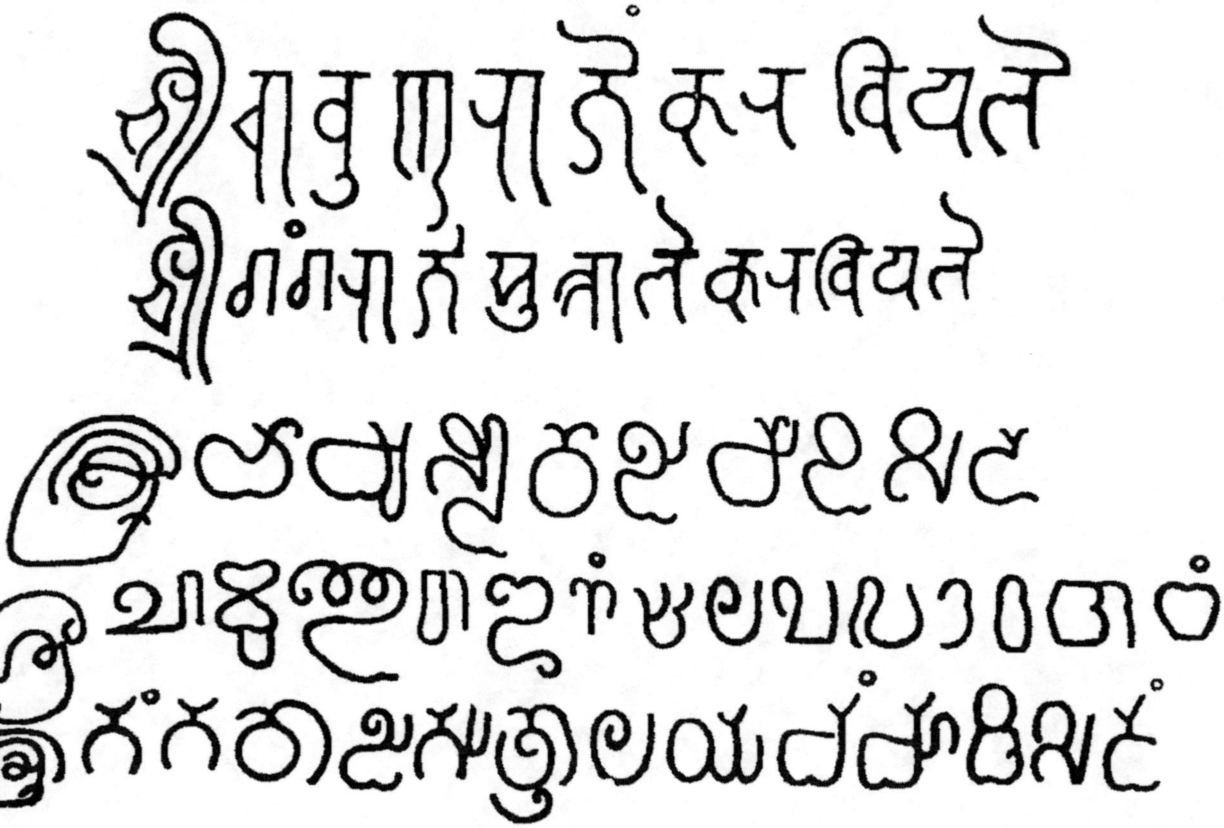

Inscriptions at foot of the image (SB 75, 76) :—

Krishnā, and included the Nolambavāḍi Thirty-two Thousand, the Gangavāḍi Ninety-six Thousand, the Banavase Twelve Thousand, the Śāntalige Thousand, and other provinces whose names are gone (*EI.* iv. 352).

His son Rāchamalla Satyavākya (IV) then came to the throne.[1] There is an inscription of his time in Cg 4, dated in 977. In this his younger brother Rakkasa appears as governing a province on the bank of the Beddore, here the Lakshmantīrtha, which is still called the Doḍḍa-hole in Coorg. For some time past there seem to have been efforts to revive the influence of the Jain religion, of which the expiring Rāshṭrakūṭa and Ganga dynasties were the principal mainstay. And under Rāchamalla was erected at Śravaṇa-Beḷgoḷa, by his minister and general Chāmuṇḍa Rāya,—who is said in TN 69 to have performed many works of merit in the land he governed,—that remarkable Jain monument and object of worship, the colossal statue of Gomaṭa. The date of its execution was about 983, and in daring conception and gigantic dimensions it is without a rival in India.

Rakkasa-Ganga Rāchamalla succeeded his elder brother, and we have a record of his reign in Sp 59. In this a chief subordinate to him is ruling the Nolambavāḍi Thirty-two Thousand. From Nr 35 it would appear that Rakkasa adopted his younger brother's daughters and son. The latter was named Rāja Vidyādhara, but may have died, as the king is represented as taking special interest in the daughters.

The only later Ganga king of whom we have certain knowledge is the Nītimārgga of Ch 10, dated in 999, in which he makes a grant along with a Pallava princess, the

[1] A certain Panchala-Dēva, with the Ganga titles, set himself up as independent in 975, but was killed in battle by the Chālukya king Taila (*EI.* v. 372). In Hr 1 he is called a *mahā-sāmantādhipati* or great feudal chief. An attempt was also made by a Ganga named Mudu-Rāchayya, who took the titles Chaladanka-Ganga and Gangara-baṇṭa, to seize the Ganga throne, but he was slain by Chāmuṇḍa-Rāya (SB 109), who thus avenged the death of his younger brother Nāgavarmma. Before the battle, the prince Rakkasa's guardian, Bāyiga of the Kakka (or Rāshṭrakūṭa) family, sent the prince away to a place of safety and rushed in to meet his own death (SB 60, 61).

elder sister of Nolamba. It is possible that Cm 3, which is of the 6th year of a Nītimārgga Rāchamalla, is of his time, as the date with a slight correction will work out, according to Dr. Kielhorn, as either 989 or 992. Then we have Md 78, in which a king called only Ganga Permmānaḍi is described as ruling Karṇṇāṭa. There are discrepancies in the date, which probably corresponds with 996. He may be the Ganga Rāja under whom Talakāḍ was lost, as SB 45, which relates how the Hoysala general Ganga Rāja in 1116 recovered Talakāḍ from the Chōlas, says he was a hundred times more fortunate than that former Ganga Rāya.

The Chōlas, who had been victorious over all the east of the peninsula, taking possession of Kānchī, the capital of the Pallavas, and reducing to submission the Eastern Chālukyas, with whom were allied the Rāshṭrakūṭas and the Gangas, now penetrated to Mysore. Ht 111 shows the Chōla king Rājarāja-Dēva ruling in the east of the State in 997. His son Rājēndra-Chōla captured Talakāḍ by 1004, and the Ganga power, which had ruled Mysore for nine centuries, was brought to an end.

But the Gangas do not disappear from history. A Ganga princess was married to the Western Chālukya king Sōmēśvara I (reigned 1042-1068), and became the mother of the kings Sōmēśvara II (reigned 1068-1076) and his celebrated brother Vikramānka (reigned 1076-1126).[1] Gangas were in authority in the Kolar District during the Chōla occupation, and were also trusted officers of the Hoysalas. It was a descendant of the Gangas, the Hoysala general Ganga Rāja, that recovered Talakāḍ from the Chōlas (Ml 31) in 1116 under Vishnuvarddhana, who then drove the Chōlas out of Mysore. The last Ganga representative was the Ganga Rāja of Ummattūr, who fortified himself on the island of

[1] It is curious that a Karṇāṭaka dynasty was set up even in distant Nepal, apparently in 1097, which was presumably of Ganga origin. The founder, Nānya-Dēva (perhaps ? Nanniya-Dēva), came from the South. He was succeeded by Ganga-Dēva and four others, the last of whom removed the capital to Khātmāndu, where the line came to an end (*Ins. from Nepal*, by Dr. G. Bühler).

Śivasamudram at the Kāvērī Falls, and assumed independence in the beginning of the sixteenth century. He was put down by the Vijayanagar king, Krishna Rāya, in 1511 (*EI.* vii. 18).

The Kalinga Ganga kings of Orissa, another branch of the Gangas, have a separate history, of which a summary may be seen in the Bangalore volume. They date by an era called the years of the Gāngēya family (*Gāngēya-vamśa-samvatsara*), the exact period of which has not been determined. They are also called the Gajapati or elephant kings. They ruled from the sixth century to the middle of the sixteenth, when the country fell a prey to the Muhammadans. One inscription of theirs, of about 700, has been obtained in Mysore (Bn 140).

The following is a table of the Ganga kings of Mysore, with dates so far as known, taken entirely from inscriptions:—

Of the Ikshvāku or Solar race, was
Dhananjaya
|
Hariśchandra,
king of Ayodhyā
:
Padmanābha
|
Dadiga — 1. Mādhava I, 103 Kongunivarmma[1]
|
2. Mādhava II,
Kiriya Mādhava
|
3. Harivarmma, . . 247-266 . .
|
4. Vishnugōpa
|
Prithivī-Ganga
|
5. Mādhava III, . . 357-370 . .
Tadangāla Mādhava,
m. Kadamba princess
|
6. Avinīta, 430-482
|
7. Durvvinīta, 482-517 . .
m. Punnād princess
|
8. Mushkara,
Mokkara,
m. Sindhu princess
|

[1] This name is applied to all the kings to the end. The Tamil chronicle says that he was ruling in 189 and reigned for fifty-one years.

9. Śrīvikrama

10. Bhūvikrama, -670,
Śrīvallabha

11. Śivamāra I, 670-713 . .
Nava Kāma,
Śishta-priyaḥ,
Pṛithivī-Koṅgaṇi I

? Ereganga

12. Śrīpurusha, 726-776 . .
Muttarasa,
Pṛithivī-Koṅgaṇi II,
Permmānadi[1]

13. Sivamāra II, -815
Saigotta

Vijayāditya,
Raṇavikrama

Mārasimha, 797
Mārasing-Ereyappa,
Lōka Trinētra

Pṛithivīpati I,
? 815

Mārasimha

Pṛithivīpati II,
Hastimalla, c. 910

14. Rājamalla Satyavākya I,[2]
m. Pallava princess

15. Nītimārgga I,[3]
Ereyanga,
Raṇavikramayya

16. Rājamalla Satya-
vākya II, 870-907

Būtugēndra, 870
Būtarasa,
Gunaduttaranga,
m. Rāshṭrakūṭa princess

17. Ereyappa, 886-913
Ereganga,
Nītimārgga II,
Satyavākya,
Mahēndrāntaka

18. Rāchamalla Satya-
vākya III, 920,
Kachcheya Ganga

19. Būtuga, 938-953
Būtayya,
Nanniya Ganga,
Ganga Gāṅgēya,
m. Rāshṭrakūṭa princess

Marula Dēva

? Sōmi Dēvi
m. to Rāshṭrakūṭa
prince

20. Mārasimha, 961-974
Guttiya Ganga,
Nolambakulāntaka

21. Rāchamalla Satyavākya
IV, 977

22. Rakkasa Ganga, 984,
Rāchamalla,

Arumuli Dēva

23. Nītimārgga III, Rāchamalla, (?) 989 or 992, 999

Rāja Vidyādhara

[1] This title is used of all the subsequent kings, often alone, without any name.
[2] These names are used as titles by all the kings that come after.
[3] This name is used as a title by the kings that follow.

These annals of the Ganga kings of Mysore present a consistent and circumstantial account that goes far to disarm criticism, and they fill up what is otherwise a blank in an interesting and important period in the history of the south. Comments casting doubt upon them have been directed mainly against minor details, that hardly affect the credibility of the chronicles as a whole. Records of so remote and lengthy a period could scarcely be expected to be free from all difficulties. But though they have been discovered in so many different parts of the country, and of such various dates, covering several centuries, they agree in giving us a generally uniform narrative, the incidents of which are corroborated by testimony from other sources, while the dates tally, and they are not discredited by anachronisms. This is the best answer to all detraction.

From one source, entitled to the highest respect,[1] an objection has been raised that the reigns of the earlier kings work out to an impossible average length for a direct succession But it is easy to imagine that some unimportant steps may have been omitted, as occurs in other known annals. That this was actually the case appears from Sh 4, which inserts a Pṛithivī-Ganga between Nos. 4 and 5. That the Gangas were long-lived is clear from the statement that the first king reigned for 51 years, and regarding Vishnugōpa, that his mental energy was unimpaired to the end of life, evidently meaning that he lived to a very advanced age, while Avinīta certainly reigned for 52 years. To take the particular reigns referred to by our critic :—From Harivarmma in 247 to Avinīta in 430 gives 183 years up to the fifth generation ; from Avinīta in 482 to Śivamāra in 670 similarly gives 188 years up to the fifth generation. And if the first five centuries of the Ganga history were occupied by even only eleven generations, this gives an average of 45 years to each, which is about the same as the above, and though high, seems by no means impossible. At any rate, apart from all theory, there they are.

[1] A scholar whose recent death cannot be sufficiently deplored.

The principal opposition, however, from another source, is based upon the sweeping dictum that all the Ganga inscriptions on copper plates are spurious, and only those on stone genuine. Merely to state this is to expose the credulous nature of this paradoxical hypothesis. And it is disproved by the fact that the ancient Āvani stone fragment (Mb 263) and Sirigunda stone (Cm 50) are contemporary with and contain records similar to those on the early copper plates. At the same time they render it probable that others on stone of like nature formerly existed, as even the Lakshmēśvara stone (*IA*. vii. 101) may bear witness. Those have been lost or destroyed, while the metal plates have survived because they were portable and indestructible and could be hidden. In view of the general consistency and veracity of the records, errors that may be detected here and there in style or orthography are of trifling importance. And the serious allegation that they are condemned by the misuse of a more modern form of a certain letter in plates professing to be ancient has been proved to have no foundation. The persistent opponent of the Gangas here referred to has lately expressed (*EI*. viii. 55) his willingness, when he feels justified, to abandon his present views and cancel anything wrong that he has written against them, but not yet. The sooner the better is the only comment one can make. The truth is bound to prevail.

6. PALLAVAS

To revert to the earlier history.—The Kadambas, as previously stated, succeeded the Śātavāhanas in the west of Mysore, but the Pallavas were their successors throughout the Telugu countries in the east of the Dekhan, and Pallava inscriptions are found as far south as Trichinopoly. These kings are first met with as the Pahlavas, who, with the Sakas and Yavanas, are said to have been destroyed (early in the second century) by Gōtamiputra Sātakarṇi (*ASIVI*. iv. 108).

A little later a Pallava named Suvisākha, the son of Kulaipa, was minister to the Kshatrapa Rudradāman (*EI.* viii. 49). Pahlava is a Prākrit form of Pārthava, meaning Parthian, here especially the Arsacidan Parthians.

According to tradition, their progenitor, descended from Śālivāhana who ruled at Pratishṭhāna (Paithan on the Gōdāvari), was a Mukunti Pallava, who introduced Brāhmans into the South in the third century. A principal seat of the Pallavas was Vengi (between the Krishnā and Gōdāvari in the east), but Kānchī (Conjeeveram, near Madras) was their chief capital. It was so in the third century when Mayūra-śarmma, the Kadamba student, went there (Sk 176), and both are mentioned in the Samudra Gupta inscription of the fourth century. The Pallavas may have ousted the Mahāvalis or Bāṇas from the coast regions, and driven them eastwards inland. The ancient inscriptions now at Mahābalipur are Pallava.

But the chief enemies of the Pallavas, to the eighth century, were the Chalukyas, who describe them as by nature hostile, as if there were some radical cause of animosity between them. If the Chalukyas, as their name suggests, were by origin Seleukian, this would account for the enmity of Arsacidans. A series of continual wars ensued. In the sixth century the Chalukyas, after defeating the powers in the west, wrested Vātāpi (Bādāmi, in the Bijāpur District) from the Pallavas, and made it their capital. Early in the seventh they captured Vengi, and established there the separate Eastern Chālukya[1] dynasty. The Pallavas now destroyed Vātāpi, but the Western Chālukyas, who had held it, before long recovered their power, and in the eighth century, inflicting a severe defeat on the Pallavas, entered Kānchī in triumph, the city, however, being spared (Kl 63). The Gangas of Mysore had also been attacking the Pallavas. They took some of their possessions in the sixth century, and completely conquered them in the seventh and eighth.

[1] After the separation the name appears with the long *ā*.

But the Western Chālukyas, shortly after they had triumphed over the Pallavas in the middle of the eighth century, were themselves overcome by the Rāshṭrakūṭas, who retained the supremacy for two hundred years. They made the Pallava king pay tribute, and imprisoned the Ganga king. Early in the ninth century, however, they released and reinstated the latter, the Rāshṭrakūṭa and Pallava (or Ganga-Pallava) kings united performing his coronation.

The earliest mention of the Pallavas in the inscriptions of Mysore is in Sk 176, which relates how the Kadamba Mayūraśarmma went to their capital to study, felt himself insulted, became an outlaw for the purpose of revenge, and was eventually recognised by them as king over a Kadamba kingdom in the west. This was in the third century. The Pallavas next appear in Dg 161, in which their king Naṇakkāsa is said to have totally defeated the army of Krishnavarmma, evidently the Kadamba king, probably in the fifth century. At the end of the same century the Ganga king Durvvinīta captured Kāḍuveṭṭi[1] on the field of battle. Narasimhapōtavarmma must have been the Pallava defeated by the Ganga king Bhūvikrama in the seventh century, and Pallava princes were in the custody of his successor Śivamāra I (Md 113). In Kl 63 Narasimhapōtavarmma is named as having erected certain of the temples in Kānchī, and Nandipōtavarmma as the Pallava who suffered a crushing defeat at the hands of the Western Chālukya king Vikramāditya Satyāśraya in about 733. The Pallava from whom the Ganga king Śrīpurusha in the eighth century took away the title of Permmānaḍi is called, as usual, Kāḍuveṭṭi. Then we have (Yd 60, Nl 60), in about 813, the Pallava king Nandivarmma, who took part (perhaps as being a Ganga-Pallava) in the coronation of the Ganga king Śivamāra II.

[1] This is the common designation in Ganga inscriptions for the Pallava king. It survives in the name of Kārvēṭi-nagara in North Arcot District. The Pallavas are also called Kāḍavas.

With him the old main line of the Pallavas perhaps ended. But the succession was maintained by the Noṇambas or Noḷambas, who claim to be Pallavas,[1] and gave their name to the Noḷambavāḍi or Noṇambavāḍi Thirty-two Thousand province, corresponding generally with the Chitaldroog District and adjacent parts north and east of it. The existing Noṇabas, a numerous and important section of agriculturists in Mysore, represent its former subjects.

The genealogy of the Noḷambas is given in the Hēmāvati pillar (Si 28). They are stated to be of the Iśvara-vaṁśa, and descended from Trinayana, through Pallava, the king of Kānchī. The first king named is Mangala or Noḷambādhirāja, praised (*nuta*) by the Karṇṇāṭas. His son was Simhapōta, whose son was Chārupponnera, whose son was Pōlalchōra Noḷamba, whose son was Mahēndra, whose son was Nanniga or Ayyapa-Dēva, whose sons were Aṇṇiga (or Bīra Noḷamba) and Dilīpa or Iṛiva Noḷamba.

Singapōta was subordinate to the Ganga king Śivamāra Saigoṭṭa, and was sent by him against his younger brother Duggamāra, who strove to set himself up as independent (Cl 8). The Rāshṭrakūṭas having imprisoned Śivamāra and assumed the government of the Ganga territory, we find (Cl 33, 34) Singapōta's son and grandson under their orders ruling the Nolambalige Thousand and other provinces. This may have been the nucleus of the Noḷambavāḍi province. On the restoration of the Gangas, their king Rājamalla Satyavākya I married Singapōta's grand-daughter, Pallavādhirāja's daughter, the younger sister of Noḷambādhirāja, and gave his own daughter Jāyabbe in marriage to Noḷambādhirāja Pōlalchōra (Si 38). The latter appears in Kl 79 as ruling the Ganga Six Thousand under the Ganga king Nītimārgga. His son by the Ganga princess was Mahēndra or Bīra Mahēndra, who in Bp 64 is ruling the same province, under

[1] A princess named in Ch 10 is said to be of the Noḷamba-*vamśa* and Pallava-*kula*.

the Gangas. In Sp 30 he appears as ruling in conjunction with two others over a territory up to the Kiṟu-tore or little river as its boundary. But Si 38 represents him as assuming independence in 878, while DB 3 says he was ruling as king, and fighting with the Ganga king. He was opposed by Būtuga, the Ganga Yuvarāja, and finally slain by Būtuga's son Eṟeyappa, who thence obtained the title Mahēndrāntaka. Mahēndra's queen was a Kadamba princess, named Dīvalabbarasi or Dīvāmbike (Mb 38), and he is called Noḷambādhirāja and the Noḷamba Nārāyaṇa. CB 26 of about 880 and Md 13 of 895 may refer to him, and show that the Noḷambas had gained considerable power.

Mahēndra's son was Ayyapa, and it is in connection with him that the Noḷambavāḍi province is first mentioned. In Jl 29 of 920 he is said to be ruling the Noḷambavāḍi Thirty-two Thousand, with Aṇṇayya (his son) as a governor under him. But as a rule all the Pallava Noḷamba inscriptions, from Mahēndra in Pg 45 of about 880 to Nanni Noḷamba in Mb 122 of 969, represent the kings as ruling the kingdom of the world, that is as independent. Noḷambavāḍi must have been the main portion of their kingdom, which seems from the inscriptions to have extended eastwards as far as the Srīnivāspur tāluq. Sb 474 of 954 speaks of the time in the (near) past when the Thirty-two Thousand was under one king.

For Ayyapa, who has the names Nanniga, Nannigāśraya, Nolipayya, and Noḷambādhirāja, we have the dates 897 in Mi 52, 918 in DB 9, 920 in Si 39, and 929 in Kd 6. His eldest son Aṇṇiga or Bīra Noḷamba, also called Aṇṇayya and Ankayya, succeeded him. For the latter we have the date 931 in Ct 43 and 44, in which he is described as being at peace, in the enjoyment of all the rights of sovereignty. Gd 4 states that Anni, a son of the Ganga prince Piḻduvipati (Prithuvīpati II), was killed in battle when fighting in his army. Aṇṇiga was defeated by the Rāshṭrakūṭa king Krishna or Kannara III in 940 (*EI.* iv. 289; v. 191). His younger brother Dilīpa or Iṟiva Noḷamba next came to the throne.

He had also the name Nolapayya. Bp 4 and Kl 198 show that he had the Vaidumbas under him, and Mb 126 that he had subjected the Mahāvalis. For him there are the dates 943 in Si 28, 948 in Si 35, 951 in Ct 49, 961 in Mb 126, and 966 in Kl 245.

In Mb 122 of 969 we are informed that Nanni Noḷamba had assumed the crown. He was Iṛiva Noḷamba's son (Hr 1). But the Ganga king Mārasimha, who ruled till 974, boasts of having destroyed the Noḷamba family, whence he had the name Noḷambakulāntaka, and he was ruling, among other provinces, over the Noḷambavāḍi Thirty-two Thousand (*EI.* iv. 352). In Mb 84 of 974 we have a record of three Noḷamba princes, who had escaped and were perhaps hiding, hearing with relief the news of his death. But the Noḷambavāḍi Thirty-two Thousand continued in possession of the Gangas, as testified by Rakkasa Ganga's inscription (Sp 59) of about 985.

The Pallava Noḷamba line, however, was not extinguished, for the kings continue to appear for a long time after, under the Chōlas and Western Chālukyas. Ht 47 informs us that when Noḷambādhirāja was ruling, Chōla fought with his army stationed at Bijayitamangala (Bētmangala, Bowringpet tāluq),[1] and Noḷambarasa was killed. But when he died, his son (? succeeded him). Ht 111 shows that in 977 the Chōla king Rājarāja had gained a footing in that part of Mysore, and Ayyapa's son Gannarasa was acting as governor under him. But a Noḷambādhirāja Chōrayya continues as a Pallava king under the Chōla king Rājarāja to 1010 (Mb 208, Ct 118). He may be the one so named in Mb 84 as having escaped the general massacre of his family, and it may be his father who is there mentioned, and who is perhaps to be identified with the Noḷambarasa above stated to have been killed in battle, leaving his son to continue the line.

But the Noḷambas seem to have gone over after this to the protection of the Western Chālukyas, who were at enmity with the Chōlas. For Mk 10 shows us a Jagadēkamalla-

[1] This indicates the direction in which they retired when driven from Noḷambavāḍi.

Noḷamba-Pallava ruling the kingdom in 1022, with the seat of his government at Kampiḷi (on the Tungabhadrā in the west of the Bellary District). Then Dg 71 shows us Udayāditya, called the Noḷamba-Pallava-Permmānaḍi,[1] ruling in 1035 under the same Chālukya king Jayasingha Jagadēkamalla. In Dg 126 is Jagadēkamalla-Immaḍi-Noḷamba-Pallava-Permmānaḍi, ruling the Kadambalige Thousand and other provinces under the same king in 1037. Dg 124 shows a Trailōkyamalla-Nanni-Noḷamba-Pallava-Permmānaḍi ruling Kadambalige in (?) 1042. The introductory part is effaced, or it might have supplied some important details. He appears again in Dg 20 with extended authority in 1045. Jl 10 shows a Nārasinga ruling the Kadambalige Thousand and other provinces under the same king in 1054, with his son Chōraya as a governor under him at Uchchangi. The Chālukya king Trailōkyamalla was Sōmēśvara I or Āhavamalla, who ruled 1040 to 1069. He married as one of his wives a Pallava princess, by whom he had his son Jayasimha, who takes the titles Vīra-Noṇamba (or Noḷamba)-Pallava-Permmānaḍi. Under his father he was governor of various provinces in 1048 and 1054 (Hl 107, 119). The next king, Sōmēśvara II, his elder half-brother by a Ganga mother, made him governor of the Noḷamba-Sindavāḍi province in 1068 (Sk 136). Mk 28 is a record of him in 1072, and Cd 82 of 1074. His other elder half-brother Vikramārka, also by the Ganga mother, on coming to the throne in 1076, made him Yuvarāja, and he won important conquests for the kingdom. In 1080 he was ruling Banavase and other large provinces for his brother (Sk 293). But eventually he rebelled against him, and was defeated and imprisoned.[2] We know that another half-brother of his, named Vishnuvarddhana Vijayāditya (see Ci 18), the son of an Eastern Chālukya princess,

[1] The title Permmānaḍi was taken by the Gangas from the Pallavas on their subjection of them in the eighth century. The Ganga power being now overthrown, the Pallavas resume the use of it.

[2] A curious inscription of his (Bn 142) is antedated in 444, and is the model on which the professed Janamējaya grants (Sk 45, Sb 183, etc.) were framed.

was ruling the Nolambavāḍi Thirty-two Thousand in 1064 and 1066, with his seat of government at Kampili. He is described as about to sink into the ocean of the Chōlas, but this was averted by Rājarāja and Chōla-Ganga of the Kalinga Gangas. Then Si 9 shows us another Udayāditya ruling in 1072 over the Noḷambavāḍi Thirty-two Thousand, and said to be extending the Pencheru kingdom on all sides. He was evidently under the Chōlas, as he has the sub-title Vīra-Rājendra, as well as Vīra-Noḷamba-Pallava-Permmānaḍi. Pencheru is Penjeṟu (or Henjeṟu), now called Hēmāvati situated on the northern border of Sīra tāluq. Apparently it was at this time the capital of Noḷambavāḍi. The same Udayāditya appears in Gd 57 in (?) 1109, and in place of bearing a Chōla title he is there styled binder of Chōla-mārāja. But meanwhile the Pāṇḍyas of Uchchangi come into view as governors of the Noḷambavāḍi province. Ci 33 shows Tribhuvanamalla-Pāṇḍya ruling it in (?) 1083, and he is described as defeater of the designs of Rājiga-Chōla. Dg 155 says he was the younger brother of Tribhuvanamalla-Noḷamba-Pallava-Permmānaḍi (Jayasimha above). Dg 3 shows that the seat of government had been moved to Beḷtūr (Bettūr near Dāvangere). In 1124 Rāya-Pāṇḍya was ruling the province from the same place (Dg 2). But next year the capital was again at Uchchangi (Ci 61), where it remained, and he had a Pallava as a feudatory under him. Dg 4, Ci 38 and 39, show Vīra-Pāṇḍya ruling the province in 1143 and 1149. Hk 56 says that at the rise of Bijjana, the Kalachurya king (in 1156), Palatta-Pāṇḍya was ruling Noḷambavāḍi. Dg 113 mentions a Pallava king in about 1160, without giving any name. Cd 13 shows Vijaya-Pāṇḍya ruling Noḷambavāḍi in 1184. But in Cd 23 we have a Pallava prince named Māchi-Dēva in 1205 as feudatory to the Hoysala king Ballāla II. His descent is given for three generations, and he was ruling in the Holalkere-nāḍ (Chitaldroog District) and adjacent parts.

8. GANGA-PALLAVAS

But while the Noṇambas or Noḷambas thus continued to represent the old Pallava dynasty, there was another branch of the Pallavas which had its origin in perhaps the eighth century. This branch has been designated the Ganga-Pallavas. For Nandivarmma from whom they descended, a contemporary of the Chalukya king Vikramāditya (reigned 733-746), though a Pallava in name, was a Ganga by descent (*EI.* iv. 182). They would seem later to call themselves the Nṛipatunga-kula, from their Rāshṭrakūṭa connection. Nṛipatungavarmma was a Pallava, the grandson of Dantivarmma and the son of Nandivarmma, but his mother was Śankhā, daughter of the Rāshṭrakūṭa king Nṛipatunga-Amōghavarsha, after whom he was probably named. At the same time he also claims to be descended from Kongaṇi, the ancestor of the Gangas. The territory of these Ganga-Pallavas lay in the east of Mysore, in the North Arcot, Tanjore, and Trichinopoly districts. Their inscriptions are in Vaṭṭeluttu and archaic Tamil characters, and their names generally have the prefix Vijaya, or, in Tamil, Ko-viśaiya.

The kings of this line of whom records have been obtained are Narasimhavarmma (about 800), his son Nandivarmma (about 820), and the latter's sons Nṛipatungavarmma or Nṛipatungavikramavarmma and Kampavarmma. Also Aparājitavikramavarmma. In Mysore we have two inscriptions of the time of these kings in the Mulbāgal tāluq (Mb 227, 211). One is of the 24th year of Narasimhavikramavarmma, and the other of the 12th year of Iśvaravarmma. As these contain references to Bānarasa and Mahēndra, they belong to about 880. Five centuries later we have representatives of perhaps the same family in the Chik-Ballāpur tāluq (CB 41, 14), who describe themselves as of the Nṛipatunga-kula and have the Ganga title Lord of Nandagiri (or Nandigiri). Vembi-Dēva was ruling in 1267 and 1270 (Dv 79, CB 14). In 1283 he has the second name Nandi-Dēva (Dv 28).

9. CHALUKYAS

The Chalukyas next claim our attention. They were in the ascendant throughout the north-west of Mysore, and the Bombay and Haidarabad Districts beyond, from the fifth to the eighth century, and from the latter part of the tenth to that of the twelfth. Their first appearance south of the Narmadā (Nerbudda) was in the fourth century, previous to which they profess to have had fifty-nine predecessors on the throne of Ayōdhyā, but of these nothing is known, not even their names. On their entering the Dekhan they overcame the Rāshṭrakūṭas, but the Pallavas effectually opposed them, and the invader, Jayasimha or Vijayāditya, was slain. His queen, being at the time pregnant, took refuge with a Brāhman, and gave birth to a son named Rājasimha, who eventually defeated the Pallavas, and then formed an alliance with them, confirmed by his marriage with a Pallava princess. In the sixth century, Pulikēśi, whose chief city was apparently Indukānta (supposed to be Ajantā or some neighbouring place), wrested Vātāpi (Bādāmi in the Bijāpur District) from the Pallavas and made it his capital. His son Kīrttivarmma subdued the Mauryas (descendants of the ancient Mauryas of Pāṭaliputra) ruling in the Konkan, and the Kadambas of Banavāsi. Another son, Mangalēśa, conquered the Kalachuryas. The Ālupas or Āluvas, ruling in Tuluva or South Kanara, were also at the same time overcome, and the next king, Pulikēśi II, came into contact with the Gangas. In about 617 the Chalukyas separated into two branches, of which the Eastern Chālukyas[1] made Vengi (near Ellore in the Gōdāvari District), taken from the Pallavas, and subsequently Rājamahēndri (Rājamundry), their capital, while the Western Chālukyas, with whom Mysore is chiefly concerned, continued to rule from Vātāpi, and eventually from Kalyāna (in the Nizām's Dominions, about 100 miles west by north of Haidarabad).

The Chalukyas were of the Sōma-vamśa or Lunar race.

[1] See note, p. 53 above.

They profess to be of the Mānavya-gōtra and Hāritīputras, nourished by the Seven Mothers (as were the Kadambas). The Varāha or Boar was the emblem on their signet. The Western Chālukyas are styled the Satyāśraya-kula, from the name of the first king of that branch. The titles on their inscriptions are nearly invariably—Samastabhuvanāśraya, Śrī-prithvī-vallabha, Mahārājādhirāja, Paramēśvara, Parama-bhaṭṭāraka, Satyāśraya-kula-tilaka, Chālukyābharaṇa.

Though these details appear very circumstantial, the origin of the Chalukyas is far from clear.[1] The name Chalukya, as I have pointed out, bears a suggestive resemblance to Seleukia, and the Pallavas being of Parthian connection, as their name implies, we have a plausible explanation of the inveterate hatred between the two, and their prolonged struggles were thus but a sequel of the contests between Seleucidæ and Arsacidæ on the banks of the Tigris and Euphrates.

The following is a table of the early Chalukyas down to the rise to power of the Rāshṭrakūṭas. A full account of the Chalukyas down to 1123, including their rise, their eclipse by the Rāshṭrakūṭas, and their revival, is given in Dg 1.

[1] They are said to have miraculously sprung from the moisture or water in the hollowed palm (*chuluka*, *chulaka*) of Hāriti's hand (see Dg 41), or, according to another account, from the libation to the gods poured from his goblet (*chulka*, *chuluka*, *chaluka*) by Hāriti. Dr. Hoernle (*JRAS.* for 1905, p. 12) says: "Despite the attempted Sanskrit derivation of the genealogists, I would suggest that the name (Chalukya) is not a Sanskritic word at all, but of foreign (Gurjara or Hunic) origin." He adds that it may be from a Turki root, *chap*, gallop, *chāpāul*, a plundering raid, a charge of cavalry (?).—Mr. V. A. Smith (*EHI.* 383) states: "There is some reason for believing that the Chalukyas or Solankis were connected with the Chāpas, and so with the foreign Gurjara tribe of which the Chāpas were a branch."

Jayasimha

Rājasimha, Raṇarāga

1. Polekēsi, Pulikēśi (I), Satyāśraya, Raṇavikrama, 550

2. Kīrttivarmma (I), Raṇaparākrama, 566-597

3. Mangalēśa, Raṇavikrānta, 597-608

4. Polekēsi, Pulikēśi (II), Satyāśraya, 609-642

Kubja-Vishnuvarddhana, 615-633, founded the Eastern Chālukya line

Ādityavarmma

Chandrāditya, queen, Vijaya-mahādēvi, 655, 659

5. Vikramāditya (I), Raṇarasika, 655-680

6. Vinayāditya, Rājāśraya, 680-696

7. Vijayāditya, Samasta-bhuvanāśraya, 696-733

8. Vikramāditya (II), 733-746

9. Kīrttivarmma (II), 746-757

Jayasimha is said to have defeated and destroyed Indra, the son of Krishna, the Rāshṭrakūṭa or Raṭṭa king. He himself, however, was slain in an encounter with Trilōchana Pallava. His queen, then pregnant, fled and took refuge with a Brāhman named Vishnu Sōmayāji, in whose house she gave birth to Rājasimha. On growing up to man's estate he renewed the contest with the Pallavas, in which he was successful, and married a princess of that race. Pulikēśi was the most powerful of the early kings, and performed the horse sacrifice. Kīrttivarmma subdued the Nalas, of whom we know no more, the Mauryas and the Kadambas. Mangalēśa conquered the island called Rēvati-dvīpa, and the Mātangas; also the Kalachurya king Buddha, son of Śankaragaṇa, the spoils taken from whom he gave to the temple of Makuṭēśvara near Bādāmi. He attempted to establish his own son in the succession, but Pulikēśi, the elder son of Kīrttivarmma, obtained the throne. Pulikēśi's younger brother Vishnuvarddhana, surnamed Kubja, on the capture of Vengi from the Pallavas, there founded the separate line of the Eastern Chālukyas, who remained in power in the Vengi and Rājamahēndri country till the eleventh century, when they were absorbed into the Chōla family.

The earliest Chālukya inscriptions in Mysore are of the time of Pulikēśi II or Satyāśraya, the first of the Western Chālukya line, of about 640. Sh 10 is a fragment, containing only his name. But Gd 48 is on copper plates, recording a grant by him to Brāhmans in the Konikal-vishaya. It begins with the mention of Polikēśi I, surnamed Raṇavikrama, who performed the horse sacrifice. It then passes to Satyāśraya (Pulikēśi II), the conqueror of Harshavarddhana. The grant was made when the king was at the Sangama-tīrtha, and on the application of his beloved daughter, called in his or her own language (*sva-bhāshayā*)[1] Amberā. Sa 79 is of the time of Vikramāditya, about 680. Then we have Sh 154, of about 685, when Vinayāditya Rājāśraya was ruling, and Pogilli-Sēndraka-mahārāja was a governor under him over Nāyar-khanda (the Shikārpur tāluq). Dg 66, the Harihara plates, are of 694, the 14th year of Vinayāditya, and so far contain information similar to that in Kl 63, but with fewer details. A grant was made in the Vanavāsi country to a Brāhman while the king was in camp near Harishapura (Harihara). Then comes Sk 278, of about 700, in the reign of Vijayāditya Satyāśraya.

But the most important of all is Kl 63, the Vokkalēri plates, dated in 757. They contain a variety of historical information of the highest value, and their publication by me in 1879 first opened the eyes of scholars to the true significance of the Pallavas, then scarcely known even by name. The plates begin with an account of the Chalukyas, and mention first Polekēśi, who performed the horse sacrifice. His son was Kīrttivarmma, who overcame the kings of Vanavāsi (the Kadambas) and others. His son Satyāśraya defeated Harshavarddhana (king of Kanyākubja or Kanōj), the warlike

[1] It is not clear what language is meant.

lord of all the north, and thus acquired the title of Paramēśvara. His son Vikramāditya Satyāśraya subdued the Pāṇḍya Chōla Kērala Kalabhra [1] and other kings, and forced the king of Kānchī (the Pallava), who had bowed to no other, to kiss his feet with his crown. His son Vinayāditya Satyāśraya quelled the power of the three kingdoms of the South—Chōla, Pāṇḍya, and Chera—and of the king of Kānchī, and levied tribute from the rulers of Kavēra, Pārasika, Simhala (Ceylon), and other islands. He also, by churning all the kings of the north, acquired the *pāli-dhvaja* and all other signs of supreme power. His son Vijayāditya Satyāśraya uprooted the enemies still left in the south, and fought for his father in the north, gaining, besides the *pāli-dhvaja*, the emblems of the Gangā and Yamunā. He was by some means taken prisoner, but escaped, and thus averted the danger of anarchy in his own country. His son was Vikramāditya Satyāśraya, who resolved to uproot the Pallavas, by nature the enemies of his family. Marching with great speed into the Tuṇḍāka-vishaya (Toṇḍa-maṇḍala), he inflicted a crushing defeat on the Pallava king Nandipōta-varmma, who fled, leaving to the conqueror his special trumpet, drum, flag, and other trophies. Vikramāditya then entered Kānchī in triumph, but spared the city, relieved the destitute, and presented heaps of gold to the Rājasimhēśvara and other temples which Narasimhapōtavarmma had formerly erected.[2] He then burnt up Pāṇḍya Chōla Kērala Kalabhra and other kings, and set up a pillar of victory on the shore of the southern ocean. His son Kīrttivarmma Satyāśraya, when only Yuvarāja, obtained permission to again attack the king of Kānchī, and forced him to take refuge in a hill fort, capturing his elephants, rubies and gold, which he delivered to his father. On succeeding to the throne he

[1] The Kalabhras are mentioned (in the Velvikudi plates) as having gained possession of the Pāṇḍya country in about the seventh century. They appear to have been Karṇāṭas (*Mad. Arch. Rep.* 1908).

[2] A pillar with an old inscription in front of the Rājasimhēśvara temple at Kānchī bears witness to his having visited it. And his queen, Lōkamahādēvi, of the Haihaya family, had a temple built at Paṭṭadkal in commemoration of his having three times defeated the Pallavas.

made a grant to Brāhmans in the Pānungal-vishaya (Hāngal in Dharwar).

But while thus triumphant in the south-east, the Chālukyas were overcome in the north-west by the original enemies whom they had subdued on first entering the Dekhan in the fourth century. These were the Rāshṭrakūṭas, who retained the supremacy for 200 years, after which the Chālukyas once more recovered their power.

10. RĀSHṬRAKŪṬAS OR RAṬṬAS

The Rāshṭrakūṭas or Raṭṭas may have existed in the Dekhan from very early times. They were perhaps connected with the Rājput Raṭhōrs, and are supposed to be represented by the modern Reḍḍis.[1] Their territory is called Raṭṭavāḍi, or, in Tamil, Iraṭṭapāḍi, and was a Seven-and-a-half Lakh country. Their capital, at first Mayūrakhaṇḍi (Mōrkhaṇḍ in the Nāsik District), was early in the ninth century established at Mānyakhēṭa (Mālkhēḍ in the Nizām's Dominions, about ninety miles west by south of Haidarābād). The earliest decided mention of them describes Indra, the son of Krishna, as overcome by the early Chalukya king Jayasimha. Then we have a Gōvinda repulsed by Pulikēśi I. But the connected table of kings is as follows:—

[1] The Rāshṭrakūṭa family was in all likelihood the main branch of the race of Kshattriyas named Raṭṭhas who gave their name to the country of Mahārāshṭra, and were found in it even in the times of Aśōka the Maurya. The Rāshṭrakūṭas were the real native rulers of the country, and were sometimes eclipsed by enterprising princes of foreign origin, such as the Śātavāhanas and the Chalukyas who established themselves in the Dekhan and exercised supreme sovereignty, but were never extirpated (Bhandarkar, *EHD.* 62).

Dantivarmma

Indra (I)

Gōvinda (I)

Karkka, Kakka (I)

Indra (II)

1. Dantidurga, 754
Dantivarmma,
Khaḍgāvaloka,
Vairamēgha

2. Krishna (I), Kannara,
Akālavarsha,
Śubhatunga

3. Gōvinda (II),
779, 783
Prabhūtavarsha,
Pratāpāvalōka

4. Dhruva, Dhōra,
Nirupama,
Dhārāvarsha

Kambha, 802
Stambha,
Raṇāvalōka

5. Gōvinda (III), 794-814
Gōyinda,
Prabhūtavarsha,
Jagattunga

Indra,
founded
Gujarat branch

6. Amōghavarsha (I),
815-877
Nṛipatunga,
Atiśaya-dhavala

7. Krishna (II), 884-913
Kannara,
Akālavarsha,
Śubhatunga

Jagattunga

8. Indra (III), 915-917
Nityavarsha

11. Baddega, Vaddiga, 937, 939
Amōghavarsha (III),
Gabhindara

9. Amōghavarsha (II)

10. Gōvinda (IV),
918 933
Prabhūtavarsha,
Suvarṇṇavarsha

12. Krishna (III), 939-968
Kannara, Iriva-Kannara,
Akālavarsha

13. Khoṭṭiga, 968-971
Nityavarsha

14. Kakka (II), 972-973
Kakkala,
Amōghavarsha (IV)
Nṛipatunga

15. Indra (IV), died 982

These kings very commonly had the title Vallabha, taken from the Chalukyas. In its Prākrit form of Ballaha, which is often used in their inscriptions in Mysore,[1] without any name. it furnishes the key by which to identify the powerful dynasty called Balharās by Arab travellers of the tenth century, and described by them as ruling from Mānkīr (Mānyakhēṭa).

Indra II is said to have married a Chalukya princess, but Dantidurga, who left no heir, and Krishna I, his uncle, who therefore came to the throne after him, were successful in overcoming the Chalukyas and establishing the supremacy of the Rāshṭrakūṭas. The beautiful Kailāsa temple of Elurā (Ellore) was probably erected by Krishna (see Gb 61).

The earliest Rāshṭrakūṭa inscriptions in Mysore are Cl 33 and 34. They are of the time of Jagattunga Prabhūtavarsha Pratāpāvalōka Śrīvallaha, which titles denote a Gōvinda. And the fact that he is called Akālavarsha's son shows that it was Gōvinda II. The Jain *Harivamśa*, composed in 783, says that Vallabha, the son of Krishna (Akālavarsha), was then ruling over the South, and this was the same person. In the above inscriptions he has the Pallava Nolamba king Singapōta's son and daughters as rulers under him. Singapōta, we know from Cl 8, was contemporary with the Ganga king Śivamāra Saigotta. The latter, having assisted Gōvinda, was seized and imprisoned by Gōvinda's younger brother Dhruva Nirupama, who had ousted his elder brother. The reason of this supersession is said in certain later grants to have been that Gōvinda was addicted to sensual pleasures, and so let the kingdom slip out of his hands. But the Paithan grant of 794 (*EI.* iii. 104), nearer to his own time, says that he brought in even the hostile Mālava and other kings to help him, who were joined by the Kānchī, Ganga, and Vengi kings. Nevertheless Dhruva defeated him, and drove these enemies away on the east and north. He then took possession of the whole kingdom, "leaping over" his elder brother.

The Rāshṭrakūṭa invasion of Mysore at the close of the

[1] Their inscriptions are often on cruciform stones, very artistic in appearance, and quite different from any others. The upper arm is deeply bevelled, and from one end to the other of the cross tree is engraved a large plough, a characteristic symbol of *rāshṭra-kūṭas* or rural headmen.

RĀSHṬRAKŪṬA STONE AT MĀVALI.

eighth century by Dhruva Nirupama profoundly disturbed the even tenor of the Ganga sovereignty, which had been maintained on the whole unimpaired for 600 years. The Gangas, it is expressly said, had never been conquered before. But now they suffered the ignominy of seeing their king (Śivamāra) led away into captivity, and their country placed under the rule of a foreign hostile prince. A motive for this procedure on the part of the Rāshṭrakūṭa king has been suggested above, but resentment at the Ganga having sided with his rival elder brother must have been a primary cause.

We thus come to Hg 93, in which we have Dhārāvarsha Śrīvallabha as the supreme ruler, and Kambharasa ruling the Ninety-six Thousand, that is, Gangavāḍi, under him. This was Dhārāvarsha's eldest son, and the first Rāshṭrakūṭa viceroy of Gangavāḍi, his claim to the Rāshṭrakūṭa throne having been set aside by his father in favour of a younger son Gōvinda. Kambhaiya appears again in SB 24, with the title Raṇāvalōka. Nl 61 shows him as Śaucha-Kambha-Dēva and Raṇāvalōka still in power, but now reconciled to his younger brother, who had assumed the crown of the whole kingdom.

The Maṇṇe plates (Nl 61) of 802 give an interesting account of the Rāshṭrakūṭas from Krishna I to Gōvinda III. Dhōra or Nirupama, besides imprisoning Ganga, hemmed in and levied a tribute of elephants from Pallava, drove Vatsa-Rāja, who had seized the Gauḍa kingdom, into the impassable desert of Mārwār, and took away from him the state umbrellas which had belonged to Gauḍa. He resolved to appoint his younger son Gōvinda as his successor, on account of his splendid form and superior abilities, thus depriving the elder son of his birthright. But when the father died and Gōvinda claimed the throne, the latter had to contend with a confederacy of twelve kings, headed, it would appear from other records, by Stambha, the Kambha above mentioned, his elder brother who had been superseded. Kambha, however, eventually submitted, and continued to rule the Ganga kingdom under his younger brother. His death may have been the occasion that led Gōvinda to release the Ganga king from "the burden of his cruel chains and restore him to his own submissive country." But Ganga in his pride having shown a return of hostility, was swiftly seized and again confined. Eventually Gōvinda replaced him on the throne, binding the diadem on his brow with his own hands, in conjunction with the Pallava (or Ganga-Pallava) king Nandivarmma.

Gōvinda's exploits are recounted—his driving away Gurjjara, and receiving the submission of Mārasarvva in the Vindhya mountains. After passing the rainy season at Śrībhavana, he came to the south and encamped on the Tungabhadrā, when Pallava paid up in full the tribute due from him. The site of the camp, as we know from *IA*. xi. 126, was at the Rāmēśvara tīrtha. This is an island in the Tungabhadrā, a few miles north of the junction of the Tungā and Bhadrā in the Shimoga District. Here the king had some sport with boars and confirmed a grant originally made by (the Western Chālukya king) Kīrttivarmma.

Of the same king's reign are the Kadab plates (Gb 61) of 812. In these the genealogy begins with Kakka, whose son was Inda, whose son was Vairamēgha. This unusual name for Dantidurga seems to be supported by an inscription in North Arcot.[1] His paternal uncle Akālavarsha, his successor on the throne, is next mentioned, and the splendid temple he erected (the Kailāsa at Ellore), dedicated after his own name to Kannēśvara. Next follow his sons Prabhūtavarsha and Dhārāvarsha, and the latter's son Prabhūtavarsha, who makes the grant from Mayūrakhanda for a temple at Mānyapura. It is in this inscription that we meet with Chāki Rāja as viceroy (the last) of the Ganga territory.

Rājamalla Satyavākya I, the Ganga king who succeeded Śivamāra II on the throne, made himself independent of the Rāshṭrakūṭas, rescuing from them his country "which they had held too long" (Yd 60). But, as we have seen above, Amōghavarsha attempted to recover it by sending a chief named

[1] *ASI.* Annual Report 1903-4, see article by V. Venkayya on *Irrigation in South India.*

Bankēśa to uproot Gangavāḍi. This project failed, and the Ganga king is described as able even to shake the world. Amōghavarsha also fought against the Ganga king Prithivipati I. The Ganga king Nītimārgga I next signally defeated the Vallabha (or Rāshṭrakūṭa) army at Rājārāmaḍu (in the north of the Kolar District). But the Rāshṭrakūṭas continued to hold the Banavase province, which they had taken over from the Western Chālukyas. Its boundaries, however, did not extend eastwards beyond the Tungabhadrā.

Amōghavarsha seems now to have adopted a different policy, and gave up his animosity in favour of alliances. For we find that his daughter Chandrobbalabbe was bestowed in marriage on Būtuga the Ganga Yuvarāja, while another daughter named Śankhā was given to the Ganga-Pallava king Nandivarmmā. We also know from the statements in the *Kavirājamārgga* that Amōghavarsha Nṛipatunga, who had a very prolonged reign of more than sixty years, from 815 to 877, came to entertain the highest admiration for the Kannaḍa people and country, their language and literature. But later on, in 930 (Dg 119), the Rāshṭrakūṭas in the reign of Suvarṇṇavarsha (Gōvinda IV) were in possession of a province called the Kadambalige Thousand, which was to the east of the Tungabhadrā and extended down to Holalkere (Hk 23). As it was in 920 that we find the Nolambavāḍi province first mentioned as such (Jl 19), Kadambalige may have been intended as a barrier between it and Banavase. Somewhat later, in the reign of Akālavarsha Kannara III, we find the Rāshṭrakūṭas established near Devanhalli (Dv 43) and Māgadi (Ma 75). These parts cannot have been gained by conquest, unless perhaps they were connected with Bankēśa's expedition (see above), or in some way with Kannara's defeat of the Nolamba Pallava king Anniga in 944. For there is no acknowledgment either now or at any time that the Gangas were subordinate to the Rāshṭrakūṭas.[1] Still less were they

[1] The single exception is the Kalbhāvi inscription (see above), but the circumstances of Śivamāra's captivity and restoration to the throne sufficiently account for this.

so at this period. On the contrary, they were in intimate alliance, and rendering each other mutual assistance. The Ganga king aided Kannara III in gaining his throne, married his sister Rēvaka or Rēvakanimmaḍi, and slew the Chōla king who was at war with him,—while, on his part, Kannara helped Būtuga to usurp the Ganga throne from Rāchamalla, and ceded to him the Banavase province, which was in addition to the districts north of it that formed the dowry of his bride. The tracts above in question may therefore have been occupied as points of communication with the east, for the Rāshṭrakūṭa dominion under Kannara III extended into North Arcot and other parts in the South even to Tanjore.

But the Rāshṭrakūṭa power was waning to its close, and feeble rulers in rapid succession occupied the throne. The Ganga king Mārasimha strove to prop it up and appears to have crowned Indra, who was his nephew, in the attempt to do so. But Kakka or Kakkala was defeated in 973, and probably slain, by the Western Chālukya king Taila, who married his daughter Jakabbe. Mārasimha died at Bankāpur in 974 at the feet of his Jain guru, and Indra, after vain efforts to recover his throne, took the Jain vow of *sallēkhana* and starved himself to death at Śravaṇa-Beḷgoḷa in 982 (SB 57), the last of his race. The Rāshṭrakūṭa rule had already been brought to an end by the Western Chālukyas, and the Gangas before long succumbed to the Chōlas. Thus fell, nearly together, the two principal Jain states of the South.

11. WESTERN CHĀLUKYAS

The Western Chālukyas, after an eclipse of 200 years by the Rāshṭrakūṭas or Raṭṭas, regained their ascendancy, as above stated, in 973. Of Taila, who restored their power, Sk 125 says: "The earth and the crown having fallen into the hands of the Raṭṭas, he drove the kings of the Raṭṭa

The genealogy of the family is given as follows in Dg 42. After many kings had ruled in succession to Krishna, the founder, there arose the celebrated Kannama-Dēva. He had two sons, Bijjala and Rāja, of whom the former came to the throne. On the other hand, Rāja had four sons—Ammugi, Śankhavarmma, Kannara, and Jōgama. The first and last of these occupied the throne in succession. Then followed Jōgama's son Permmāḍi, whose son was Bijjala-Dēva. He made the whole earth his own, even as Agastya swallowed up the ocean. Another account (Sk 236) says the Kalachurya line gave light to the world through Sōma; through Pemma it became spotless; through Gorvappa it was distinguished for enjoyment; through Vajra it acquired might of arm; king Yōga gave it stability; and through king Bijjala it gained power.

Bijjala was a Jain by religion. Though he had usurped the throne, he did not assume the royal titles till six years afterwards, in 1162. A minister named Rēcha claims (Sk 197) to have obtained the empire for him and his successors. He then marched to the south, whither the Chālukya prince had retired, and proclaimed himself supreme. During his reign Basava, the son of an Ārādhya, came to settle in Kalyāna, where he became the son-in-law of the chief minister. He had a very beautiful sister named Padmāvatī, whom Bijjala, having seen, became enamoured of and married. Basava was thus in course of time appointed chief minister and general. The Rāja gave himself up to the charms of his beautiful bride and left all power in the hands of Basava, who employed the opportunity thus afforded him to strengthen his own influence, displacing the old officers of State and putting in adherents of his own, while at the same time he sedulously cultivated the favour of the king. By these means, and the promulgation of the new Lingāyit faith, he increased rapidly in power. At length Bijjala's fears were aroused, and he made an attempt to seize Basava; but the latter escaped, and afterwards dispersed the party sent in

Iriva-Nolambādhirāja. Satyāśraya also had a son, Kundamarasa or Kundaka-Rāja, who was viceroy and governor of Banavase in 1012 (Sk 287), with the seat of his government at Balipura or Belgāmi (Sk 125). He was still in the same position in 1025 (Sa 7). Jayasimha Jagadēkamalla, Satyāśraya's younger brother, next came to the throne. He caused the lotus king Bhōja to shut up, and was a lion to the elephant Rājēndra Chōla. In 1032 he was enjoying sports at Etagiri (Yatagiri in the Nizam's Dominions). In 1036 he was at Pottalakere (Sk 126), and made a grant to Vādi-Rudraguṇa or Lakulīśvara-paṇḍita for repairs to the temple of the Pancha Linga at Balligāve, which had been set up by the Pāṇḍavas when they came there after performing the Rājasūya sacrifice. This Lakulīśvara has been supposed to be the same as the founder of the Pāśupata sect, whose career it had appeared began at Mēlpāḍi in North Arcot in 1020 (*SII*. iii. 27). But Lakulīśa, according to Si 28, must have lived at an earlier period than 943. And it is now discovered that the original Lakulīśa (whose name means Śiva with the club) belongs to the first century.[1] The king in 1039 was at Ghaṭṭadakere (Sk 153). In 1042 an agrahāra was established at Andhāsura, the place still so called near Anantapur, but first mentioned in connection with Jinadatta-Rāya, who belongs to the eighth century. A glowing description is given in Sa 109 *bis* of the Sāntalige-nāḍ, of which Andhāsura was apparently the capital at that time. Such was its fertility that hunger was unknown there. Meanwhile, in 1042 we have notices (Si 40, 37, 25) of certain Chōla chiefs connected with Irungōla-Dēva ruling under this king in the north of Sīra tāluq.

Jayasimha's son Sōmēśvara I next came to the throne, and is styled Trailōkyamalla and Āhavamalla. His governor of Banavase in 1046, among other titles, is called "guardian of Kollipāke, the door of the South." This place, which is frequently referred to as a chief seat of the Lingāyit faith,

[1] See *JBoRAS*. xxii, 151; *JRAS*. for 1907, p. 419.

has unfortunately not been identified. In 1046 Chāmuṇḍa-Rāyarasa was governor of Banavase (Sk 160), and in the following year of other provinces as well, as far as the western ocean (Sk 151). He erected the elegant monolith *gaṇḍa-bhēruṇḍa* pillar at Belgāmi, surmounted by the image of Bhēruṇḍēśvara in human form with double eagle's head. He himself is called *gaṇḍa-bhēruṇḍa*, and a *bhēruṇḍa* pole, perhaps the length of the pillar, was established as a measure for land. In Sk 152 is the record of a man who thirteen years afterwards climbed to the top of the pillar and committed suicide by throwing himself down on to a row of spear-headed stakes. The king's son by his Pallava wife appears as governor under him in 1048 and 1054 (Hl 107, 119). An inscription of the latter year (Sk 118) says that the Chōla king valiantly fell in a battle with him, a reference to the death of Rājādhirāja. Sb 325 says that Āhavamalla slew the warlike Chōla. In 1051 the king visited Bandanikke (Hk 65). In 1058 his son Vikramāditya, who is given all the Ganga titles, was ruling in Balligāve as viceroy over the Banavase, Sāntalige, and Nolambavāḍi provinces (Sk 83). Two years later he was ruling Gangavāḍi (Sk 152, Dg 140). In 1063 and 1065 the king's son Vishnuvarddhana Vijayāditya was ruling the Nolambavāḍi kingdom (Si 18, Dg 111), with the seat of his government at Kampili (Mk 29). Meanwhile, in 1062, the Śāntara kings were ruling in Pomburchcha. The king also had a notable master of the robes in Lakshma or Lakshmaṇa, to whom he gave rank next to the royal princes, and entrusted him with the government of the Banavase province (Sk 136). In 1068 the king came to a tragic end by drowning himself, when smitten with deadly fever, in the Tungabhadrā at Kuruvaṭṭi (Sk 136).

His eldest son Sōmēśvara II Bhuvanaikamalla succeeded to the throne. He was a Ganga on his mother's side, and had as minister the powerful Ganga prince Udayāditya. The latter was governor of the Gangavāḍi, Banavase, and Sāntalige provinces from 1070 (Sk 109) to 1075, and had the seat of his government at Balligāve (Sk 130). The king himself made his chief residence at Bankāpura (Sk 129, 128). He was attacked at the beginning of his reign by the Chōla king Vīra Chōla, who was put to flight. He then formed three provinces, extending from coast to coast, to protect himself against Chōla invasions. These were Banavase, Nolamba-Sindavāḍi, and a territory beginning (it says) at Alampura. This last may be a place to the south of the mouth of the Pālār river. The three were placed respectively in charge of the viceroys Lakshmana, Vikrama-Nolamba, and the Ganga maṇḍalika, perhaps Udayāditya (Sk 136).

His younger brother, the distinguished Vikramāditya or Vikramānka, also a Ganga on the mother's side, next came to the throne. He set aside the Śaka era and established a new one, called the Chālukya Vikrama era, from the beginning of his rule. It is in this reign that we have the inscriptions giving an account of the origin and genealogy of the Gangas (Nr 35, Sh 64, 4, etc.). The king appointed as Yuvarāja his half-brother Jayasingha, the son of a Pallava mother, and called Vīra-Nolamba-Pallava (Sk 297). In 1074 the latter has the epithet *aṇṇa-niśśīmam* (Cd 82), which may mean either that his elder brother placed no restraint upon him, or that he had unbounded confidence in him. In 1080 he was on the most affectionate terms with his brother (Sk 297). He was ruling the Banavase and other provinces, all the lands as far as the southern ocean, in 1079 and 1080 (Sk 109, 293, 297). The last two contain a record of his exploits. The king was residing at Etagiri in 1077 and 1078 (Sk 124, 135), and his valour is extolled, especially in victory over Chōla and Lāla. From 1106 the Pāṇḍyas of Uchchangi became the rulers under him of the Nolambavāḍi and other provinces (Dg 139, Hl 68). Tribhuvanamalla Pāṇḍya is said in Dg 155 of 1124 to be Vīra-Nolamba's younger brother. He may have been related by marriage. He had the seat of his government at Beḻtūr (Bettūr near Dāvangere), and he claims (Dg 139) to be the emperor's right hand, and

(Dg 3) to have made important conquests for him. The Hoysalas were in power in Gangavāḍi, but in SB 45 and 59 a spirited account is given of a night attack made on Vikrama's army by the Hoysala general Ganga Rāja, at Kannegāla, and the Hoysalas soon assumed independence. Sāntalige was being governed by the Śāntaras, and feudatory Chōla chiefs ruled the territory on the north-east (Cl 43).

Vikrama's son Sōmēśvara III Bhūlōkamalla was the next ruler, and was called Sarvajna, or all-wise, by other kings. In 1129 he came on an expedition to the South and encamped at Hulluni-tīrtha. Banavase in his time was ruled by Kadambas (Sb 141), while the Pāṇḍyas continued to govern Nolambavāḍi, and Chōla kings—Irungōla and others—the parts in the north-east.

Jagadēkamalla is said (Ci 277) to have slain the generals of the hostile Chōla and Gurjjara kings, and captured their wealth and troops of horse. Of the same reign is Pg 43, in which we have Irungōla's son ruling in the Henjeru city. The latter (in Si 23) makes a grant there in the Nonambēśvara temple, which, it is interesting to note, is called the great *ghaṭika-sthāna* of the city. The exact signification of this term is not known, but here it seems to indicate the chief place of assembly for Brāhmans. The word occurs in the Tālgunda inscription (Sk 176), as well as in Cn 178 and Sk 197.[1]'

Under Nūrmmaḍi Taila or Trailōkyamalla, the Chālukya dynasty, which had reached its zenith with Vikramāṅka, began rapidly to decline. A powerful noble named Bijjala, of the Kalachurya family, had been appointed as general and minister, and the influence thereby obtained he turned against his sovereign and expelled him from the throne. This event occurred in 1156. The Chālukya king retired south and maintained himself in the Banavase country. The religious feuds which raged at Kalyāna in connection with the establish-

[1] See Dr. Kielhorn's article on the subject (*Göttingen Nachrichten* for 1900, *Heft* 3), and foot-note to p. 8 of Introd. *EC.* vol. vii.

ment of the new Lingāyit creed kept the hands of the Kalachuryas fully occupied. The Chālukya influence, therefore, was not extinguished, and Sōmēśvara, the last of his race, succeeded to the fallen fortunes of his house in 1162. He seems to have had his residence at Annigeri in Dharwar, and on the extinction of the Kalachuryas in 1183 an attempt was made to recover the Chālukya power, but in vain. What ultimately became of him does not appear. The latest record of him is Hl 46, dated in 1189. The Hoysalas of Dōrasamudra from the south, and the Sēunas or Yādavas of Dēvagiri from the north, had now closed in upon the disputed dominions, and the great and powerful Chālukya name disappears from history as that of a dominant race. But certain descendants of the line appear to have ruled in some parts of the Konkan till the middle of the thirteenth century.

12. KALACHURYAS

The Kalachuryas or Kalabhuryas were one of the lines of kings subdued by the Chalukyas on their first arrival in the south. They were apparently connected with the Haihayas in descent. The founder of the line was named Krishna, said to have been born of a Brāhmani girl by Śiva. In the guise of a barber, he slew in Kālanjara an evil spirit of a king who was a cannibal, and took possession of the Nine-lakh country of Ḍahala (Chēdi or Bandelkhand). A Chēdi or Kalachuri era, dating from A.D. 248,[1] is used in their inscriptions in the north, and is evidence of the antiquity of the family. Their inscriptions in Mysore, some seventy in number, are principally confined to Belgāmi in Shikarpur tāluq, Harihar in Dāvangere tāluq, and some places in Sorab tāluq. Among their titles are: Lord of the city of Kālanjara (in Bandelkhand), having the flag of a golden bull, Śanivārasiddhi, Giridurgamalla.[2]

[1] As determined by Dr. Kielhorn (*EI.* ix. 129).
[2] The last two were adopted by Vīra Ballāla of the Hoysala line.

The genealogy of the family is given as follows in Dg 42. After many kings had ruled in succession to Krishna, the founder, there arose the celebrated Kannama-Dēva. He had two sons, Bijjala and Rāja, of whom the former came to the throne. On the other hand, Rāja had four sons—Ammugi, Śankhavarmma, Kannara, and Jōgama. The first and last of these occupied the throne in succession. Then followed Jōgama's son Permmāḍi, whose son was Bijjala-Dēva. He made the whole earth his own, even as Agastya swallowed up the ocean. Another account (Sk 236) says the Kalachurya line gave light to the world through Sōma; through Pemma it became spotless; through Gorvappa it was distinguished for enjoyment; through Vajra it acquired might of arm; king Yōga gave it stability; and through king Bijjala it gained power.

Bijjala was a Jain by religion. Though he had usurped the throne, he did not assume the royal titles till six years afterwards, in 1162. A minister named Rēcha claims (Sk 197) to have obtained the empire for him and his successors. He then marched to the south, whither the Chālukya prince had retired, and proclaimed himself supreme. During his reign Basava, the son of an Ārādhya, came to settle in Kalyāna, where he became the son-in-law of the chief minister. He had a very beautiful sister named Padmāvatī, whom Bijjala, having seen, became enamoured of and married. Basava was thus in course of time appointed chief minister and general. The Rāja gave himself up to the charms of his beautiful bride and left all power in the hands of Basava, who employed the opportunity thus afforded him to strengthen his own influence, displacing the old officers of State and putting in adherents of his own, while at the same time he sedulously cultivated the favour of the king. By these means, and the promulgation of the new Lingāyit faith, he increased rapidly in power. At length Bijjala's fears were aroused, and he made an attempt to seize Basava; but the latter escaped, and afterwards dispersed the party sent in pursuit. His adherents flocked to him, and Bijjala, advancing in person to quell the insurrection, was defeated and compelled to reinstate the minister in all his dignities. Basava not only resumed his former power and authority, but formed a plot against the life of the king, probably in the hope of becoming supreme in the State as regent during the minority of his nephew, the son of Bijjala and Padmāvatī. Accounts differ as to the mode in which the king was killed. According to the Jain version, he was poisoned on the banks of the Bhīma when returning from a successful expedition against the Silāhāra chief of Kolhāpur; while the Lingāyits state that he was assassinated by three of Basava's followers.

Rāyamurāri Sōvi, the son of Bijjala, resolved to avenge his father's death, and Basava fled to Ulive or Vṛishabhapura on the Malabar coast. Thither the king pursued him and laid siege to the place. It was reduced to extremities, and Basava in despair threw himself into a well and was drowned. But according to the Lingāyits he disappeared into the linga at Sangamēśvara, at the junction of the Malprabhā and Krishnā.

The remaining three kings of this line were brothers of Sōvi, and during this period the last Chālukya regained a certain portion of his kingdom. But the territories of both towards the south were absorbed into the dominions of the Hoysalas, who had by this time risen to power in Mysore.

The following is a table of this short-lived but eventful Kalachurya[1] dynasty:—

1. Bijjala, Bijjana, Nissankamalla, Tribhuvanamalla, 1156-1167

2. Rāyamurāri Sōvi, Sōmēśvara, Bhuvanaikamalla, 1167-1176	3. Sankama, Nissankamalla, 1176-1181	4. Āhavamalla, Apratimalla, 1181-1183	5. Singhana, 1183

The first appearance of Bijjala in our inscriptions is in 1156 (Sk 104, 108). In these, which acknowledge the

[1] The name also appears in the form Kalatsurya (Sb 131, 267).

Chālukya supremacy, Bijjala is styled a mahā-maṇḍalēśvara, but in the first he is significantly said to be ruling all the countries. From 1158, described as his 2nd year (Sb 255), he is entitled *bhujabala-chakravartti*[1] or mighty emperor, and invested with a number of epithets (Sk 18). In the next year, 1159, the dominion appears as his (own) victorious kingdom (Sk 123). On the other hand, Sb 328 of the same year begins with a genealogy of the Chālukyas down to Nūrmmaḍi Taila, and merely adds "at that time" was Bijjala king (*kshōnipāla*). Sk 102 of 1162 relates how he came to subdue the southern region and encamped at Balligāve. The next year he is said (Sk 242) to have extended his territory to the shore of the ocean, while Sk 123 says he subdued from the ocean in the south to the Chālukya capital in the north. In 1164 and 1165 raids by the Hoysalas are mentioned (Dg 42, Sb 372). In 1168 Bijjala has all the Chālukya supreme titles (Sk 92). Sk 197 says that the king of Simhala carried his tray, the Nepāla king was his perfumer, Kērala was his betel-bearer, Gurjjara was his artificer, Turushka was his groom, Lāla was his valet, Pāṇḍya was his crutch, and Kalinga the attendant on his elephant.[2]

He was succeeded by his son Sōmēśvara or Rāyamurāri Sōvi-Dēva, who is said (Sb 389) to have exacted tribute from Lāla, Chōla, and Gurjjara. Kadamba kings had for some time at this period been governors of the Banavase province, and of interest is the statement in Sb 345 of 1171 that Sōvi-Dēva, the Kadamba governor in that year, had put the Changālva king[3] into chains, as he had vowed. Sb 139 of 1173 shows how the despatch of a military force was needed to collect the fixed land rent.

Sankama-Dēva, a younger brother, next came to the

[1] This title was also taken by the Hoysalas.

[2] Certain inscriptions (Hl 50, Sk 197, 119) introduce Bijjala's younger brother Mailugi-Dēva and his son Kali-Dēva or Kandara, and a Mailugi-Dēva, younger brother (probably cousin) of Rāyamurāri Sōvi-Dēva, as if they had sat on the throne. They may perhaps have been associated in the government.

[3] For the Changālva kings, see section under that head below.

throne. Of him it is said (Sk 96) that twice five heralds were continually heard proclaiming in his court how Gaula had sent (as tribute) elephants ; Turushka, horses ; the Simhala king, pearls ; Chōla, white cloths ; Magadha, musk ; the Malaya king, sandal ; and the Lāla king, young girls. In this year, 1179, Sankama paid a visit to Balligrāme, accompanied by the chief officers of his court, and being greatly impressed with the munificence and charities of the Kēdārēśvara temple, and with the erudition of its high priest, the rāja-guru Vāmaśakti, made a grant for it.

Āhavamalla, another brother, succeeded, but may have been associated in the government with Sankama for some time before. Sk 119 says he was a lion to the elephant Gaula, a net for the shoal of fish the Chōlika army, a south wind to the rain-cloud the Āndhra king, and a continual thunderbolt to the royal swan the Mālava king. The latest date we have for him, 1183, is described as his 4th year or his 8th year (Sk 245, 159). With him the Kalachuryas came to an end, though there is no record of how this happened. But a chief named Brahma or Bomma is credited (*IA.* ii. 299) with destroying the Kalachuryas and restoring the Chālukyas. He was eventually defeated by the Hoysala king Ballāla.

13. CHŌLAS

While, after the overthrow of the Rāshṭrakūṭas in 973, the Western Chālukyas and the Kalachuryas in succession dominated the north-west of the Mysore country for 210 years to 1183,—after the overthrow of the Gangas by 1004,[1] the Chōlas dominated the south and east of the country for 112 years to 1116. The Chōlas[2] were one of the oldest royal lines known in the south of India, being mentioned in

[1] The exact date of the event is not known, but the earliest mention I have met with of the conquest of Gangavāḍi is in the 19th year of Rājarāja (Mb 123).

[2] The name as written in Tamil is Śōḻa or Śōṟa ; in Kannaḍa it is Chōḷa ; and in Telugu appears as Chōḍa (for the Eastern Chālukya kings).

the edicts of Aśōka in the third century B.C. They were Tamil, and their original capital was at Oreiyūr (now known as Warriore), near Trichinopoly. But the later capital, which is the one principally identified with them, was Tanjore.

Of their early history little or nothing has been recovered, but a few details for the first and second centuries appear in a recent publication.[1] It is not till the tenth century that anything definite is known about them, and even then their practice of dating inscriptions only in the regnal year of the king afforded no basis for framing the chronology of the line; while the names adopted by many of the kings were themselves misleading, being mere royal titles. The first actual date which gave a clue was in a Ganga inscription of 950 in Mysore (Md 41). This contained the statement that the Ganga king Būtuga, who was aiding the Rāshṭrakūṭa king Kannara or Krishna III in his war against the Chōlas, slew the Chōla king Rājāditya at Takkolam (near Arkonam), thus bringing the war to a close. Chōla inscriptions dated in the Śaka era were also found in other parts of Mysore, and eventually in the Madras country too. A chronology of the Chōlas from the tenth century, when they first came into prominence, has thus been constructed, the calculations being made by Dr. Kielhorn (see *EI.* viii. App. ii. 21), and it would seem that contact with the Gangas and other powers to the north first led them to adopt the Śaka era in dating their inscriptions.[2] After the twelfth century the Chōlas ceased to be formidable.

The following is a table of the Chōla kings thus deduced. They had the titles Parakēsarivarmma and Rājakēsarivarmma alternately, beginning with the first :—

[1] See note 2, p. 19 above.

[2] Unlike those of other royal lines, the Chōla inscriptions, instead of being on separate slabs of stone set up at the site of a grant, are mostly inscribed on the basement and outer walls of temples, in long single lines that go right round the building. The earlier ones in Mysore are generally in Kannaḍa, but the majority are in Tamil, and there are even some in the Tamil language but in Kannaḍa characters.

1. Vijayāditya

2. Āditya I

3. Parāntaka I, Vīra-Nārāyaṇa, 907-

4. Rājāditya, -949 Mūvaḍi-Chōla

5. Gaṇḍarāditya

9. Madhurāntaka, Uttama-Chōla

6. Arinjaya

7. Parāntaka II

8. Āditya II

10. Rājarāja I, 985- Mummaḍi-Chōla, Rājāśraya

11. Rājēndra-Chōla I, 1012- Muḍikoṇḍa-Chōla, Gangaikoṇḍa-Chōla, Nikarili-Chōla

Kundavvā, m. to E. Chālukya king Vimalāditya

12. Rājādhirāja I, 1018- Jayangonda-Chōla

13. Rājēndra-Dēva, 1052-

14. Rājamahēndra

Madhurāntakī, m. to Rājēndra-Chōla II (No. 17)

15. Vīrarājēndra I, 1063 Vīra-Chōla, Karikāla-Chōla

16. Adhirājēndra

Ammāngā, m. to E. Chālukya king Rājarāja

17. Rājēndra-Chōla II, Kulōttunga-Chōla I, 1070-

18. Vikrama-Chōla, 1118-

19. Kulōttunga-Chōla II, -1143-

20. Rājarāja II, 1146-

21. Rājādhirāja II

22. Kulōttunga-Chōla III, 1178- Kōnērinmaikoṇḍān, Tribhuvanavīra, Vīrarājēndra-Chōla

23. Rājarāja III, 1216-

24. Rājēndra-Chōla III, 1246-1267

The first event which brought the Chōlas into contact with Mysore was in 921. At that time they had uprooted the Bāṇas, and the Chōla king Parāntaka conferred the Bāṇa sovereignty on the Ganga prince Prithivīpati, giving him the name Hastimalla (*SII.* ii. 387). The next event was the death of the Chōla king Rājāditya in 949 by the hand of the Ganga king Būtuga. This, according to Md 41, may have been effected by an act of treachery, but the large Leyden plates give a different version (*ASI.* iv. 207). The occasion was war between the Chōlas and the Rāshṭrakūṭas, in which Krishna or Kannara III, the Rāshṭrakūṭa king, was aided by Būtuga, who was his brother-in-law. The scene of the tragedy was at Takkolam (near Arkonam), and it brought the war to an abrupt termination. Krishna-Rāja, thus victorious, assumes in Tamil inscriptions the title *Kachchiyun-Tanjaiyun-koṇḍa* (capturer of Kānchī and Tanjore), and seems to have established his power for a time over the Chōla territories. He also rewarded Būtuga by giving him the Banavase Twelve-Thousand province, the north-west of Mysore, which, added to the provinces north of it that formed the dowry of his bride, carried the Ganga territories once more far up towards the Krishna river.

But the tide turned in the time of Rājarāja. The Chōlas had by that time carried their arms up to Kalinga on the east coast, and made Vengi, the Eastern Chālukya territory, an appanage of the Chōla empire, Rājarāja's daughter being married to the Eastern Chālukya king Vimalāditya. The wave of conquest was then directed to the west, against the Western Chālukyas, in the course of which the Ganga territory in Mysore was invaded. We accordingly find Rājarāja established near Hoskōte in 997 (Ht 111). But by 1004 his son Rājēndra-Chōla, who was in command of the Chōla army, succeeded in capturing Talakāḍ, the Ganga capital, and brought the Ganga power to an end. The conquest of the south and east of Mysore, in an arc extending from Arkalgūḍ in the west, through Seringapatam, north by Nelamangala to Niḍugal, was speedily effected, and Rājendra-Chōla gained the title Gangaikoṇḍa-Chōla. The Changāḷvas, whose kingdom was in the Hunsūr tāluq and Coorg, were at the same time brought under Chōla subjection, and the Chōla general Panchava-mahārāya, who had overcome the Changāḷvas in the battle of Panasoge, was rewarded by Rājarāja with the Arkalgūḍ and Yēlusāvira country, together with the title Kshattriya-śikhāmaṇi Kongāḷva. In the extreme north-east, connected with Niḍugal, was Henjeṟu (now Hēmāvati, on the northern border of Sīra tāluq), a subordinate Chōla kingdom. These were the outposts of the new conquest.

There is little doubt that the Chōlas contemplated the entire subjugation of Mysore. But in this they were foiled to the westward by the Hoysalas, who were now rising to power. Thus, Rājarāja's general Apramēya is said, in 1006, to have encountered Poysala's minister Nāgaṇṇa (TN 44), and to have won a battle over other Hoysala leaders at Kalavūr (Kaleyūr near Mālingi, opposite to Talakāḍ, on the other side of the river). Then, Panchava-mahārāya, another of Rājarāja's leaders, who had distinguished himself in the battle of Panasoge (Cg 46), and been invested with the title of Kongāḷva, conducted victorious expeditions along the west coast (Sr 140). But in Mysore the Kongālvas were opposed by the Hoysala king Nṛipa-Kāma in 1022 and 1026 (Mj 43, Ag 46), and made no way in extending the Chōla conquests in this country.

The territory actually acquired by the Chōlas in Mysore was parcelled into provinces, which, according to their usual policy, were named after Chōla kings. The south of Gangavāḍi, or that part of Mysore District, thus received the name Muḍikoṇḍachōla-maṇḍala ; the north of Bangalore District was the Vikramachōla-maṇḍala ; Kolār District was the Nikarilichōla-maṇḍala. The sub-divisions of these large provinces were termed valanāḍ. Thus, the southern portion of the first above named was the Gangaikoṇḍachōla-valanāḍ, while that of the third was the Jayangoṇḍachōla-valanāḍ. Towns were treated in the same way, so that Talakāḍ became Rājarājapura ;

Manalūr (Malūrpaṭṇa, near Channapaṭṇa) became Nikarili-chōlapura; Kuningil (Kunigal) became Rājēndrachōlapura. But Kolār retained its original name of Kuvalāla.

The conquests of Rājarāja's reign, as detailed in various inscriptions, are thus described in Cp 128, of his 23rd year. He destroyed the ships at the Kāndalūr Śālai (on the west coast), and with his victorious army conquered Vengai-nāḍ (the Eastern Chālukya territory on the east coast, between the Krishnā and Gōdāvari rivers), Gangapāḍi (the Ganga territory in the south and east of Mysore), Nulambapāḍi (the Nolamba Pallava territory in the north of Mysore), Taḍigaivali (the west of Bangalore District), Kūḍa-malaināḍ (the Coorg hill country), Kollam (Quilon), Kalingam (the Kalinga Ganga territory on the east coast, up to Orissa), Īlā-maṇḍalam (Ceylon), the Iraṭṭa-pāḍi Seven-and-a-half Lakh country (the Raṭṭa or Rāshṭrakūṭa territory in the Dekhan), twelve thousand ancient islands of the sea (perhaps the Laccadives and Maldives), and deprived the Sēliyar (or Pāṇḍyas) of their glory at the very time when it was at the highest. In Mysore both he and his son specially patronised the temple of Pidāriyār in Kolār, now known as the Kolāramma, and repeatedly endowed it, while Rājēndra-Chōla had the brick parts rebuilt in stone (Kl 109).

Many of these conquests were really effected by Rājarāja's son Rājēndra-Chōla, who was in command of his father's army. But the conquests made by Rājēndra-Chōla and the trophies acquired by him in his own reign are thus described (among other records) in Nj 134 of 1021, his 9th year. They were—Yedatore-nāḍ (the north of Mysore District); Vanavāsi (Banavāsi, on the north-west frontier of the Mysore country); Kollipāke (a celebrated Saiva place, not identified); Manne (in Nelamangala tāluq, the Ganga royal residence); the crown of the king of Īlā (Ceylon), and the more beautiful crown of its queen; also the crown of Sundara and the necklace of Indra which the king of the South (Pāṇḍya) had given up to the kings of Īlā; the whole of Īlā-maṇḍala (Ceylon); the famous crown and the ruby necklace which were heirlooms worn by the Chēralas or Kēralas (kings of Malabār); many ancient islands; the superb crown of pure gold which Paraśurāma, when he uprooted the race of kings twenty-one times, had deposited in the inaccessible Chandimat island. He moreover defeated Jayasinga (the Western Chālukya king), who turned his back at Muśangi or Muyangi and fled. To these achievements are added in Kl 44 of ? 1023, his 12th year,—the Iraṭṭapāḍi Seven-and-a-half Lakh country (the Raṭṭa territory in the Dekhan); great mountains filled with the nine treasures; Śakkaragoṭṭam (Chakrakoṭṭa in Central India); Madura-maṇḍala (the Pāṇḍya territory of Maḍura); Nāmanaigakkonai, Panjappalli, and other places whose names are gone. But the information is supplied in Cp 82 of 1034, his 23rd year, or Nl 7 of 1038, his 27th. The above list of conquests is there extended as follows. He took Maśuni-dēśam; defeated Indiraviratan of the Lunar race in a great battle at Ādinagaravai, capturing his relations and family treasures; Oṭṭa-vishaiyam (Orissa); Kōsalai-nāḍ (in the Central Provinces); Taṇḍabutti (Daṇḍabhukti), after destroying Danmapāla (its king Dharmapāla) in a fierce battle; Dakkana-Lāḍam (southern Lāṭa), after a vigorous attack on Iraṇaśūram; Vangāla-dēśam (Bengal) from which Gōvindaśandan (Gōvindachandra), dismounting from his horse, fled; terrified Mayipāla of Sangottal in battle, capturing his elephants, women and treasures; and took Uttira-Lāḍam (northern Lāṭa), and even Gangai (the Ganges). He also sent many ships over the billowy ocean and captured Śangirāma-Viśaiyōttungapanman (Changirāma-Vijayōttunga-varmma), the king of Kiḍāram (near Prome in Burma), seizing his fine elephants and the jewelled archway of his fort and palace gates; gained Śrivijaiyam, Pannai, Malaiyūr, Māyiruḍingam, Ilangaśōbam, Mā-Pappālam (in the Andaman islands), Mevilipangam, Valarppandār, Kulaittakolam, Mādamalingam, Ilāmuri-dēśam, Mā-Nakkavāram (the Nicobar islands), and Kiḍāram (in Burma). A good many of these names of persons and places are not identified, but the enumeration suffices to show the wide range of Rājēndra-Chōla's victorious expeditions. His son boasts (Nl 25) that his father had conquered from Gangai (the Ganga territory[1]) in the north to Ilangai (Ceylon) in the south, and from Mahōdai (Cochin) in the west to Kaḍāram (Burma) in the east. Few of the parts, however, thus attacked were retained. The invasions were evidently mere raids on a large scale, whose object was booty, especially crowns, crown jewels, and jewelled trophies of all kinds.

Rājādhirāja-Dēva had been associated with his father in the government for more than a quarter of a century, or (as Nl 25 and CB 21 say) had planted his own umbrella under the white umbrella of his father, and had shared in his career of conquest. He next succeeded to the throne, and the events of his reign are recounted in Dv 75. He bestowed crowns and the kingdoms subdued in the last two reigns on his uncles, brothers and sons. His treatment of captive kings was bloodthirsty and cruel, while he was as eager as his father to amass crowns and jewels. He beheaded the Pāṇḍya king Mānābaranan on the field of battle, taking his golden crown set with large gems; had the Kērala king trampled to death by his elephant; sent Sundara-Pāṇḍiyan flying, and seized his state umbrella, his big fans made from the tail of the yāk, and his throne. He slew the king of Vēnāḍ, destroyed the three kings of Irāmakum, and wrecked the ships of Villavan (the Chēra king) at Kāndalūr Śālai. He routed the army of Āhavamalla (the Western Chālukya king) and forced him to retreat, burnt Kollipākkai, and openly seized the jewelled crown of Vikramabāhu, the king of Ilangai (Lanka). When Vīra-Sālamēgan invaded the country from Īlam (Ceylon), he drove him off, took his sister and wife prisoners, and cut off the nose of his mother. And on his returning to revenge them, he slew him on the battlefield, and seized his golden crown set with large jewels. He also took the crown of Śrīvallavan Madanarāja, a king of Īlam descended from Kannara (? Rāshṭrakūṭa

[1] This might perhaps be taken to mean the Ganges, but Rājendra-Chōla is commonly described as the conqueror of Gangai and the East country, in which the former is unquestionably the Ganga territory, from the conquest of which he had the title Gangaikoṇḍa-Chōla.

king) ; and leading the army a second time to the north, chased away Gaṇḍan, Dinakara-Nāranan, Ganavati and Madiśūdanan, and burnt the palace of the Śalikkiyar (Chālukyas) at Kampili (on the Tungabhadrā, north of Bellary). Dv 76 adds a few more details. The tribute paid by the Villavar (Chēras), Mīnavar (Pāṇḍyas), Śalikkiyar (Chālukyas), Vallavar (Pallavas), Kōśalar, Vanganar, Konganar, Śintukar, Ayyanar, Śingalar (Singalese), Pangalar, and Āntarar (Āndhras), together with the revenue he obtained from one-sixth share of the produce of the land, he distributed among the Brāhmans, and performing the horse-sacrifice, seated himself on the throne with the name Jayangoṇḍa-Chōla. But he died in fighting against the Chālukya king Āhavamalla in the battle of Koppam (perhaps Kopana in the south-west of the Nizam's Dominions[1]) in 1052. An inscription at Annigere in Dharwar[2] says that the wicked Chōla (Rājādhirāja), who had abandoned the religious observances of his family, penetrated into the Belvola country and burnt the Jain temples erected there by (the Ganga king) Ganga-Permāḍi, but that he eventually yielded his head to (the Chālukya king) Sōmēśvara (Ahavamalla) in battle and forfeited his life. On the other hand, a Chālukya inscription in Mysore (Sk 118) says the Chōlika (or Chōla king) valiantly died on the battlefield.[3]

Rājēndra-Dēva, his younger brother, backed by the elder brother's army, had invaded the Iraṭṭapāḍi Seven-and-a-half Lakh country and erected a pillar of victory at Kollāpuram (Mb 107, Kl 107). It was in revenge for this that Āhavamalla attacked the Chōlas at Koppam. Rājēndra-Dēva was present at the battle, and when his brother died took command of the army and secured the throne. Notwithstanding that his brother the king had fallen, and that he himself was severely wounded and had lost many of his principal leaders, he contrived to slay the Chālukya king's younger brother Jayasinga, Pulakēśi, Daśavarmma, Nanni-Nulamba, and other princes

[1] See note, p. 16, Introd. to vol. ix. [2] *KD.* 441.
[3] *āhavānganadoḷ Chōlikan ammi sattan.*

without number, so that Āhavamalla fled in terror (Bn 108). Rājēndra followed the example of his brother in bestowing royal titles on his uncle, his brothers, his sons and grandsons (Bn 108).

Of the time of Rājamahēndra, probably his son, perhaps the one to whom he gave the title Uttama-Chōla, there is only one inscription (Ht 36), of his 2nd year. It contains no historical information, and the reign was a very short one.

We then come to Vīrarājēndra, of whom a long account is given in Cp 85, of his 4th year. He was a younger brother of Rājēndra-Dēva. He routed the army which had been sent against him into Vengai-nāḍ (the Eastern Chālukya territory); beheaded the great chief Śāmundarājan and cut off the nose of the beautiful Nāgalai; when Vikkalan and Singalan (the Western Chālukyas Vikrama and Jayasimha) engaged him in battle at Kūḍal-Sangamam (the junction of the Tungabhadrā and Krishnā), hoping to wipe out the disgrace of their former defeat, he gained the victory. He overcame Śingan of Kōśalai, Kēṫaraiyan, Māraiyan, Iraśayan, and others; and when Maduvanan fled, along with the other chiefs who had dismounted from their elephants, Āhavamalla also fled, leaving his wives, treasure, elephants, and other valuable spoils to the victor. He beheaded on the battlefield the king of Pottappi, Vāran, Kēralan, and Jananāta's brother; had the king of the South (Pāṇḍya), Śrīpallava's son Siruvan, and Vīrakēsari trampled to death by elephants, seizing all their crowns and jewelled decorations; drove the family of the Śengiraiyas and Śeralas into the western ocean; subdued the Iraṭṭas and captured their elephants; in a fresh battle cut off the heads of the chiefs Val . . ., Vanjipayyan, Piramadēva, Baṇḍāra-Toraiyan, Śattiyaṇṇan, Pattiyaṇṇan, Vīmanayan, and Vangāran; also of the Ganga, Nulamba, Kāḍava, and Vaidumba kings; and returned to his great city Gangai (perhaps Gangaikoṇḍaśōlapuram), near the great river.

The next inscriptions are those of Rājēndra-Chōla II, Eastern Chālukya king on his father's side, but through his mother a grandson of the Chōla king Rājēndra-Chōla, and by his wife a son-in-law of Rājēndra-Dēva, who was also his uncle. He is better known as Kulōttunga-Chōla, the title he afterwards assumed in his 7th year. He is the Rājiga-Chōla whose designs are said to have been frustrated by the Chālukya prince Vikramāditya and the Pāṇḍyas of Uchchangi. Kl 108 of his 2nd year, and Cp 77 of his 17th, say that when still Yuvarāja he wedded the goddess of Victory by his heroic deeds at Chakrakoṭṭa, where he took tribute from the king of Dhārā, and captured troops of elephants at Vayirāgaram. He also routed the army of the kings of Kuntala (the Western Chālukyas), and put on the garland of victory over the North, while he inherited at the same time the crown of the South and of the country adorned with the Ponni (or Kāvērī). His white umbrella shone like moonlight all over the earth, and his tiger banner fluttered on mount Mēru. Many rows of elephants stood before him, sent as tribute by kings of remote islands, while outside his splendid capital lay the head of the runaway Pāṇḍya king, pecked by kites. He inflicted a total defeat on Vikkalan (the Chālukya), forcing him to retire in disorder to the west, his retreat being marked by dying elephants all the way from Nangili (in the east of Mulbāgal tāluq) to Manalūr and the Tungabhadrā. By this victory the Chōla acquired the two countries Ganga-maṇḍalam and Śinganam, a statement which, together with the line of the Chālukya retreat, indicates that the Chōlas had temporarily lost the Ganga country. He then resolved to take the Pāṇḍi-maṇḍalam, and when his armies marched forth for this purpose, it was as if the northern ocean was about to overflow the southern ocean. The five Panjavas (Pāṇḍyas) fled in terror to the forests. These he destroyed, planted pillars of victory in all directions, took possession of the pearl fisheries, the Podiyil mountain, where the three forms of Tamil (prose, poetry, and the drama) flourished, the central Śayyam (the Sahya mountains) where elephants are captured, the (river) Kanni and Gangai. He established colonies in all parts of the conquered country as far as Kottāru. He then seated himself on the throne solely for the receipt of tribute. Later inscriptions, down to Kn 12 of his 49th year, say that he caused the wheel of his authority to roll over all regions, so that the Mīnavar (Pāṇḍyas) lost their position, the Villavar (Chēras) became disconcerted, and the other kings retreated in disguise.

By 1116, near the close of his reign, Talakāḍ, the old Ganga capital, had been retaken [1] by the Hoysalas, and Chōla dominion in the Mysore country brought to an end. This important capture was effected by Ganga-Rāja, a general of the Hoysala king Vishnuvarddhana, and probably a descendant of the old Ganga Rājas, being (as SB 45 says) a hundred times more fortunate than that former Rāja of the Gangas (under whom Talakāḍ and the kingdom were lost). Farther point is given to the event by his original name Rājēndra-Chōla being used for the Chōla king in Bl 58. A spirited account is contained in SB 90 and Ml 31 of how Ganga-Rāja summoned the fort to surrender, and how the Chōla governor Adiyama returned a defiant answer, saying, Fight and take it (if you can). This Ganga-Rāja did, driving out the Chōla chiefs who were present, and followed up his success by bringing under one umbrella all the districts which had become Chōla nāḍs. Putting to flight the Tigulas (the Tamil people) of Gangavāḍi, he caused Vīra-Ganga (the Hoysala king) to stand erect (or assert his independence).

Some relics of Chōla dominion lingered on in the north-east of the Kolar District, where we have inscriptions of Vikrama-Chōla down to his 12th year (Ct 70). They are chiefly in the Chintāmani and Śrīnivāspur tāluqs. In Ct 160 of his 5th year, he is credited with the destruction of Kalinga and the conquest of Kaḍalmalai.

At a still later period Kōnērinmaikoṇḍān made some

[1] The date is determined by Yd 6, the first to give Vishnuvarddhana the title Talakāḍu-goṇḍa, dated Saka 1038 (expired), Durmukhi, and Ch 83, which describes him as in the same year ruling in Talakāḍu and Kōlāla over the whole of Gangavāḍi as far as Kongu. Moreover, a village which Ganga-Rāja received as a reward for his exploit he made over to a Jain priest in 1117 (Ml 31).

arrangements connected with the Marudūr (Maddūr) agrahāra, through his agent there (Md 3, 7). But the Chōla authority in Mysore had long ceased, and the tables were now turned, for the Hoysalas became protectors of the Chōlas. One of the titles of Nārasimha II, the Hoysala king who came to the throne in 1220, was *Chōla-rājya-pratishṭhāchārya* (setter up of the Chōla kingdom). This was justified by the aid given to the Chōla king Rājarāja III, who in 1232 had been taken captive by the Kāḍava (Pallava) king Perunjinga at Śendamangalam in South Arcot. Nārasimha, on hearing of it, sent an army and set him free (*EI.* vii. 160; Gb 45). The next Hoysala king, Sōmēśvara, had also by 1237 entered into the Chōla country, defeated Pāṇḍyá, and restored Chōla to his hereditary kingdom (Md 122). According to Ak 123 this was a Rājēndra-Chōla. But two years later he had himself taken possession of the Chōla country and was ruling from there (TN 103), his residence being at Kannanūr (Nj 36) or Vikramapura (to the north of Śrīrangam in Trichinopoly), which, it is said (Bn 6), he had created for his pleasure in the Chōla-maṇḍala conquered by the might of his own arm, and there, with an interval in 1252, he was till 1254. Kp 9 of 1257 describes him as the talisman (*rakshāmaṇi*) or protector of Chōla.

14. POYSALAS OR HOYSALAS

On the subversion of the Gangas by the Chōlas in 1004, the Poysalas or Hoysalas rose to power in the west of Mysore, and eventually, in 1116, expelled the Chōlas and became rulers of the whole country, which they held till the middle of the fourteenth century. They were of indigenous origin, and Sosevūr or Sosavūr—the Śaśakapura of Sanskrit writers—named as their birthplace, has been identified with Angaḍi in the Western Ghats, in Mudgere tāluq (see Mg 9, 15, 16, 18). They claim to be Yādavas and of the Lunar race, and bear the

SALA AND THE TIGER.

Size of Original 5ft. × 3ft.

title Lord of Dvārāvatī-pura (which represents both Dvāraka in Kathiāwār, the reputed capital of Krishna, the hero of the Yādavas, and their own capital Dōrasamudra). They were Jains, and the progenitor of the family was Sala. On a certain occasion when he went to worship at the temple of his family goddess Vāsantikā-dēvī at Sosevūr (still represented by that of Vasantamma) and was receiving instruction from the yati there, a tiger bounded out of the forest, glaring with rage. The yati[1] hastily snatched up his rod[2] and handed it to the chief, saying *poy Sala* (strike, Sala!). Whereupon Sala hit at and killed the tiger, finishing it off perhaps with his dagger (see Bl 1/1). Moreover, from the rescued yati's exclamation, he assumed the name Poysala, of which Hoysala is the more modern form.[3] This story is repeated in all the accounts of the origin of the dynasty, and their crest on temples exhibits a free standing group of Sala stabbing the tiger (see frontispiece, vol. v.), while the seal of copper-plate grants shows a dead tiger and the rod (as in Bn 6).

Of the time of Sala no records have been found, but the name Poysala occurs in an inscription of 1006 at Kaliyūr, on the opposite side of the river to Talakād (TN 44). From that time onwards Hoysala inscriptions become more and more frequent until they mount up to bewildering numbers, down to the establishment in 1336 of the Vijayanagar empire, the founders of which were probably connected with the Hoysalas. The Hoysala inscriptions are found from Tanjore in the south to Sholapur in the north, and from Coorg in the west to the east coast in South Arcot. They are mostly on prepared slabs of black hornblende, and are remarkable for their beautiful and artistic execution, the whole being so skilfully engrossed that,

[1] According to Sb 28 his name was Sudatta, and Nj 39, 38 state that he had been brought by the king from some other place and established there. Nr 46 calls him Vardhamāna-munīndra.

[2] Though described as a cane (*betta*) and in other ways (see vol. v. Introd. 10), it was no doubt really the usual stout rod of an ascetic, made of the solid or male bamboo.

[3] The name also appears as Poysaṇa and Hoysaṇa. In Tamil it is written as Poyichala or Pochala.

notwithstanding ornamental flourishes and pictorial initials, no space is left for the insertion of a single additional letter.

The Hoysalas at first acknowledged the supremacy of the Western Chālukyas, the chosen enemies of the Chōlas, but the bond was a loose and friendly one, and in the time of Vishnuvarddhana they became independent. Their capital was Dōrasamudra (now Halebīḍ in Bēlūr tāluq), which appears in Sanskrit as Dvārasamudra and Dvārāvatīpura. But while this was under preparation and being adorned with splendid buildings by Vinayāditya (see SB 53), the capital was at first at Sosevūr and then at Beluhūr, Bēlāpura or Vēlāpura (Bēlūr). Among the usual titles of the Hoysalas were (besides the one mentioned above),—*Yādava-kulāmbara-dyumani* (sun in the sky the Yādava family), *samyaktva-chūḍāmani* (crest-jewel of perfect devotion), *Maleparoḷ-gaṇḍa* (champion among the Malepas or hill chiefs), *bhujabala-pratāpa-chakravartti* (strong-armed illustrious emperor), and frequently, from the time of Ballāla II., *dakshina-chakravartti* or *tenkana-chakravartti* (emperor of the South). But the special titles and conquests of any one king are often carried on and attributed to his successors.

The following is a table of the Poysalas or Hoysalas as derived from their inscriptions:—

1. Sala, Poysala, Hoysala, 1006

2. Nṛipa-Kāma, Kāma-Poysala, . . 1022-1027 . .
? Rāchamalla-Permmāḍi

3. Vinayāditya, Tribhuvanamalla-Poysala, . . 1047-1100

Ereyanga (Yuvarāja from 1063 to 1095)

4. Ballāla I, 1100-1106
Tribhuvanamalla-Ballāla-Poysala

5. Biṭṭi-Dēva, Biṭṭiga, . . 1111-1141
Vishnuvardhana,
Vīra-Ganga, Vikrama-Ganga,
Tribhuvanamalla, Talakāḍu-goṇḍa

Udayāditya
died 1123

6. Nārasimha I, Pratāpa-Nārasimha, 1141-1173
Jagadēkamalla-Nārasimha

7. Ballāla II, Vīra-Ballāla, 1173-1220
Śanivāra-siddhi, Giridurgamalla, Yādava-Nārāyaṇa

8. Nārasimha II, Vīra-Nārasimha, 1220-1235
Magara-rājya-nirmmūlana, Pāṇḍya-disāpaṭṭa, Chōla-rājya-pratishṭhāchārya

9. Sōmēśvara, Vīra-Sōmēśvara, Soi-Dēva, 1233-1254

10. Nārasimha III, Vīra-Nārasimha,
1254-1291

11. Ballāla III, Vīra-Ballāla,
1291-1342

12. Ballāla IV, 1343
Vīra-Virūpāksha-Ballāla

Rāmanātha, Vīra-Rāmanātha,
1254-1295

Viśvanātha, 1295-1297

Nṛipa-Kāma or Kāma-Poysala is not included in the Hoysala genealogy as usually given in their numerous inscriptions, which proceeds from Sala to Vinayāditya. The reason of this omission is not evident, as Ak 157 and 141 say that he was Vinayāditya's father. He cannot have been Sala himself, or this would have leaked out in some of the numberless inscriptions which contain the pedigree. On the contrary, he is said to have been known as Rāchamalla-Permmāḍi, which connects him with the Gangas, due perhaps to intermarriage. That he ruled there can be no doubt, for, among others, Mg 19 is of his 7th year, and in Mj 43, dated in 1022, and Ag 76, dated in 1026, we find him opposing the Kongālva king, and next year aiding Banavase (Mj 44). Moreover, SB 44 describes him as the patron of Ēcham or

Ēchiga, the father of Ganga-Rāja, the Hoysala general who captured Talakāḍ in 1116. How he was related to Sala does not appear, but if the Poysala of 1006 was Sala, there was very little distance between them.

Vinayāditya was the first notable king of the line. He was born in Sosavūr (SB 56) and ruled from there. He is styled Tribhuvanamalla-Poysala-Dēva, from the Western Chālukya king Tribhuvanamalla Vikramāditya (reigned 1076-1126) being his overlord, but Hl 1 shows that before this Hoysala-Dēvī was the queen in 1055 of Trailōkyamalla, Vikramāditya's father. Vinayāditya also had the six letters *Ra-kka-sa Po-ysa-la* inscribed on his flag, a possible reference to connection with the Ganga king Rakkasa. In what year Vinayāditya came to the throne we do not know. The earliest date we have for him is 1047 (Ng 32, Cm 160). The boundaries of the kingdom in his time are given in the former as—Konkaṇa (North Kanara), Ālvakhēḍa (South Kanara), Bayalnāḍ (Waināḍ), Talekāḍ (in the south-east of the Mysore District), and Sāvimale (somewhere to the north), and he is said (Bl 200, etc.) to be ruling the Gangavādi Ninety-six Thousand. The latest date we have for him is 1100 (Bl 141). His wife was Keleyabbarasi, and they had a son Eṟeyanga.

Whether the latter ever occupied the throne seems doubtful, and he probably died before his father. Kd 142 shows him to be only Yuvarāja or heir-apparent up to 1095. At the same time, Kd 33, without date, and Cn 148 of 1093 represent him as ruling (also SB 144), which must have been in conjunction with his father. He was a general under the Western Chālukyas, and is described as a powerful right arm to the Chālukya king. He trampled down the Mālava army, burnt Dhārā and laid it in ruins, dragged down Chōla and plundered his camp, broke and ruined Kalinga (Sh 64, etc.). By his wife Ēchala-Dēvī he had three sons—Ballāla, Biṭṭi-Dēva, and Udayāditya.

Of these, Ballāla I succeeded his grandfather on the throne in 1100 (Bl 199), and his reign was a short one, but there are inscriptions of his up to 1106 (Cn 169). He is styled Tribhuvanamalla-Ballāla-Poysala, and visited Sosavūr in 1100 (Bl 199), but made Beluhūr (Bēlūr) his capital (Ng 32, Cm 160). The inscriptions tell us of his marrying in one day in 1103 the three beautiful and accomplished daughters of Mariyāne-daṇḍanāyaka. In 1104 he led an expedition against the Changālva king (Hn 161, 162), and together with his brothers repulsed an attack made by Jagaddēva (Śāntara king) on Dōrasamudra, capturing his treasury and the central ornament of his necklace (Bl 58, Ng 30).

Biṭṭi-Dēva, Ballāla's brother, next came to the throne, and is celebrated as the rescuer of his country from the Chōlas and the establisher of the independence of the Hoysalas, whose kingdom he greatly extended. In what year his reign began has not been discovered. DB 11 might have decided the question, being of his 12th year, but unfortunately no year is named. The earliest actual date that can be cited for him is 1111 in Sh 89, but Kd 164 represents him as ruling in 1100: this must have been in association with Ballāla, his elder brother. An important event in his career was his exchanging the Jain faith for that of Vishnu, which took place (before 1116) under the influence of the reformer Rāmānuja, who had fled from persecution by the Chōla king, a rigid Śaiva, and taken refuge in the Hoysala country. This change was signalised by Biṭṭi-Dēva calling himself thenceforward Vishnuvarddhana, the name by which he is best known. He now entered upon an extensive range of conquests. Talekāḍ was captured by his general Ganga-Rāja in 1116, and this was immediately followed up by the expulsion of the Chōlas from Mysore and the recovery of all the provinces there which they had previously taken. These Ganga-Rāja loyally made over to his king. He also in a night attack drove off the Chālukya army encamped at Kannegāla (near Hassan). By these operations he caused Vishnuvarddhana, who now took the title Vīra-Ganga, to stand erect, that is, enabled him to assume independence (SB 90, etc.). Thus in

1117 Ch 83 says that he was ruling in peace in Talakāḍ and Kōlāla, having under his sole umbrella the kingdom of the Gangavāḍi Ninety-six Thousand, including Kongu (Salem and Coimbatore). The conquest of the Nīlagiris and Malabār, according to the same inscription, was effected by the general Punisa, who, among other exploits, is said to have frightened the Todavar, the earliest mention that has been found of the Todas as the settled tribe inhabiting the Nīlagiri mountains. While these expeditions were being carried out in the south and west, the king's attention was directed to the north, and in the same year as the capture of Talakāḍ, 1116, the Pāṇḍyas of Uchchangi were attacked and defeated in a battle at Dumme, which is on the border of Shimoga and Chitaldroog Districts (Cm 99). According to Ck 29 and 30, the conquest of Uchchangi was effected for him by Chāma-Dēva, a son of the Orissa king Chōla-Ganga, and born in the Mysore country. Pages might be filled with the details of Vishnuvarddhana's conquests as given in various inscriptions. Suffice it to say that the boundaries of the kingdom in his reign extended (Mg 22, Kd 102, etc.) on the east to Nangili (the eastern portion of Kolar District); south to Kongu, Chēram, and Ānemale (Salem, Coimbatore, and Travancore); west to Bārakanūr (in South Kanara); north to Sāvimale (somewhere towards the Krishnā). The southern boundary is given in Ak 30 as Rāmēśvara (on the east coast in the Madura District). Hn 119 says: east, south and west three oceans being the boundaries of the land he ruled, on the north he made the Perddore (or Krishnā) his boundary. The course of his victories is thus graphically put in Kd 69: the lion the Hoysala king's valour, having sported in plunder at Talakāḍ, attacked the lofty elephant Uchchangi, calmly marched by Banavase, daringly seized on Belvala, and sprang forward with joy to the Perddore (or Krishnā), planting his feet on Hānungal. Bl 58 describes his conquests in general, and Ng 70 gives a list of important forts which he captured. The provinces over which he ruled were (Cm 160, Kd 80, etc.)—Kongu,

Nangali, Talakāḍ, Gangavāḍi, Nolambavāḍi, Banavase, Hānungal, Huligere, Halasige, and Belvala. Gold coins of his have been found, on the reverse of which appear the titles *Talakāḍu-goṇḍa* or *Noṇambavāḍi-goṇḍa*. His own country (says Hn 119) he gave to Brāhmans and the gods, and himself ruled over the foreign countries won by his sword. Dōrasamudra was the recognised capital (Bl 147, Md 29, etc.), but he made his residence at various places. In 1128 he was at Yādava-pura or Tonnūr (My 16). In 1137 Bankāpura on that side (the north) and Talavana-pura (Talakāḍ) on this side (the south) are stated (Ak 144) to be his capitals (*rājadhāni*). He took up his abode in the former in 1139 (Cm 199, 200), and there he died in 1141 (Cm 96), his body being conveyed to Sosavūr. His first wife was Śāntala-Dēvī, a strenuous upholder of the Jain faith, but she died in 1131 (SB 53), and by a subsequent marriage with Lakkumā or Lakshmī-Dēvī he had the son who succeeded him, born in 1133 (Bl 124), and crowned from the day of his birth (Bl 93).

This was Nārasimha I, who must have been a boy when he came to the throne. His reign was on the whole uneventful, but the boundaries of the kingdom were maintained. He is said in 1145 to have slain Changālva in battle, and seized his elephants, horses, gold and new jewels (Ng 76). He is also said to have been a terror to most of the kings of the South (Sr 74, Kd 51, Hs 137), and in 1161 to have defeated a Kadamba force that threatened Bankāpura (Bl 193). But his power was sustained mainly by his father's reputation and the devotion of his father's generals. Of these, Chokimayya (Hn 69) calls himself king Vishnu's Garuḍa, and in Bp 9 of 1155 appears as if ruling at Nangali over part of Gangavāḍi. Then there were Huḷḷa (SB 137[a], 138), who was one of the foremost upholders of the Jain faith, and Biṭṭiga (Hs 137). The Chālukya king Jagadēkamalla attacked Hoysala in 1143 (Dg 85), and seems to have asserted his supremacy by 1149 (Ck 29, 30). Thus Nārasimha has the prefix Jagadēkamalla in 1153 and 1155 (Kl 100[a], 169), but immediately after this the Chāluḳya throne was usurped by Bijjala and the Kalachuryas. The Hoysala king eventually lapsed into a voluptuary. For Bl 193 informs us that he had three hundred and eighty-four well-born women in his female apartments, and Bl 114 contains statements that bear this out. He died in 1173, being, it would seem, only forty years of age. His chief queen was Ēchala-Dēvī, and they had a son Ballāla.

The reign of Ballāla II or Vīra-Ballāla vied in glory with that of his grandfather Vishnuvarddhana, and the whole dynasty is in consequence sometimes called the Ballālas after him. He was crowned on the 22nd of July 1173 (Kd 4, 136, 129) in the capital Dōrasamudra. In Bl 86 an account is given of a royal progress made by him in his father's lifetime through the hill countries in the west. On this occasion Tantrapāla-Hemmāḍi claims to have induced Kongālva, Changālva, and the other chiefs of Male to do homage, and eventually to have gained the crown for Ballāla, himself being made minister. But Hs 20 shows that in 1174 Ballāla had to send an expedition under his general Beṭṭarasa against the Changālva king Mahadēva, who had retired to Pālpare, a fort in Kiggaṭnāḍ in south Coorg. Beṭṭarasa destroyed him and made Pālpare the seat of his own government. But the Changālva Pemma-Vīrappa later on attacked him, aided by the Koḍagas (or Coorgs) of all the nāḍs, and was near gaining the victory, when Beṭṭarasa eventually triumphed. This is the earliest specific mention that has been found of the Koḍagas or people of Coorg. But Ballāla's great victories were to the north. An early conquest was that of Uchchangi, the Pāṇḍya fortress. This had been besieged by the Chōlas for twelve years and abandoned as hopeless; but Ballāla easily overcame it, and when Kāma-Dēva, the Pāṇḍya king, threw himself on his mercy, restored him to his kingdom. This was before 1177 (Ck 36), and he, in consequence, assumed the titles Giridurgamalla and Śanivāra-siddhi. A battle with Sankama-Dēva (the Kalachurya king) is mentioned in 1179 (Mg 33). But his great decisive victory was one gained at

HOYSALA STONE INSCRIPTION.

Size of Original, 4 ft. 7 in. × 1 ft. 9 in.

Soraṭūr (near Gaḍag) over the formidable Sēuna army. Though he came with as many as 200,000 infantry (says Dg 25), armed with thunderbolts, and 12,000 cavalry, conspicuous with high saddles and jewelled breastplates, Ballāla-Rāya on his one elephant charged the Sēuna king's army, put them to flight, and slaughtered them all the way from Soraṭūr to the bank of the Krishnavēni river. According to Bl 77 he moistened his sword with the blood of the Pāṇḍya king, whetted it on the grindstone the head of Bhillama, and sheathed it in the mouth of Jaitugi (Sēuna kings). He followed up this great victory by the capture of a number of forts north of the Mysore country, all these successes being accomplished before 1190 (Cn 179). By 1193 he had taken up his residence at Lokkigondi or Lakkundi in Dhārwār (Sk 105). His northern boundary was advanced to the Bhīmarathī (Tp 43). He was now sole ruler of the Seven-and-a-half Lakh country (Ci 64), and styled emperor of the South (Sb. 140). During this period he lived at various places, but eventually established the royal residence (*rājadhāni*) at Hallavūr, also called Vijayasamudram (Hn 139, Cn 172) and Vijayapura (Cn 244). This place was the modern Hulloor, on the Tungabhadrā in the Rāṇi-Bennūr tāluq of Dhārwār. He was there in 1180 (Ci 73), but from 1200 (Hn 139) seems to have been living there almost continuously till 1211 (Ak 137). His senior queen Umā-Dēvī, mentioned in 1209 (Ak 40), appears in many records for a long time. His son Nārasimha was apparently associated with him in the government in 1205 (Cd 23). He was Yuvarāja in 1210, and had a sister named Sōvala-Dēvī, celebrated for her beauty and virtues (Cn 243).[1] At the same date the king, his crowned queen Padmala-mahādēvī, and their son Nārasimha are represented as all ruling together (Hk 13, 14). In 1218 the king was encamped at Niḍugal-durga (Hn 61). At length,

[1] She established the agrahāra of Sōmanāthapura, which was equal to Valabhi, at Hāruvanahalli (Hāranhalli in Arsikere tāluq), where there is a fine temple of Sōmēsvara (Ak 123).

being of full age, Ballāla established Nārasimha in the kingdom and went to heaven (Cn 211[b]). This was in 1220, as Nārasimha was crowned in that year (Cn 172[b]). Thus closed an energetic and distinguished reign of forty-seven years, during which the Western Chālukyas and the Kalachuryas came to an end, the Sēunas were driven back, and the Hoysalas remained as a dominant power in the South. Coincident with the king's death was the self-sacrifice of the prince Lakshma, recorded on a pillar by the side of the Hoysalēśvara temple at Halebīḍ (Bl 112). He was of royal blood, and perhaps a half-brother. He and a thousand warriors had vowed themselves, as Garuḍas, to live and die with the king, and at his death took their own lives as a sign of undying devotion to him.

Nārasimha II was crowned on the 16th of April 1220 (Cn 172[b]). His distinctive titles are—uprooter of the Magara kingdom, displacer of Pāṇḍya, establisher of the Chōla kingdom (Cn 197). Saying, "Why am I called master of elephants when there are no troops of elephants of which I am master?"—he marched, without stopping, for a hundred *gāvudas* to the east, and uprooting the Magara king, captured the hundreds of elephants he had brought against him (Ci 72). By this expedition he became possessed of a wealth of elephants, horses, jewels, and other valuables, such as had never been acquired before (Cn 197). In connection with this an incident related in Cn 203 of 1223 deserves notice. When marching against Magara, the king encamped at Chūḍavāḍi and gave a feast to celebrate the adding to his necklace of an emerald received from Munivarāditya. This must have been a stone of unusual size and value. Chūḍavāḍi is no doubt the Chūḍa-grāma (Muḍiyanūr in Mulbāgal tāluq) mentioned in 338 (Mb 157). Munivarāditya was an old title belonging apparently to a landed chief in Mēlai (or western) Mārāyapāḍi (Ci 162), and the Magara kingdom may have been identical with the Mahārājavāḍi of which the Bānas were in possession in the ninth century (see above, p. 43; also below, p. 164). The boundaries of the Hoysala kingdom are given in 1228 as Nangali on the east, Kongu on the south, Ālvakhēḍa on the west, and the Heddore on the north (Cn 204). But the next year Nārasimha is said to be ruling from Kānchī, with the surrounding ocean as his boundary (Tp 42). The Sēunas had again attempted to press to the south, but their multitudinous army was routed (Md 121), and their leaders Vikramapāla, Pāvusa, and others were slain (Dg 25). In South Arcot the Kāḍava (or Pallava) king Perunjinga had meanwhile taken the Chōla king prisoner. On hearing of it, Nārasimha vowed that the trumpet should not sound until he had released him. He accordingly sent an army, which forced the Kāḍava king to surrender, and set free Chōla, to whom Nārasimha restored his crown, thus justifying his title of setter up of the Chōla kingdom (*EI.* vii. 160 ; Gb 45). A pillar of victory was also erected at Sētu (Dg 25), as far as which he brought the land under his control (Cn 203). By his wife Kālale-Dēvī he had the son Sōyi-Dēva or Sōmēśvara (Cn 203), who was tended like a mother by the king's sister Sōvala-Dēvī (Ak 123).

Sōmēśvara came to the throne in 1233, as 1254 is given as his 21st year (Sr 110). Of him it is said (Kp 12) that when he first began to walk, Chēra went before him, calling out, "Bravo! mind your steps, Dēva!" while the Chōla king and Pāṇḍya, one on each side, held his hand. The boundaries of his kingdom are given (Md 122) as Kānchī on the east, Vēlāvura (Bēlūr) on the west, the Peddore (or Krishṇā) on the north, and Bayalnāḍ (Wainād) on the south. He is represented as first fighting against Krishna-Kandhara (the Sēuna king), but he was principally engaged in conquests to the south, while the Sēunas continued to make incursions in the north-west.[1] In 1236 he is said (Kp 63) to be living in the Pāṇḍya-maṇḍala, which he had acquired by his strength and

[1] An inscription at Pandharpur (near Shōlāpur) states that the Hoysala king Sōmēśvara made a gift to the god there in Saka 1159, or A.D. 1236 (*Bo. Archl. Rep.* 1897-8).

valour. Jl 33 says he marched into the Chōla-Pāṇḍya kingdom, and Ak 123 that he had uprooted Rājēndra-Chōla on the field of battle, but when he threw himself on his mercy, gave him his protection. He now took up his residence permanently at Kannanūr or Vikramapura (north of Śrīrangam in Trichinopoly), which he had created for his pleasure in the Chōla-maṇḍala acquired by his own arm. Here, with a short interval in 1252, he remained till 1254 (Ak 108), being styled *Sārvvabhauma* or universal emperor. In 1252 he revisited Dōrasamudra,[1] and the two Cĥangālva kings then ruling conducted him to Rāmanāthpura (Ag 53).

On his death in 1254 a division was made of the Hoysala territories. The ancestral Kannaḍa kingdom, with its capital at Dōrasamudra, was given to Nārasimha III, his son by his wife Bijjala-Rāṇi, while the Tamil districts in the south and Kolar fell to the share of Rāmanātha, another son by his wife Dēvala-Dēvī.[2] Nārasimha was born perhaps on the 12th of August 1240 (Kd 100), and his *upanayana* was performed on the 25th of February 1255 (Bl 126). He now paid a visit to the Vijaya-Pārśva Jain temple at Halebīḍ and read the genealogy of his line as recorded in the inscription there (Bl 124). He signs himself *Malaparoḷ-gaṇḍa* in Md 79 and TN 100. In 1271 the Sēuna king Mahadēva came forth to battle, but fled in a single night (Ng 39). In 1276 a more formidable invasion took place by the Sēunas under Sāluva-Tikkama, the general of Rāma-Dēva. Assisted by Irungōla and other powerful local chiefs, he advanced against Dōrasamudra. But in a great battle fought at Belavāḍi on the 25th of April the Sēuna army was utterly routed and driven beyond Dummi with great slaughter (Bl 164, 165). The rival king Rāmanātha continued to rule throughout the reign of Nārasimha, and collisions occasionally took place between their followers. But he mostly remained in his own territory, and

[1] As stated in an inscription lately discovered at Kondajji agrahāra in Gubbi tāluq.

[2] Inscriptions of the Hoysala kings Sōmēśvara and Rāmanātha are found as far south as Tanjore, at Sendalai and Mannārguḍi (*Mad. Archl. Rep.* 1896-7).

probably had his capital at Kannanūr in Trichinopoly, as Ballāla (his successor) is represented as marching from Kannanūr (Ck 4). In the Mysore country he seems to have had a residence at Kundana, perhaps the place of that name near Devanhalli. The southern boundary of his kingdom in Mysore extended from about Honnudike in Tumkūr tāluq to Lakkūr in Mālūr tāluq, the western being east of the range of hills north from Dēvarāyadurga. He survived Nārasimha and was succeeded for a short time by his son Viśvanātha, but the Hoysala dominions were again united under Nārasimha's son Ballāla III.

The latter was crowned on the 31st of January 1292 (Cn 36). In 1301 he appears issuing his orders to the temple priests throughout the districts in Kolar resumed from Rāmanātha's kingdom (Bn 51, etc.). In 1305 we find him marching against the Sēuna king, who was desirous of capturing him (Sa 156). In this reign began the Musalmān invasions from Delhi which brought the Hoysala empire to an end. The earliest notice of these is in 1310, when the Turukas are said to have marched against Dōrasamudra (Hn 51, 52). This was the first invasion, under Kāfūr, the general of Alā-ud-dīn of the Khilji or second Pathān dynasty. The king was defeated and taken prisoner; Dōrasamudra was sacked, and the enemy returned to Delhi literally laden with gold. The king's son, carried off as a hostage, was restored in 1313 (Sh 68). By 1316 the capital was rebuilt (Md 100). But a later expedition in 1326, sent by Muhammad III, of the house of Tughlak, completely demolished the city. The king seems to have retired to Toṇḍanūr (Tonnūr near Seringapatam), but eventually went to live at Unnāmale (Tiruvannāmalai or Trinomalee in South Arcot). He was there in 1328 (DB 14) and frequently afterwards up to 1342 (Bn 21). But in 1329 he had a residence in Mysore, called by various names—Virūpākshapura (Ht 43), Hosavīḍu, Hosanāḍ, Hosadurga, and so on. It is uncertain what place this was. But in 1340 he performed an anointing to the kingdom (Bn 111), which must have been that of his son, who is called (Cm 105) Vīra-Virūpāksha-Ballāla-Dēva. The ceremony therefore probably took place at Virūpākshapura. In 1341 he is said to have erected a pillar of victory at Sētu (Mr 82). At length he fell fighting against the Turukas in a battle at Beribi on the 8th of September 1342 (Kd 75). His son was wearing the crown in 1343 (Cm 105), but the Hoysala power was at an end. The latest date that has been found in inscriptions for Ballāla is 1346 (Bn 120).

15. SĒUNAS

The Sēunas (also called Yādavas of Dēvagiri), who were the great rivals of the Hoysalas in contending for the possession of the Western Chālukya and Kalachurya dominions, claim descent from Krishna through Subāhu, a universal monarch, who divided his empire between his four sons. The second son, Driḍhaprahāra, obtained the south, and his descendants ruled over the Sēuna country, in Central India, probably corresponding in great part with the modern Khāndēsh. He was succeeded by twenty-two kings of his line down to Bhillama, who was the contemporary of the Hoysala king Ballāla II, and from whose time alone the history of Mysore is concerned with the dynasty. Their inscriptions are confined to the north of the Shimoga District and the Dāvangere tāluq, and range in date from 1212 to 1300. They had titles such as Yādava-Nārāyaṇa, bhujabala-pratāpa-chakravartti, etc., which were appropriated by the Hoysalas on the latter defeating them. Their standard bore the device of a golden *garuḍa*. Having overcome the Kalachuryas, they became masters of all the western Dekhan, with their capital at Dēvagiri, now known as Daulatabad. Their destruction was due to the same Musalmān invasions from Delhi that brought the Hoysala power to an end. The following is a table of the kings :—

1. Bhillama, 1187-1191
|
2. Jaitugi, Jaitrapāla, 1191-1210
|
3. Singhana, 1210-1247
|
Jaituga
|
4. Kandhara, Kanhara, Krishna, 1247-1260 — 5. Mahadēva, 1260-1271
|
6. Rāmachandra, Rāma-Dēva, 1271-1309
|
7. Sankara-Dēva, 1309-1312

The immense army of Bhillama was totally routed by Ballāla II at Soraṭūr, as previously related, and slaughtered all the way to the Krishnā river. Jaitugi is also mentioned as defeated by him. Singhana took advantage of Ballāla's death to seize some part of Mysore in the extreme north-west. According to Sb 319 an army of 30,000 horse sent by him captured the hill fort of Gutti (that is, Chandragutti) in 1239. His attempts to collect the local revenue, however, seem to have been resisted by force (Sb 425, 217), and about the same time battles were fought against his army by the Sindas at Nēmatti (Hl 54, 55). The Sēuna kings, among other epithets, are generally described as destroyers of Mālava-Rāya, terrifiers of the Gurjjara Rāya, and establishers of Telunga-Rāya. The Hoysala king Sōmēśvara, as we have seen above, is said to have fought against Krishna-Kandhara. But in Mahadēva's time the Sēuna general Sāluva-Tikkama claims to have won important victories over the Hoysalas, in connection with which, apparently, he made some additions to the temple of Harihara, which the king had himself visited, and where he remitted all the taxes of the agrahāra (Dg 59). But Hg 39 says, on the other hand, that Mahadēva fled in a single night. In the time of Rāma-Dēva the seat of the Sēuna government in Mysore was fixed at Bettūr, close to Dāvangere on the east. But in 1276 an invasion of Dōrasamudra by Sāluva-Tikkama was entirely defeated at the battle of Belavāḍi, as related in Bl 164, 165. The

Musalmān invasions from Delhi began in the reign of Rāma-Dēva and before long extinguished the Sēuna power. Finally, in 1338, Muhammad Tughlak removed the capital of his empire from Delhi to Dēvagiri, giving it the name of Daulatābād.

16. VIJAYANAGAR

The Vijayanagar empire was founded in 1336, immediately on the disappearance of the Hoysalas from the stage of history. The founders were two princes named Hakka and Bukka, sons of Sangama. The former became the first king, taking the name of Harihara, and his brother succeeded him. They were probably subordinates of or connected with the Hoysalas,[1] and were aided in their enterprise by the head of the *maṭha* at Śringēri (in the Kaḍūr District) founded by the reformer Śankarācharya in the eighth century. The name of this guru was Mādhava, and he is known as Vidyāraṇya. He became the first minister of the new State.

The Vijayanagar inscriptions in Mysore are nearly as numerous as those of the Hoysalas. There is one (Bg 70) which actually professes to be of the date 1336, and relates a story as to how the site of Vijayanagar was selected. But it cannot be relied on, no original being forthcoming. Then, Mg 25 contains some statement, which, owing to gaps in the inscription, cannot be fully made out, that Bukka-Rāya's chief councillor was unwilling to give up Sosavūr. This was the birthplace of the Hoysalas. By 1539 its name had been changed to the present Angaḍi (Bl 197).

But Sg 1 of 1346 is genuine and undoubted, and one

[1] A Ballappa-dannāyaka, described as a son of the Hoysala king Ballāla III, appears in several inscriptions at the close of the Hoysala period, down to Mr 16 of 1343. And in Sg 1 of 1346 we find Ballappa-dannāyaka as a son-in-law of the first Vijayanagar king, Harihara I. Moreover, in Yd 29 appears a son of Ballāla, called Hampe-Vodeyar. Now Hampe (the ancient Pampa) is still the name for the site of Vijayanagar.

of the earliest known inscriptions of the Vijayanagar kings. After obeisance to Vidyātīrtha, the guru of Vidyāraṇya above mentioned, it states that Harihara, having conquered the earth from the eastern to the western ocean, resolved to make a grant to celebrate the festival of his victory. Accordingly, he, with his four brothers, his son-in-law and other relatives, made grants to Bhāratītīrtha-śrīpāda and his disciples, as well as to forty Brāhmans living in the holy place Śringēri, for the maintenance of the rites and services. Another interesting inscription is Sk 281 of 1368, which contains particulars regarding Mādhava, then minister to Bukka-Rāya, and he is described as the guru who cleared and made plain the ruined path of the *upanishads*. It is unique in being dated by the Śātavāhana-śaka, for the Śālivāhana-śaka, a reminiscence of the origin of the latter. And it is of interest to note that the grant made in it consists of a village which was the object of the grant in the Kadamba Prākrit inscription of about the third century on the Malavalli pillar (Sk 264), and connected with a preceding inscription on the same pillar (Sk 263) recording a grant in about the second century by the (Śātavāhana) king Sātakarṇṇi.

The first or Sangama dynasty of Vijayanagar, who were Yādavas, held the throne from 1336 to 1478, and consisted of nine kings. The throne was then usurped by a Sāluva chief, who was succeeded by his son. There were thus only two kings of the Sāluva dynasty, also Yādavas, and they occupied the throne from 1476 to 1496. Then followed the Narasinga dynasty from Tuluva, which ruled from 1496 to 1567, and had six kings. The fourth and last dynasty was the Rāma-Rāja or Karṇāṭa. It was in power from 1567 to 1644, and numbered six kings.

The following is a table of the Sangama dynasty :—

[TABLE

Sangama,
m. Kāmāmbikā

1. Harihara I, Hariyappa-Oḍeyar, 1336-1353 | Kampa, Kampaṇṇa — Sangama | 2. Bukka-Rāya, 1353-1377, Bukkaṇṇa-Oḍeyar, m. Gaurāmbikā | Mārapa | Muddapa

Harihara II, 1377-1404 | Virūpanna, Virūpāksha, 1354-1377 | Mallinātha, 1363 | Kampaṇṇa, 1365, 1371 | Jannāmbikā

By Pampā-Dēvī, 4. Bukka-Rāya II, 1405-1406 | By Mēlā-Dēvī or Mallā-dēvī, 5. Dēva-Rāya I, Pratāpa-Dēva-Rāya, 1406-1416 | Chikka-Rāya-Oḍeyar, 1379, 1381 | Virūpanna, Virūpāksha, 1384, 1404

By Malliyavve, Mallaṇṇa, 1412 | By Dēmāmbikā, 6. Vijaya-Rāya, 1416-1417,[1] m. Nārāyaṇāmbikā | Harihara-Rāya, 1422

7. Dēva-Rāya II, 1419-1446, Prauḍha-Dēva-Rāya, Pratāpa-Dēva-Rāya II, Gaja-bēṇṭekāra | Pārvyati-Rāya, Śrīgiri, 1424, 1425

By Ponnala-Dēvī, 8. Mallikārjuna, 1446-1467, Immaḍi-Dēva-Rāya, Immaḍi-Prauḍha-Dēva-Rāya | By Simhala-Dēvī, 9. Virūpāksha, 1467-1478

Of Sangama's five sons, the eldest, called according to tradition Hakka, assumed the name Harihara, and was the first king of the new empire. Kampa or Kampaṇṇa became ruler of a kingdom in the east, in the direction of Nellore, and had Śāyana, the commentator on the Vēdas,[2] brother of Mādhava, as his minister. Bukka succeeded Harihara on the throne, and was the most distinguished of the brothers. Mārapa obtained a kingdom in the west (Sb 375), with the seat of his government at Gōmantaśaila or Chandragupti (Chandragutti). He subdued the Kadambas.

The Vijayanagar kings had Virūpāksha for their family

[1] Certain inscriptions represent him as ruling in 1422 (An 79, Sk 93).

[2] Some copper-plates of 1386 in the Inām office name Nārāyaṇa-vājapēya-yāji, Narahari-sōmayāji and Paṇḍari-dīkshita as the scholars who assisted him in his commentaries, and their families still receive special honours at the Sringēri maṭha (*Mys. Arch. Rep.* of 1908).

god, and their grants are usually signed in his name. Their crest was the Varāha or Boar, which had been that of the Chālukyas. Their capital was situated on the Tungabhadrā, in the west of the present Bellary District, near the Pampā lake, on a remarkable site covered with immense boulders, and their stronghold was the hill Hēmakūṭa. In Mysore, the king's eldest son was as a rule a viceroy in Muluvāyi (Mulbāgal) in the east, while another son was viceroy in Āraga in the Male-rājya or hill kingdom in the west. Another son was at times governor of the Terakanāmbi kingdom in the south. But from the end of the fifteenth century the chief representative of the empire in the south was a viceroy called the Śrī-Ranga-Rāyal, whose seat of government was at Seringapatam.

Of Harihara I not much is known beyond what has been stated above. But Bukka-Rāya, whom he appointed as his Yuvarāja (Cn 256), was famous. With the assistance of Vidyātīrtha-muni he became very great, and having freed from enemies a hundred royal cities, counting from Dōrasamudra, ruled over an empire perfect in its seven parts (Yd 46). Though the establishment of the capital is attributed to Harihara, and his naming it Vidyānagarī after Vidyāranya-śrīpāda (Cd 46), the building of the city and the transformation of its name to Vijayanagari, or city of victory, are said to have been the work of Bukka-Rāya (Cn 256). The latter has the special titles *ari-rāya-vibhāḍa* (destroyer of hostile kings), *bhāshege-tappuva-rāyara-gaṇḍa* (champion over kings who break their word), *Hindū-rāya-Suratrāṇa* (Sultān over the Hindū kings), *pūrva-paśchima-dakshiṇa-samudrādhīśvara* (master of the eastern, western, and southern oceans). He was a terror to the Turushkas, the Konkana (king) Śanka-pārya, the Āndhras, Gurjaras, and Kāmbhōjas, and defeated the Kalingas. An interesting event of his reign, showing his liberal-mindedness, was his reconciliation of the Jainas and the Vaishnavas in 1368. The latter had been persecuting the former, who in a general body appealed to the king for protection. He summoned the leaders of both sects before him, and declared that no difference could be made between them. Then (as graphically described in Sb 136), taking the hand of the Jainas and placing it in the hand of the Vaishnavas, he ordained that they should each pursue their own religious practices with equal freedom. Copies of this decree were to be set up in various places, and besides the one at Śravaṇa-Beḷgoḷa (SB 136), there is still one at Kalya in Magadi tāluq (Ma 18), the Kallehada-paṭṭana mentioned in them.

In 1355 Bukka-Rāya is said (Cd 2) to be ruling from Hosapaṭṭaṇa in the Hoysana country, and Hosapaṭṭaṇa is mentioned in connection with the Jains who appealed to him as above mentioned, who are said to have come from districts included within Āneyagondi, Hosapaṭṭana, Penugoṇḍa, and Kallehada-paṭṭana. It may be the place called Hosavīḍu, Hosadurga, and by other names, which was a residence of the last of the Hoysala kings. I have thought it might be Hosūr in Goribidnūr tāluq, or Hosadurga in Chitaldroog District. But this is uncertain, and its identification would be of interest. It is described as having been the capital of Nijagali-Kaṭaka-Rāya, but unfortunately this does not help us. It was apparently the same place as Virūpākshapura (see vol. x. Introd. 32).

Harihara II, Bukka-Rāya's son by Gaurāmbikā, succeeded him on the throne. But he also had other sons—Virūpaṇṇa-Oḍeyar by Jommā-Dēvi, whose succession was apparently desired in the west (Kp 6); Mallinātha or Mallappa-Oḍeyar, who was ruling in the east of Mysore; and Kampanna-Oḍeyar or Chikka-Kampaṇṇa, ruling in the south of Mysore. Harihara II is principally praised for making the sixteen great gifts at various sacred places, localities which show that his territories extended from the Krishnā at Kurnool to Kumbhakōna or even farther south. But severe struggles were going on with the Sultāns of the Bahmani kingdom of Gulbarga, which was founded in 1347, or only eleven years after Vijayanagar. Thus, in 1380, when the Turushkas were swarming over the Ādavani (Adōni) hill-fort and kingdom, Mallappa-Oḍeyar's son defeated them, took possession of the fort and kingdom, and handed them over to Harihara (Kg 43). In 1384 the Turukas are said to have come and attacked Kottakoṇḍa when the army had gone to the Orugal country (Ck 15). In 1397 we are informed of the exploits of the general Guṇḍa (Bl 3), into the flames of whose valour the Yavanas, Turushkas, and Āndhras fell like moths. He conquered the Kēralas, Taulavas, Āndhras, and Kutakas, seized their wealth, and gave the spoils to the king. Dragging the elephant-like Saipa, Patheya, and other proud Turushkas along by their hair in battle, he tied them up in his stables like monkeys; and besides them, seized by the throat the two great tigers known as Jyēshṭha and Kanishṭha. He set up pillars of victory in all the fifty-six countries, and restored the tower at the gateway of the Bēlūr temple, which Ganga Sālār, the Turushka from Gulbarga, had come and burnt. Harihara was a cultivator of Karṇāṭaka learning[1] (Kp 34). He died on the 30th of August 1404 (Tl 129, SB 126), and his virtues, it is said (Si 95), are sung in pleasant stories by the Nāga maidens in Pātāla, listening to which the serpents there are filled with delight.

He had a son by Pampā-Dēvī, who appears to have reigned next, under the name of Immaḍi-Bukka-Rāya or Bukka-Rāya II. But the reign was a very short one, of little more than a year. Dēva-Rāya or Pratāpa-Dēva-Rāya then succeeded, Harihara's son by Mēlā-Dēvī or Malla-Dēvī, of the family of Rāma-Dēva, probably the Sēuna king.. He also had the sons Chikka-Rāya-Oḍeyar, ruling in Āraga in the hill country to the west; and Virūpaṇṇa or Virūpāksha, who conquered the eastern countries down to and including Ceylon (*EI.* iii. 225), and in 1404 appears as if ruling in Vijayanagar (Tl 13). Perhaps he was a candidate for the throne on the death of his father. But Pratāpa-Dēva-Rāya gained it, and was crowned on the 7th

[1] *Karṇāṭaka-vidyā-vilāsa.*

of November 1406 (Hn 133). Some inscriptions seem to represent him as the founder of a Pratāpa dynasty. An interesting account is given in Dg 23 and 29 of the construction of a dam at Harihara in 1410 across the Haridrā. The struggles with the Musalmāns to the north continued unabated, and the pages of Firishta are filled with details relating to them. According to him, Dēva-Rāya, whom he calls Dewul-Roy, was forced to give his daughter in marriage to the Bahmani Sultān Fīrōz Shāh. At the end of his reign Dēva-Rāya inflicted a severe defeat upon the Sultān. A great slaughter of the Muhammadans followed, and the Bijāpur country was laid waste with all the treasured resentment of many years. These reverses killed Fīrōz Shāh. But his successor, Ahmed Shāh, drove back the Hindus, and desolated the possessions of Vijayanagar, massacring women and children without mercy. Whenever the number came to 20,000, he halted for three days and made a feast. The Hindus, in desperation, formed a plot against him, from which he escaped by a hair's breadth. Terms were then agreed to, and he retired to his own country, the capital of which he shortly removed from Gulbarga to Bīḍar, a hundred miles to the north.[1] Of these affairs there is little indication in our inscriptions, which generally represent the king as ruling a peaceful kingdom.

Dēva-Rāya was succeeded by Vijaya-Rāya, his son by Dēmāmbikā, but the history is not very clear at this period, and Vijaya-Rāya's reign was a short one. He was followed by his son Dēva-Rāya II, also called Prauḍha-Dēva-Rāya, who had the special title Gaja-bēṇṭekāra or elephant hunter. His mother was Nārāyanāmbikā, and one inscription (Ml 121) describes him as having received the throne from his elder sister (*nijāgrajā*), which may perhaps refer to the princess married into the Bahmani family. The kings of Anga, Kannōja, Kāmbōja, Vanga, and Nēpāla are said (Tl 200) to have

[1] The Bahmani empire was finally dismembered in about 1489, and broken up into the five States of Bijāpur, Ahmednagar, Golkoṇḍa, Berār, and Bīḍar.

acted as his servants, carrying his umbrella, his chāmara, his stick, or his goblet. He also had 10,000 Turushka horsemen in his service (Sr 15). He died on the 24th of May 1446 (SB 125, 127). He had a brother Pārvvati-Rāya-Oḍeyar, who in 1425 ruled the Terakanāmbi kingdom, in the south of Mysore District (Ch 195, 105), and is no doubt the Śrīgiri, who was ruling in North Arcot in 1424 (*EI.* viii. 308).

Dēva-Rāya's son by Ponnalā-Dēvī, Mallikārjuna, also called Immaḍi-Dēva-Rāya, next came to the throne, and he was followed by Virūpāksha, the son of Dēva-Rāya by Simhalā-Dēvī. These were reigns wanting in vigour. Mallikārjuna is said (Md 12, 59) to be in Penugoṇḍa in 1459, along with his minister, engaged in affairs connected with Narasinga's kingdom. This was the chief next to be mentioned.

Sāluva-Nṛisimha, also called Narasinga-Rāya-Oḍeyar, the most powerful noble in Karṇāṭa and Telingāna. He was general of the armies of Vijayanagar, and successfully defended it against the Muhammadans. But the influence he thus gained enabled him in 1478, in the reign of Virūpāksha, to usurp the throne. When he was thus king,[1] the Bahmani Sultān again invaded the Vijayanagar territories, and was over-running the whole country, having advanced so far as to lay siege to the strong fort of Mālūr (Kolar District). Nṛisimha took to flight, but afterwards came to terms with the Sultān, who nevertheless marched on to Kānchī (Conjeeveram), "situated in the centre of the dominions of that malignant one," and plundered the town and temples, which were "the wonder of the age." Nṛisimha's distinctive titles were—*mēdinī-mīsara-gaṇḍa* (champion over the mustaches of the world), *kaṭhāri-sāluva* (dagger falcon). He was succeeded by his son Immaḍi-Nṛisimha or Immaḍi-Narasinga-Oḍeyar, for whom the earliest date seems to be 1493.

This king, however, was murdered in 1496 by their general Narasa or Narasinga. He was of Tuluva descent,

[1] He was the tenth king of Vijayanagar, and his son the eleventh.

and became the founder of the Narasinga dynasty of Vijayanagar. The following is a table of this dynasty :—

Timma,
m. Devaki
|
Iśvara,
m. Bukkamma
|
12. Narasa, Narasinga, Nṛisimha, 1496-1503

By Tippāji,	By Nāgalā-Dēvī,	By Ōbāmbikā,	
13. Vīra-Narasimha or Nṛisimha, Bhujabala-Rāya, 1504-1509	14. Krishna-Rāya, 1509-1529	15. Achyuta-Rāya, 1530-1542	Ranga, m. Timmāmbā
	Tirumalāmbā, m. to Rāma-Rāja (see Karṇāṭa dynasty)	16. Venkaṭa-Dēva-Rāya, 1542	17. Sadāśiva-Rāya, 1543-1567

Narasa is said in several inscriptions (Sk 234, etc.) to have quickly dammed the Kāvērī when in full flood, crossed over and seized his enemy alive in battle. Then, taking possession of Śrīrangapaṭṭaṇa (Seringapatam), he made it his own abode. Having conquered Chēra, Chōla, and Pāṇḍya, as well as the proud lord of Madhura, the fierce Turushka, the Gajapati king and others; from the banks of the Ganges to Lankā (Ceylon), and from the eastern to the western mountains, he imposed his commands upon all kings. In Rāmēśvara and other sacred places he from time to time bestowed the sixteen great gifts. He died in 1503 (Kr 64).

He was succeeded in turn by three sons, born to him by different mothers. The first of these, Vīra-Narasimha or Nṛisimha, also called in a few cases Bhujabala-Rāya,[1] drew to himself, it is said, the hearts of all from Sētu to Sumēru, and from the eastern to the western mountains, and made all manner of gifts in all the sacred places. The Anga, Vanga, Kalinga, and other kings addressed him with such words as, "Look on us, great king! Victory! Long life!" His half-brother Krishna-Rāya next came to the throne, and was one of the most powerful and distinguished of the Vijayanagar monarchs. About 1520 he inflicted a severe defeat upon the Muhammadans, in consequence of which a good

[1] The Busbalrao of the Portuguese historian Nuniz.

understanding prevailed between the courts of Vijayanagar and Bijāpur for a considerable time. One of the earliest expeditions of the reign was against Ganga-Rāja, the chief of Ummattūr (in Mysore District), who had rebelled and claimed Penugonda, perhaps as being a Ganga. His main stronghold was on the island of Śivasamudram,[1] at the Falls of the Kāvērī, and parts of the Bangalore District were known as the Śivasamudram [1] country. Krishna-Rāya captured his fort at the Falls, and also took Seringapatam. He extended the limits of the empire until they reached to Cuttack on the east and to Salsette on the west. In capturing Koṇḍaviḍu in 1516, he took prisoner Vīrabhadra, son of the Gajapati king Pratāpa-Rudra, and Dg 107 relates that he granted him the Malcya-Bennūr country (in the west of Mysore) as an estate. Krishna-Rāya was a great patron of Sanskrit and Telugu literature, and had at his court eight celebrated poets, distinguished as the *ashṭadiggaja*. On his death, Achyuta-Rāya, his half-brother, succeeded to the throne. He was profuse in gifts to the Brāhmans, the records of which are commonly surmounted by a figure of the Vāmana or dwarf incarnation. He established in 1539 a sort of bank for the benefit of Brāhmans, called the Ānanda-nidhi. Two verses celebrating this event are repeated in Dg 24 and Hk 123, as well as in eight other places in Hampi and Kamalāpura.[2]

Achyuta-Rāya's son, perhaps an infant, was next crowned as king, but died in a short time. Sadāśiva Rāya, the son of Ranga, a deceased brother of Achyuta by the same mother, was then raised to the throne by the great minister Rāma-Rāja (who was his brother-in-law) and the councillors. He is said to have subdued all his enemies in Suragiri (Penugoṇḍa), and brought the whole land into subjection to his commands, while the Kāmbōja, Bhōja, Kalinga, Karahāṭa and other kings acted as servants for his female apartments.

But Rāma-Rāja himself wielded the chief power in the State, and is called the ruler of the great Karṇāṭa kingdom

[1] Properly Śivanasamudram. [2] For the latter see *Mad. Arch. Rep.* for 1903-4.

(Ng 58). Though possessed of commanding abilities, so great was his arrogance that the Musalmān States of Bijāpur, Golkoṇḍa, Ahmednagar, and Bīḍar were provoked to combine in an attack on Vijayanagar as their common enemy. In the battle of Talikota, near Raichūr, on the 23rd of January 1565, Rāma-Rāja was slain, on which the Hindu army fled panic-stricken, and the royal family escaped to Penugoṇḍa. The victorious Muhammadans marched to Vijayanagar, which they utterly sacked and destroyed. Thus fell this once great and populous capital, the ruins of which are still a source of admiration to visitors.

From Rāma-Rāja was descended the last Vijayanagar dynasty, styling themselves kings of Karṇāṭa. Their capital was at first at Penugoṇḍa, which was attacked in 1577 by the Muhammadans, but successfully defended by Jagadēva-Rāya, whose daughter was married to the king, and who became chief of Channapaṭṇa. In 1585 the capital was again removed to Chandragiri, and later still to Chingalpat (Chingleput). These were, however, captured by the forces of Golkoṇḍa, and the king fled to the protection of Śivappa-Nāyak, the chief of Bednūr in the west of Mysore.

The following is a table of the Karṇāṭa or Rāma-Rāja dynasty :—

Bukka, Aravīti-Bukka,
protector of Sāluva-Nṛisimha,
m. Ballāmbikā
|
Rāma-Rāja,
m. Lakkāmbikā
|
Śrī-Ranga,
m. Tirumala-Dēvī
|

Rāma-Rāja, killed 1565, m. Tirumalāmbā, dr. of Krishna-Rāya (No. 14)
|
Śrī-Ranga

18. Tirumala-Rāya, 1567-1571, m. Vengalāmbā
|
19. Śrī-Ranga-Rāya I, 1573-1584
|
22. Vēnkaṭapati-Rāya II, Peda-Vēnkaṭa, 1626-1640
Pina-Venkaṭa
|
Śrī-Ranga-Rāya (No. 23)

20. Vēnkaṭapati-Rāya I, 1586-1615
|
Śrī-Ranga
|
21. Rāma-Dēva, Rāmachandra-Rāya, 1615-1625

Vēnkaṭādri
|
Aravīti-Rangapa-Rāja
|
Gōpāla-Rāja
|
(adopted)
23. Śrī-Ranga-Rāya II, 1643-1664

The descent of this dynasty, who call themselves kings of Karṇāṭa or Karṇāṭaka, is elaborately traced back (as in Tm 1) to the Lunar line, through Yayāti and Puru. In that race was Bharata, in whose line was Santanu, fourth from whom was Vijaya, whose son was Abhimanyu, whose son was Parīkshit. Eighth from him was Nanda, ninth from whom was Chālikka, seventh from whom was Rāja-Narēndra. Tenth from him was Bijjalēndra, third in whose line was Vīra-Hemmāḍi-Rāya, who prostrated himself before Murāri (Vishnu), and was lord of Māyāpuri. Fourth from him was Tāta-Pinnama, whose son Sōma-Dēva took from the enemy seven hill-forts in one day. His son was Rāghava-Dēvarāṭ, whose son was Pinnama. He was lord of Aravīṭi-nagari and had a son Bukka, who assisted in firmly establishing even the kingdom of Sāluva-Nṛisimha. Bukka's wife was Ballāmbikā, and their son was Rāma-Rāja. He gained a victory over Sapāda's army of 70,000 horse, took the hill-fort of Ādavani (Adoni), and driving away Kāsappuḍaya, captured Kandana-vōli-durga (Kurnool), and owing to his faith drank with impunity the water from the feet of Hari there, although his kinsmen had put poison into it. His son, by Lakshmyāmbikā, was Śrī-Ranga-Rāya, whose wife Tirumalāmbikā bore to him three sons—Rāma-Rāja, Tirumala-Rāya, and Vēnkaṭapati.

Aliya[1]-Rāma-Rājaya-Dēva having (in 1565) suddenly set (or died) owing to acts of State by the kings of the Turukas, the city, throne, and countries of the realm were destroyed and in ruins (Hk 6, Hl 7). On the death of Sadāśiva-Rāya, the brother of Rāma-Rāja, named Tirumala-Rāya, was anointed to the throne, and ruled from Penugoṇḍa (Anantapur District), which now became the capital. He subdued all his enemies and made all the great gifts in the various sacred places. He captured the eighty-four hill-forts (the Mahratta country), put down the pride of Avahala-Rāya, subdued the Utkala (Orissa) king, and styled himself the Tribhuvanamalla of Vengi, and

[1] Son-in-law, that is of Krishna-Rāya.

the Suratrāna (or Sultān) of Urigōla (Ōrangal). He reduced to submission the Raṭṭas, and called himself lord of Kalyāna-pura, Chālikka emperor, victor over Gonga of Komarānikōṭa, and displacer of the Rāya of Rodda. The Kāmbhōja, Bhōja, Kalinga, Karahāṭa and other kings were his door-keepers.

He was succeeded in order by his sons Śrī-Ranga-Rāya I and Vēnkaṭapati-Rāya I. The former, halting in Uddagiri (? Udayagiri), captured the hill-forts of Koṇḍavīḍu and Vini-koṇḍa (both in the Krishna District), and took up his residence in Penugoṇḍa. Vēnkaṭapati-Rāya, his brother, was next anointed to the throne in Suragiri (Penugoṇḍa) by Tātāchārya, the family guru, but removed the capital to Chandragiri (in North Arcot). Immediately after his accession he dispersed the hosts of Yavana fiends. His army also plundered Malik Ibrāhim's son Muhammad Shāh (both kings of Golkoṇḍa) of horses, elephants, and white umbrella, so that he returned home in disgrace. Among other titles, Vēnkaṭapati has those of Manniyān and Sāmūla, and displacer of Oḍḍiya-Rāya (the Orissa king). It was during his reign, and apparently with his consent, that the Rājas of Mysore gained Seringapatam, and thus became independent.

Vēnkaṭapati's grandson Rāma-Dēva or Rāmachandra-Rāya next came to the throne, and was followed by Vēnkaṭapati II, grandson of the original Rāma-Rāja, and called Peda-Vēnkaṭa. His younger brother Pina-Vēnkaṭa's son, Śrī-Ranga-Rāya, adopted by Gōpāla-Rāja, grandson of the original Rāma-Rāja's brother Vēnkaṭādri, was next placed on the throne as Śrī-Ranga-Rāya II. In 1644 his capitals Chandragiri and Chingalpat being taken by the forces of Golkoṇḍa, he fled to the protection of Śivappa-Nāyak of Bednūr, in the west of Mysore, who installed him at Bēlūr and neighbouring parts, and even laid siege to Seringapatam on the plea of restoring his sovereignty. But in this he was defeated. Śrī-Rānga-Rāya's inscriptions continue to 1664, and with him ended the Vijayanagar empire. According to Kg 46 he had a son

Dēvadēva who was ruling in that year, and in Gu 64 and 65 we have a still later Vēnkaṭapati ruling in 1668, who may have been the same. The line eventually merged in that of the chiefs of Ānegundi, who were subdued by Tipū Sultān. Some members of the family, however, still continue there.

17. BIJĀPUR SULTĀNS

But it was in 1644 also that, as the result of the Bijāpur conquests in the late Vijayanagar possessions in Mysore and adjacent countries, the Carnatic Bijāpur Balāghāṭ and Pāyanghāṭ provinces were formed under the governorship of Shāhji, father of the celebrated Mahratta leader Śivaji. The latter, after his father's death, overran all these *jāgīr* provinces to enforce his claim to a half-share. Records of this Mahratta domination are found in inscriptions of Śivaji's son Sambhōji or Sambhāji, dated 1663 and 1680 (Kl 219, CB 32), of Sambhāji's wife (Kl 227, 224, 254), and Sambhāji's sons (Mb 154, Ct 54), down to 1693. The most interesting is the one on the wall of a temple on the summit of Nandidroog (CB 32), which gives a brief but graphic description of this great stronghold.

Meanwhile we have records of the Ādil Shāhi kings of Bijāpur themselves. They were of high birth, being descended from a prince said to be the son of the Ottoman Sultān Amurāth or Murād, and brother of Muhammad the Great, the conqueror of Constantinople. He escaped to Persia and was transported to the Bahmani court in India, where he rose to power, and ended by establishing this line of kings, the constant rivals of Vijayanagar.

A fine Arabic and Persian inscription of 1632 (Sk 324) is of the reign of Muhammad-Ādil-Shāh, son of Ibrāhim-Ādil-Shāh, and records the erection of a fort on the hill at the Māsur-Maḍag tank on the northern frontier of Mysore in the Shikarpur tāluq, as a memorial of victory to that point over the wicked infidels. Other inscriptions of the same reign are Ci 43 and 44 of 1653, relating to the formation of a tank by the local governor under circumstances of special interest. In 1648 was built by the local chief the fort at Channarāyapaṭṭaṇa in the Hassan District, apparently in pursuance of a treaty with Bijāpur (Cn 158, 160, 165), no doubt to mark the limits of the two territories. At Sīra is an inscription on the tomb of Malik Rihān, Subahdār of Sīra, who died in 1651 (Si 66[b]). In 1703 and 1712 are records of the governor Gulām Ali Khān, in the former of which he decided a dispute between two Hindu gurus as to their respective disciples (Mb 98, Kl 74).

18. MUGHALS

Of the Mughal period there are a few inscriptions. The most interesting is one of the time of Aurangzeb relating to the grant of Doḍ-Ballāpur in 1691 (DB 31). In 1696 was erected the big mosque at Sīra (Si 66[a]). There are also records of the Navāb Durga-Kūli-Khān in 1720 (Si 112), and of the Navāb Dilāvar-Khān in 1742 and 1745 (Si 13, Ht 19).

19. MYSORE RĀJAS

It was their acquisition of Seringapatam in 1610, and the retirement from it then of the Vijayanagar viceroy, that brought the Rājas of Mysore into prominence as independent rulers. But the family traces its origin to the beginning of the fifteenth century, and after the catastrophe which befell the Vijayanagar empire at the battle of Talikota in 1565, the Rājas of Mysore, in common with its other feudatories, had been preparing to cast off the Vijayanagar yoke.

They are of the Lunar race, and their origin is thus related in Ch 92 and other inscriptions. Certain Yādava princes from Dvāraka (the capital of the hero Krishna in

Kathiāwār) came to the Karṇāṭa country, either led by fancy, according to some accounts, which seems natural, or, according to others, in order to visit their family god Nārāyaṇa on the peak of Yadugiri (Mēlukōṭe). Seeing the beauty of the land, and being pleased with it, they took up their abode in Mahishapura (Mysore), and became the progenitors of the existing royal family. Tradition alleges that there were two princes, named Vijaya and Krishna. Espousing the cause of a distressed maiden, the daughter of the Woḍeyar or chief of Hadana (now Hadināḍ, to the south-east of Mysore), they saved her from a forced marriage with the chief of Kārugahalli, who was of inferior caste, by secreting themselves at the wedding banquet and slaying him. She then became the willing bride of Vijaya, who assumed the government of Hadana and Kārugahalli, adopting the title of Oḍeyar or Woḍeyar,[1] along with a profession of the Jangama or Lingāyit creed. From them was descended Hire-Beṭṭada-Chāma-Rāja (the third of those named Chāma-Rāja), to whom are assigned the dates 1513 to 1552, previous to which no annals have been preserved. He, during his lifetime, made a partition of his dominions between his three sons. To Timma-Rāja he gave Hemmanhalli, to Krishna-Rāja he gave Kembala, and to Chāma-Rāja, surnamed Bōl (the Bald), he gave Mysore. No male heir surviving to either of the elder brothers, the succession was continued in the junior or Mysore branch. The following is a table of the kings :—

[1] A title of all the Rājas of Mysore. It was also a title of the early Vijayanagar kings, and of various lines of chiefs in the South. It signifies lord or master (being the honorific plural of Oḍeya), and appears in Tamil as Uḍaiyār. As *vaḍēr* it is the term applied to Jangama or Lingāyit priests.

[TABLE

Hire-Beṭṭada-Chāma-Rāja (1513-1552)

Timma-Rāja (1552-1571) Krishna-Rāja 1. Bōl Chāma-Rāja IV, 1571-1576

2. Beṭṭada-Chāma-Rāja V, 1576-1578 3. Rāja-Woḍeyar, 1578-1617 Dēva-Rāja, m. Kempamāmbā Channa-Rāja

6. Kanṭhīrava-Narasa-Rāja I, 1638-1659 Narasa 5. Immaḍi-[1] Rāja-Woḍeyar, 1637-1638 Dēva-Rāja, m. Amritāmbā 7. Doḍḍa-Dēva-Rāja,[2] 1659-1672

4. Chāma-Rāja VI, 1617-1637 8. Chikka-Dēva-Rāja, 1672-1704, m. Dēvamāmbā Kanṭhīrava

9. Kanṭhīrava-Narasa-Rāja II, 1704-1713, m. Chelvājamāmbā

11. Chāma-Rāja VII, 1731-1734

12. Immaḍi[1]-Krishna-Rāja, 1734-1766 10. Doḍḍa-Krishna-Rāja, 1713-1731, m. Dēvājamāmbā

13. Nanja-Rāja, 1766-1770 14. Chāma-Rāja VIII, 1770-1776

15. Chāma-Rāja IX, 1776-1796

16. Mummaḍi[1]-Krishna-Rāja, 1799-1868

(adopted)

17. Chāma-Rājēndra X, 1868-1894

18. Krishna-Rāja IV, 1894-

Timma-Rāja is said (Sr 14) to have gained the title Antembara-gaṇḍa,[3] distinctive of the Mysore Rājas. Chāma-Rāja IV defeated in battle Rēmaṭi-Vēnkaṭa, the general of Rāma-Rāja. He also, as we know from history, withheld the tribute due to Vijayanagar, and set at defiance the viceroy at Seringapatam, who in vain attempted to arrest him. He was succeeded by his eldest son, Beṭṭada-Chāma-Rāja, who, though conspicuously brave, had no capacity for government. His younger brother, Rāja-Woḍeyar, was therefore raised to the

[1] Immaḍi means second; Mummaḍi, third.

[2] His elder brother, as the senior, was originally called Doḍḍa-Dēva-Rāja, but as he did not come to the throne, the designation is applied to the junior who actually ruled.

[3] "Champion over those who say they are such and such." A more intelligible form is *Birud-ant-embara-gaṇḍa*, "champion over those who say they have such and such titles."

throne by the elders. He, it is said (Sr 14, 64, TN 63), according to his vow, thrashed the proud lord of Kārugahalli on the field of battle with his riding-whip. But, far more important, he overcame Tirumala-Rāya (the Vijayanagar viceroy) and seated himself on the jewelled throne in Seringapatam. Whatever were the means by which this was accomplished, it is undoubted that the aged viceroy retired to Talakāḍ in 1610, where he shortly after died, and that Rāja-Woḍeyar took possession of Seringapatam and made it his capital in place of Mysore.[1] From this time dates the independence of the Mysore Rājas, though it is curious that some of their inscriptions still acknowledge the Vijayanagar supremacy down to as late a period as 1668 (Gu 65), and Narasa-Rāja of Maisūr is said (Yd 5) to be the right hand of the Vijayanagar sovereign in 1642. But, at the same time, they make numerous grants by their own independent authority, one of the earliest that can be cited being of the date 1612 (Ch 200).

All the sons being dead, Rāja-Woḍeyar was succeeded by a grandson, Chāma-Rāja VI, in whose time (1630) we know that Channapatna and its possessions were added to Mysore. A posthumous son born to Rāja-Woḍeyar was next placed on the throne as Immaḍi-Rāja-Woḍeyar (Yd 17), but he was shortly poisoned, at the instigation, it appears, of the Dalavāyi.[2]

Kanṭhīrava-Narasa-Rāja I, son of the gallant Beṭṭada-Chāma-Rāja, then obtained the crown, and had a distinguished reign. He successfully repelled the Bijāpur invasions, and extended the kingdom on all sides, gaining great booty, some of which he applied to strengthening the fortifications of

[1] This seems to have been countenanced by the Vijayanagar sovereign Vēnkaṭa-pati-Rāya, who is said (TN 62) to have confirmed Rāja-Woḍeyar in 1612 in the possession of Ummattūr and Seringapatam; and Nj 198 implies that he considered the Mysore kings to have a right to the throne of Karṇāṭa.

[2] The title of the chief officer of the State, who was at the head of the army but was also a minister. The office was mostly hereditary, the Mysore and Kalale families having entered into an alliance according to which the former provided the Kartar (Curtur in the English records) or ruler of the State, and the latter the Dalavāyi or commander-in-chief.

Seringapatam. He was the first to establish a mint, at which were coined the Kanthirāya (Canteroy) *huns* and *fanams* named after him (Ag 64), which continued to be the current national money until the Muhammadan usurpation. According to Sr 103 he was Krishna himself, born to give peace to the world when it was troubled by the Turushkas and resounded with the noise of horse hoofs. While he ruled, all the land was prosperous. When he went forth to war, the Vangas, Hūnas, and Konkanas were terrified, the Saurāshṭras lost their kingdom, the Gurjara horse bolted, the Mlēnchhas fell down in a swoon. He established many agrahāras, bestowed numerous gifts, and revived the observance of the *ēkādaśi-vrata*, or eleventh day vow in honour of Lakshmī-Nṛisimha (Vishnu), like Ambarīsha and other kings of old (Ag 64).

He died without issue, and Doḍḍa-Dēva-Rāja, a grandson of Chāma-Rāja IV, was selected to succeed him, a rival claimant, afterwards Chikka-Dēva-Rāja, being sent, with his father, into confinement at Hangala (Gundalpet tāluq). This reign was occupied in repulsing invasions from Bednūr by Śivappa-Nāyak, who attempted to restore the authority of the Vijayanagar king, a fugitive at his court. Doḍḍa-Dēva-Rāja extended the Mysore territories to the south and north-west. All those who were persecuted by the Mlēchchas, who had seized upon the land, flocked (says Yd 54) to him for protection. The Pāṇḍyas lost their kingdom, the Chōlas sailed away with all their forces to the islands, the Kēralas took poison, the Haivas were smitten by the gods, the Konkanas lost heart, the Hūnas sought only to save their lives, the Habbusikas were pierced all over with wounds, the Lāṭas were driven to wander in the forests, the Gurjaras were paralysed, the Rānas obtained *nirvāna*, while the Kurus, Maravas, Mudgalas and Jangālas, the Angas, Vangas, Kalingas, the Magadha king, with the king of Madhura and others, threw themselves at his feet. Several uncouth Mahratti and Hindu-stāni words are given as specimens of the exclamations heard on all sides from those who fell in his wars. He made all the gifts described in the *Hēmādri* and other sacred books, and established in every village inns (*chatra*) for the distribution of food. Dividing his kingdom into four parts, he gave the first to the Brāhmans, the second to the gods, the third to charity, and reserved the fourth for his own use. Details of his conquests are also thus given (Sr 14). He defeated the army of the lord of Madhura in Īrōḍu (Coimbatore District), slew Damaralaiyappēndra, and put to flight Anantōji. He captured the elephant named Kulaśēkhara, and took by assault Śāmballi (in Bhavāni tāluq, Coimbatore), Ōmalūr (near Salem), and Dhārāpuram (in south of Coimbatore District). He defeated the army of the Keladi kings (Shimoga District), captured the elephant called Gangādhara, and seized Hāsana (Hassan) and Sakkarepaṭṭaṇa. The territories thus acquired extended from Sakkarepaṭṭaṇa (near Chikmugalūr) in the west to Sēleyapura (Salem) in the east, and from Chikkanāyākapura (Chiknāyakanhalli) in the north to Dhārāpuram in the south, between all which places he established an inn for travellers at every *yōjana* (about nine miles) along every road. He died at Chiknāyakanhalli.

Chikka-Dēva-Rāja, great-grandson of Chāma-Rāja IV, previously passed over and sent into confinement, was now elevated to the throne, and is one of the most celebrated of the Mysore Rājas. Many important administrative changes were made by him, some of which created serious discontent. This was suppressed by a treacherous massacre of Jangama priests, who had fomented it. But at his death in 1704, notwithstanding the troublous times, he had built up a secure and prosperous kingdom, stretching from Palni and Ānemale (Madura District) in the south to Midagēśi (north of Tumkūr District) in the north, and from Carnatic Garh in the Bāramahāl (Salem District) in the east to the borders of Coorg and Balam (Manjarābād) in the west.

The inscriptions are chiefly concerned with his successes in war. One of the earliest (Ch 92 of 1675) describes him as seated on the throne of the Karṇāṭa dominion like the great Indra. In the east, defeating the Pāṇḍya king Chokka

(Nāyak of Madura), he seized Tripura and Anantapuri; in the west, smiting the Keladi kings, with the Yavanas, he took Sakalēśapura and Arakalgūḍu (both in Hassan District); in the north, defeating Ranadulha-Khān (the Bijāpur general), he captured Kētasamudra, with Kandikere, Handalakere, Gūlūr, Tumukūr, and Honnavalli (all in Tumkūr District). Defeating in battle Mushtika, who was aided by the Morasas (people of Kolar District) and Kirātas, he captured Jadagana-durga and changed its name to Chikkadēvarāyadurga (now Dēvarāyadurga). The Varāha (or Boar) which was lost in the Yavana invasion, he brought from Śrīmushna (South Arcot) and set it up with devotion in Śrīrangapaṭṭaṇa (Seringapatam—it is now in Mysore, where it was removed in the time of Pūrnayya). He also (Sr 151) conquered Timmappa-Gauḍa and Rāmappa-Gauḍa and took Maddagiri, Midagēśi, Bijjavara and Channarāyadurga. Then he is said (in Sr 14 of 1686) to have defeated the Mahrattas from Panchavaṭī (Nāsik, in the north of the Bombay Presidency), and of their leaders he slew Dādōji and cut off the limbs and noses of Jaitaji and Jasavanta.[1] He also reduced to abject terror Śambhu (Sambhōji, son and successor of the celebrated Sivaji), Kutupu-Shāh (one of the Sultāns of Golkoṇḍa), Ikkēri Basava (Basavappa-Nāyak, adopted son of Channammāji, widow and successor on the throne of Sōmaśēkhara-Nāyak), and Ekōji (or Venkōji, the half-brother of Sivaji, who seized Tanjore and founded the line of Mahratta rulers there). We are also informed (in Sr 64 of 1722) that he conquered the lord of Madhura, and withstood Sivaji at the time when the rulers of the countries around Āgra, Delhi, and Bhāgānagara (Haidarābād) were falling down before him and presenting tribute. He

[1] *Dādōjī bhidi Jaitajī-Jasavatōs sarvānga-nāsā-chhidi.* The latter part of the phrase might possibly be rendered—"cut off the noses of all arms." This was a practice adopted by the Mysoreans in order to instil terror into the enemy. See Manucci, *Storia do Mogor* (Irvine's translation and additional notes, vol. iv.) But may it not have been the survival of an old Indian custom? For Professor Macdonell, in writing of early Sanskrit medical works (*Imp. Gaz. Ind.*, vol. ii.), says—"Probably the only valuable contribution to surgery to which India can lay claim is the art of forming artificial noses. This operation has been borrowed in modern times from India, where Englishmen became acquainted with it in the 18th century.

thus acquired the title Apratima-vīra (unrivalled hero), which is one of the distinctive epithets of the Mysore Rājas. He is moreover said to have defeated attacks from every point of the compass, made by Turukas (or Muhammadans), Morasas (Telugu people of the Kolar District and north-east), Āreyas (or Mahrattas), Tigulas (Tamil people), Koḍagas (Coorgs), and Malegas (hill tribes in the west). In addition to Kutupu-Shāh (of Golkoṇḍa), he is said to have driven off Edulu-Shāh (Ādil-Shāh of Bijāpur).

Kanṭhīrava-Narasa-Rāja II, the son of Chikka-Dēva-Rāja, was born deaf and dumb, and thence called Mūk-arasu. But through the influence of the eminent minister Tirumalārya he succeeded to the throne. There are no inscriptions of his time.

His son, Doḍḍa-Krishna-Rāja, followed, during whose reign frequent invasions took place by the Muhammadans and the Mahrattas, who had to be bought off. The king being immersed in his own pleasures, all power began to fall into the hands of the ministers.

With him the direct descent ended. Ag 62 gives a list of the kings down to 1811, but (to complete the chronicle from history) Chāma-Rāja VII, a member of the Hemmanhalli family, was next elected. He was eventually deposed by the dalavāyi Dēvarāj and the minister Nanjarāj, and died a prisoner at Kabbāldurga in 1734. Immaḍi-Krishna-Rāja of Kenchangōd, a younger and distant branch, was put on the throne in that year, and died in 1766. His eldest son Nanja-Rāja was directed by Haidar-Ali to be installed, but finding him not sufficiently subservient, Haidar turned him out of the palace in 1767. He was strangled in 1770, being nominally succeeded by his brother Chāma-Rāja VIII, who died childless in 1775. An inscription of the previous year (Bl 65) truthfully represents Chāma-Rāja as the king, but the excellent Haidar-Ali as the ruler. Chāma-Rāja IX, a member of the Kārugahalli family, was next selected by Haidar in a dramatic manner. He died in 1796 and Tīpū-Sultān appointed no successor. On the capture of Seringapatam by the British in 1799 and the death at the same time of Tīpū-Sultān, the Muhammadan usurpation of Haidar-Ali (1761-1782) and Tīpū-Sultān (1782-1799[1]) being brought to an end, the British Government restored the Hindu dynasty, and placed on the throne Mummaḍi-Krishna-Rāja, son of the last-named Chāma-Rāja. His inscriptions run from 1800 (Sr 8) down to near the end of his life in 1868. One in the Lakshmīramaṇa temple at Mysore commemorates his installation there on the throne of his ancestors on the 30th of June 1799. Another, of 1829, in the Kṛishna-svāmi temple, ascribes to him nine modes of service, called the nine jewels, for the pleasure of the goddess Chāmuṇḍēśvari. These were—the jewel of adornment, in presenting crowns for the gods at Mēlukōṭe and other places; the jewel of love of country, in founding Chāmarājnagar and other towns; the jewel of devotion, in building temples; the jewel of their consecration, in completing their towers; the jewel of public good, in erecting dams and bathing-places; the jewel of charity, in establishing inns for feeding pilgrims at various sacred places; the jewel of fame, in issuing gold and silver coins; and the jewel of language, in publishing commentaries on the sacred books. Ch 86 of 1828 and Nj 8 of 1845 contain a list of the titles and emblems of the Rājas of Mysore. Krishna-Rāja was deposed in 1831 for continued misrule, and during the next fifty years Mysore was administered by British Commissioners. In 1881 it was again restored to the Mysore family in the person of Krishna-Rāja's adopted son Chāma-Rājēndra, and he was succeeded in 1894 by the present Mahārāja, Krishna-Rāja IV, at first under the Regency of the Mahārāni his mother. On attaining majority in 1902 he was installed in power.

20. COORG RĀJAS

The Kongālvas, who had been installed by the Chōlas in 1004 or 1005 (Cg 46) as rulers of Kongal-nāḍ—the Yēlusā-vira country in Coorg and the Arkalgūd tāluq in Mysore—

[1] Examples of Haidar-Ali's inscriptions are Cp 146, 18, and 114; of Tipū-Sulṭān's, for the most part characteristically bombastic, Sr 23, 159, Bn 7, and My 54.

and of whom there are a dozen or more inscriptions in Coorg (see Cg 30-50), disappeared on the expulsion in 1116 of the Chōlas from Mysore by the Hoysalas, their latest inscription being dated in 1115 (Cg 33). But the Changālvas, who ruled over the other parts of Coorg and Changa-nāḍ—the Hunsūr tāluq in Mysore—continued in power, in subordination to the Hoysalas, and subsequently, as the Rājas of Nanjarāyapaṭṭaṇa or Nanjarājapaṭṭaṇa, to Vijayanagar, till nearly the middle of the seventeenth century (Hs 36). The earliest express mention of the Koḍagas or Coorgs in the inscriptions is in 1174 (Hs 20), when Bāḍagaṇḍa Nandi-Dēva, Udeyāditya-Dēva of Kuruche, and others, the Koḍagas of all the nāḍs, are said to have assisted the Changālva prince Pemma-Vīrappa in his attack on the Hoysala army at Pālpare, an enterprise that was not successful. The Changālva line became extinct in 1644 by the death of the last king at the capture of Piriyapatna or Periapatam by the army of the Mysore Rāja. The latter did not, however, follow up the victory into Coorg, owing to the forces of Bednūr having entered the country under Śivappa-Nāyaka, who was engaged in invading Malayāla. The Koḍagas later on may have attempted to recover Piriyapatna, as they are mentioned (Sr 64) among the assailants from all quarters who were overcome by Chikka-Dēva-Rāja of Mysore.

The throne of Coorg left vacant by the overthrow of the Changālvas did not remain long unoccupied. A prince of the Bednūr family, who may have been related to the Changālvas in some way, having settled at Hālēri (called Kshīranagara in Sanskrit), to the north of Mercāra, in the garb of a Jangama or Lingāyit priest, gradually brought the whole country under his authority. His descendants continued as Rājas of Coorg till 1834, when the country was annexed by the British.

The following is a table of the Coorg Rājas, whose history is contained in the *Rājēndranāme*, compiled by order of Vīra-Rājēndra, and translated into English by Lieut. Abercromby at Mangalore in 1808 :—

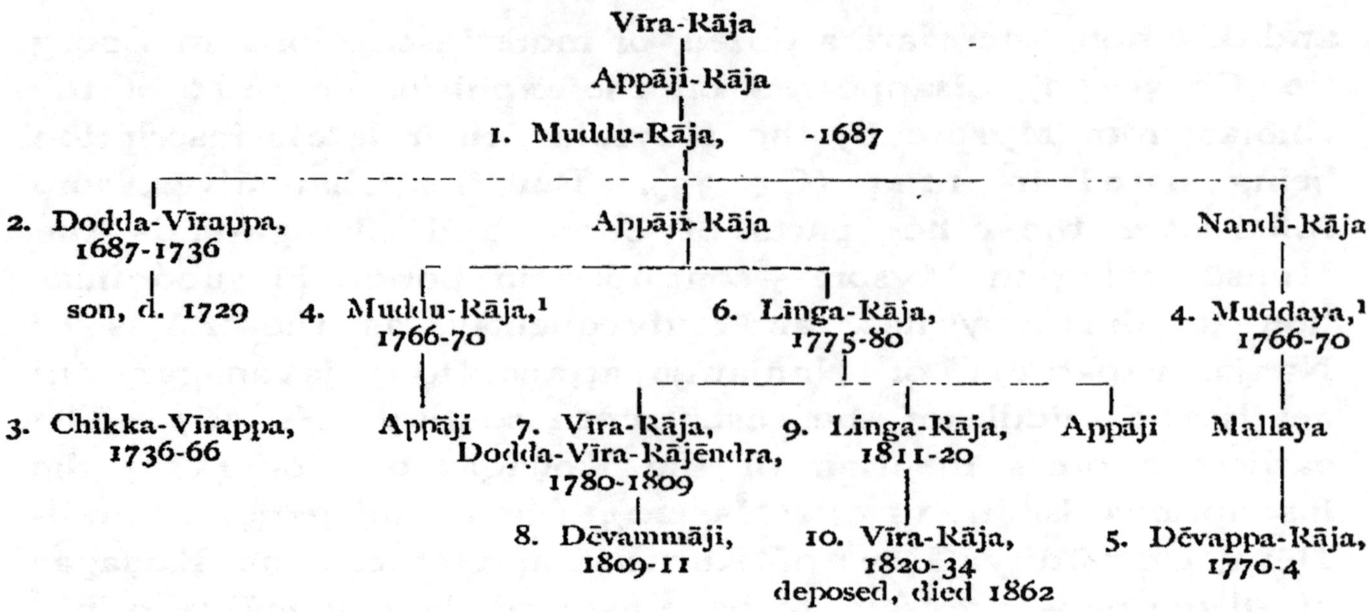

The first Muddu-Rāja removed the capital from Hālēri to Madikēri (Mercāra), where he built a fort and palace in 1681. The second Muddu-Rāja and his cousin Muddaya ruled together at the same time, and died in the same year. The succession was then disputed. Dēvappa-Rāja at first secured the throne, but Linga-Rāja, the rival candidate, gained possession by seeking the support of Haidar Ali, who had usurped the throne of Mysore. Linga-Rāja died in 1780, and his tomb was erected in Mahadēvapura, the northern quarter of Mercāra (Cg 12). Haidar then took possession of Coorg under the pretext of being guardian to the sons until they should come of age. But the princes were confined at Gorūr (in Hassan tāluq) and then at Piriyapatna (Periapatam). In 1782 the Coorgs rose in rebellion, and Haidar Ali died. But Tīpū-Sultān, his son, re-established his power, and when the Coorgs again rebelled, deported them wholesale to Seringapatam, and parcelled out the country among Musalmān landlords, who were enjoined to exterminate all the Coorgs that might remain. In 1738 Vīra-Rājēndra, with his wife and brothers, made his escape from Piriyapatna, and before long was able to regain a measure of power. Through the support of the British, who were now at war with Tīpū-Sultān, he was at

[1] Joint rulers.

length securely seated on the throne, and a large body of Coorgs escaped to their own country during the siege of Seringapatam by Lord Cornwallis in 1792. Vīra-Rājēndra had a romantic career and was the most distinguished of the Coorg Rājas. Cg 13 and 14 are grants made by him in 1796 for Śivāchāra maṭhas, and they direct that at the time of Śiva-pūjā blessings may be invoked with the following hymn of benediction :—

jāti-smaratvam pṛithvī-patitvam saubhāgya-lāvannyam atīva-rūpam |
tvad bhakti vidyā paramāyur ishṭam tvam daś cha mē Śankara janma janmani ||

(Recollection of former births, dominion of the world, the glory of good fortune, surpassing beauty,
Faith in thee, knowledge, long life, (objects of) desire, —(of these) be thou giver to me, Śankara, from age to age.)

And the witnesses are thus described :—

āditya chandrō anilō nalaś cha dyaur bhūmir āpō hṛidayam Yamaś cha
ahaś cha rātriś cha ubhayaś cha sandhi dharmasya janati narasya vṛitah.

(Sun and moon, wind and fire, sky, earth and water, heart (or conscience) and Yama, day and night, morning and evening; these know the deeds of a righteous man.)

In Cg 17 are recorded the erection and endowment of the Ōnkārēśvara temple at Mercāra in 1820 by the first Linga-Rāja. The building was commenced, it is said, on the 1,796,362nd Kali day, and completed on the 1,797,421st. A curious account of an elephant hunt in the time of the last Vīra-Rāja is given in Cg 25. Elephants having increased in numbers to such a degree that they were destroying fruit trees and crops, killing travellers, and damaging houses, the king considered it part of his duty as protector of his people to rid them of these troubles. He therefore, after invoking the aid of Śiva, entered into the forests in a chariot made and painted like a lion (according to Hindu belief the natural enemy of the elephant), and in the course of 2 years, 1 month and 25 days, between 1822 and 1824, disposed of 414 elephants. The actual days on which they were hunted were

38, and in those days he claims to have shot with his own hand 233, while his trained soldiers captured 181 alive, and "it was a marvel that men should catch stout and lofty rutting elephants as if they were mice."

But this king was a monster of sensuality and cruelty, and by wholesale murders had established a reign of terror in the country. In 1832 his sister and her husband escaped to the Resident at Mysore for British protection, and the Rāja's insolent and defiant conduct led to an expedition being sent against him. As the result, he was deposed in 1834, and at the request of the people the country was taken over by the British. The Rāja was deported to Vellore, but afterwards lived at Benāres. In 1852 he was allowed to go to England, where he sought to gain the favour of Queen Victoria by having his daughter baptized and brought up as a Christian. He then commenced a Chancery suit against the East India Company, which dragged on till the affairs of the Company passed over to the Crown. He died in England in 1862, and was buried in Kensal Green Cemetery in London.

Among later inscriptions is Cg 29 of 1857. This relates to the restoration of a temple of Mahadēva on the Kunda hill. The work, to which a number of prominent men contributed, including a Brāhman, Coorgs, and even a Muhammadan, was commenced, it is said, on the 1,810,060th Kali day.

II. RULERS OF MINOR STATES

1. ĀLUPAS OR ĀLUVAS

Of the rulers of the principal minor States, we may begin with the Ālupas or Āluvas (also called Ālu and Ālva). They are mentioned in connection with the Chalukyas in the seventh century, who describe them along with the Gangas as an ancient family (Dg 66), and under the Rāshṭrakūṭas in the eighth (Sb 10). Their original estate seems to have been Eḍevolal, to the north-east of Banavāsi. But their regular kingdom was called Ālvakhēḍa or Āluvakhēḍa, which was one of the boundaries of the Hoysala kingdom in the eleventh century (Mg 32). It was a Six Thousand province (Sb 10), situated chiefly in South Kanara, and it has been suggested that it corresponds with the Olokhoira mentioned by Ptolemy so far back as the second century. The inscriptions of the Āluvas have been found at Kigga (Koppa tāluq) and at Udayāvara, near Uḍipi (South Kanara), while it appears that Pomburcha (Humcha in Nagar tāluq) was at one time in their possession (Kp 37).

No connected genealogy of the line has been obtained, nor any account of their origin. But the names of certain kings occur. Thus we have Guṇasāgara as governor of the Kadamba-maṇḍala in about 675 (Kp 38), and his son Chitravāha (Chitravāhana) in 692 in the time of Vinayāditya (Sb 571). Then in about 800 we have a later Chitravāhana, ruling the Āluvakhēḍa Six Thousand under the Rāshṭrakūṭa king Gōvinda III (Sb 10). The Udayāvara inscriptions (*EI.* ix. 15) supply Raṇasāgara and Śvētavāhana as the names of other kings; also Pṛithivīsāgara and Vijayāditya or Māramma.

2. ŚĀNTARAS

The earliest mention of these kings is in the time of (the Chalukya) Vinayāditya, the end of the seventh century.[1] With the approval of the brother's son of the Chānta king Jayasangraha, who was lord of the city of Madhura encircled by the Kālindī, and of the Ugra-vamśa but connected with the Yadu-vamśa by marriage, a grant was then made by the wife of the Pāṇḍi yuvarāja; and it is said to be under the protection of "the three hundred of the children of the house of the Chāntas." That this was the original form of the name appears also from Sk 283 of about 830, where too the king is said to be a Chānta. According to Nr 35 and 48, the Śāntara kingdom was founded by Jinadatta-Rāya, lord of the northern Madhura (Muttra), who was of the Ugra-vamśa. The Śāntaras are identified with Paṭṭi-Pomburcha,[2] the modern Hombucha or Humcha in Nagar tāluq, as their capital, which may previously have been in the possession of the Āluvas. The remote progenitor of the line was Rāha, from whom was descended Sahakāra, who became a cannibal. He was the father of Jinadatta, who escaped from him in disgust and came to the South, bringing an image of the Jain goddess Padmāvatī. She bestowed on him the power to transmute iron into gold, as exemplified in his horse's bit being turned into a golden bit on touching it with her image. Thus aided, he subdued the local chiefs around, and established his capital at Pomburcha (supposed to mean golden bit) and took the name Śāntara. His descendants the Śāntaras ruled over the Sāntalige

[1] Plates lately discovered in Tarikere tāluq (*Mys. Arch. Rep.* of 1908).

[2] Paṭṭi was apparently the name of the country in which Pomburchcha was situated. The Hoysala king Vishnuvarddhana is said (Sr 49, Bl 58) to have set up Paṭṭi Perumāla.

Thousand, which corresponds generally with the present Tīrthahalli tāluq and neighbouring parts. Jinadatta conquered the country southwards as far as Kalasa (Mudgere tāluq), and northwards fortified Gōvardhangiri (Sāgar tāluq), which he named after the famous hill near Muttra in the north of India. At a later period the capital was removed to Kalasa and then to Kārakala (in South Kanara). The rulers eventually became Lingāyits and adopted the title of Bhairarasa-Woḍeyars, but they probably had Jain wives. They continued beyond the fall of Vijayanagar in the sixteenth century, and were finally absorbed into the Keladi State.

Among the early Śāntara kings are mentioned the brothers Śrīkēśi and Jayakēśi, and the son of the former, Raṇakēśi. We have the Chānta king Jagēśi in Sk 283 ruling the whole of Sāntalige under the Rāshṭrakūṭa king Nṛipatunga Amōgha-varsha. He may therefore be placed in about 830. But a connected genealogy begins with Vikrama-Śāntara, who had the titles Kandukāchārya and Dāna-vinōda. He is credited with forming the Sāntalige Thousand into a separate kingdom, of which the boundaries were the Sula river on the south, Tavanasi on the west, and Bandige on the north. No eastern boundary is named (Nr 35). In about 920 a Śāntara king, whose name is not given, was defeated in a battle with the Nolambas, and slain and beheaded by the Ganga prince, the son of Pilduvipati or Prithuvipati (Gd 4). In 1062 and 1066 Vīra-Śāntara and his son Bhujabala-Śāntara are said (Nr 47, 59) to have freed the kingdom from those who had no claim to it. The reference may be to certain Chālukya princes, Bijjarasa and his brother Gōna-Rāja, who are stated (in Sa 109 *bis*) to be in full enjoyment of the Sāntalige-nāḍ in 1042. A glowing description is given of the fertility of the province, which was such that hunger was unknown there, and grass, firewood, and water were so abundant that many learned Brāhmans were induced to make it their abode. The Sāntalige-nāḍ, it says, had been ruled by many, but among them none was more famous than Gōna-Rāja. He established an agrahāra for the Brāhmans at Andhāsura (still so called, near Anantapur). Andhāsura is named among one of the first conquests of Jinadatta.

After this the Śāntaras completely recovered their power and influence. For of Nanni-Śāntara, the brother of Bhujabala, it is said (Nr 36) that he gained much greater distinction than even Būtuga-Permmāḍi (the Ganga king) had obtained, as the emperor came to meet him half way, and, giving him half the seat on his metal throne, placed the valiant Śāntara, whom he had protected, at his side. In the third generation from this we have Jagadēva, who must be the king that attacked the Hoysalas in Dōrasamudra and was beaten off by Ballāla I and Biṭṭi-Dēva in 1104, as his nephew Jayakēśi is given the date 1159 (Sa 159).

The centre of the State was later removed southwards to Kalasa (Mudgere tāluq), and from 1209 (Mg 65) to 1516 (Mg 31) it is called the Kalasa kingdom. Inscriptions at Kalasa give us the names of its rulers, two of whom, from 1246 to 1281, were queens, Jākala and Kālala-mahādēvīs; then Vīra-Pāṇḍya and Bhairarasa-Woḍeyar alternately recur. In 1292, at the time of the coronation of the Hoysala king Ballāla III, Kālala's son Pāṇḍya-Dēva successfully defended his country from an attack (Cm 36). But for the fourteenth century there are no inscriptions; it was the time of the Musalmān invasions from Delhi. In 1432 was erected the gigantic image of Gōmaṭa at Kārakala by Vīra-Pāṇḍya. From 1516 the State is called the Kalasa-Kārakala kingdom (Mg 41), and is described (Mg 62) as the kingdom below and above the Ghats. Kalasa is above the Ghats, in Mysore, and Kārakala below the Ghats, in South Kanara, both in about the same latitude. In 1530 the king is only said to be on the throne of Kārakala (Kp 47). The extension of the kingdom below the Ghats probably took place in the fifteenth century, when the kings had the title (Mg 42) *ari-rāya-gaṇḍara-dāvani* (cattle-rope to the champions over kings). The Vijayanagar king Krishna-Rāya soon after invaded the Tulu country and encamped near Mangalūr (Mg 41).[1] Bhairarasa fled, but made a vow that if the imperial army should retire and he return in peace to his country, he would repair the temple at Kalasa. What he wished for happened, and his right to the territory which he had occupied may then have been recognised. In 1542 and 1555 the crown is said (Mg 40, 60) to be that of Keravase, which may have been then the capital. It is near to Kārakala, on the east. The latest grant we have by the Bhairarasa-Woḍeyars is dated 1598 (Kp 50). But another colossal image of Gōmaṭa was erected at Yenūr (in South Kanara) by the brother of a king named Pāṇḍya in 1603 (see SB, Introd. 31, 32; *EI.* vii. 110, 112).

3. CHANGĀLVAS

The Changālvas or Changāluvas were a line of kings ruling for a long period in the west of the Mysore District and in Coorg. Their original territory was Changa-nāḍ (Hs 97), corresponding chiefly with the Hunsūr tāluq. They claim to be Yādavas (Hs 63, Yd 26) and of the Lunar race, descended from a king named Changālva, who was in Dvarāvatī, and having defeated Bijjalēndra, seized his titles. What these were does not appear, but the kings are generally styled mahā-maṇḍalika-maṇḍalēśvara. This Bijjala might perhaps be an early king of that name among the Kalachuryas (see above, p. 79), or one of the Śāntaras. The Changālvas became devoted Śaivas, and had as their family god Annadāni-Mallikārjuna on the Beṭṭadpur hill (in Hunsūr tāluq), which they called Śrīgiri, perhaps with reference to the Śaiva sacred place Śrīparvata or Śrīśaila in the Kurnool District. But they are first met with in Jain inscriptions at Panasoge or Hanasoge, to the south of the Kāvērī river in the Yedatore tāluq, where there are many ruined *basadis.* These, according to Yd 26, were sixty-four in number, and were set up by Rāma, the

[1] The invasion is said to have been made by Bhujabala-Rāya. If this be taken as a name and not a title, it may refer to Krishna-Rāya's elder brother Narasimha, who is called Buśbalrao by Nuniz (see *Mys. Arch. Rep.* of 1908).

son of Daśaratha, the elder brother of Lakshmaṇa, and husband of Sītā. The Jain priests of the Hottage (or Pustaka) gachcha claim exclusive jurisdiction over basadis at Panasoge and at Tale-Kāvērī (in Coorg), which may perhaps have been the limits of the Changālva kingdom east and west.

One of the basadis or Jain temples at Panasoge set up by Rāma had been endowed by the Gangas, and was rebuilt by the king Nanni-Changālva. The Ganga gifts are ascribed in Yd 25 to Mārasimha-Dēva, and he ruled from 961 to 974. Nanni-Changālva, from his prenomen Rājēndra-Chōla, belongs to the beginning of the eleventh century. He is the first Changālva of whom we have any certain knowledge. But as their kingdom was conquered by the Chōlas at the time when the Ganga power was overthrown in 1004, the Changālvas must have been an established line of kings prior to that. Their inscriptions are found mostly in the Hunsūr and Yedatore tāluqs and in Coorg, where they occur as far west as Yedava-nāḍ and Beṭṭyet-nāḍ.

The subjugation of the Changālvas by the Chōlas seems to have been effected by their defeat at Panasoge by the Chōla general Panchava-mahārāya (Cg 46). The subsequent Changālva kings all had Chōla prenomens for nearly two centuries. But on the expulsion of the Chōlas from Mysore by the Hoysalas in 1116, the Changālvas came into collision with the latter. Ballāla I had led an expedition against them in about 1104 (Hn 162). Vīra-Ganga was applied to for a grant by their *purānika* in 1139 (Cn 199, 200). In 1145 Nārasimha is said (Ng 76) to have slain Changālva in battle, and seized his elephants, horses, gold, and new jewels. In 1155 Nārasimha's general Chokimayya is said (Hn 69) to have brought the Changa king's territory into subjection to his king, and in 1171 Sōvi-dēva, the Kadamba ruler of Banavase, having vowed to do it, put the Changālva king into chains (Sb 345). Changālva is named as one of the kings who paid homage to Nārasimha's son Ballāla when as a prince he made a tour in the hill countries to the west (Bl 86). But

Ballāla, when on the throne, had to send an expedition in 1174 under his general Beṭṭarasa against the Changālva king Mahadēva, who had retired to Pālpare, a fort in Kiggaṭnāḍ in south Coorg. Beṭṭarasa destroyed him, and made Pālpare the seat of his own government. But the Changālva Pemma-Vīrappa afterwards attacked him, aided by the Koḍagas (or Coorgs) of all the nāḍs (the earliest express mention of the Coorgs). Beṭṭarasa was near being totally defeated, but contrived to gain the victory (Hs 20). After this the Changālvas appear to have submitted to the Hoysalas. In 1245 they had their capital at Śrīrangapaṭṭaṇa, not Seringapatam, but the place in Coorg known as Koḍugu-Śrīrangapaṭṭaṇa, situated to the south of the Kāvērī, near Siddapur (Ag 53), and two kings, Sōma-Dēva and Boppa-Dēva, were ruling conjointly. In 1252 the Hoysala king Sōmēśvara was received by them on a visit (Ag 53) to Rāmanāthpura (on the north bank of the Kāvērī in Arkalgūd tāluq). Changālvas named Mali-Dēva and Harihara-Dēva are mentioned in 1280 and 1297 (Bl 89, Cg 54, 45, 59), but during the fourteenth century none are met with.

At the end of the fifteenth century they again appear, and Nanja-Rāja, who ruled from 1502 to 1533, was the founder of their new capital Nanjarājapaṭṭaṇa or Nanjarāyapaṭṭaṇa. It is in Coorg, to the north of the Kāvērī, where it turns north and becomes the common boundary of Mysore and Coorg. The kings now called themselves kings of Nanjarāyapaṭṭaṇa or Nanjarājapaṭṭaṇa, and this place still continues to give its name to the northern tāluq of Coorg. Nanja-Rāja's younger brother Mahadēva is mentioned in Hs 63 and SB 103, but a genealogy of the Changālvas at this period is given in Hs 24 and 63. Mangarasa in his *Jayanṛipa-kāvya*, written in about 1509, says that his father was descended from the minister of the Changālva kings, and that the latter derived their origin from Krishna, that is, were Yādavas. Śrīkanṭha-Rāja, ruling in 1544 (Cg 26) seems to have been an important personage, and is distinguished by supreme titles (Hs 24). Piriya-Rāja, surnamed Rudragaṇa, who ruled from 1586 to 1607, rebuilt Singapaṭṭaṇa and named it after himself Piriyapaṭṭaṇa (Hs 15), the Periapatam in Hunsūr tāluq. In 1607 Tirumala-Rāja, the Vijayanagar viceroy at Seringapatam, made a grant of the Malalavāḍi country (Hunsur tāluq) to Rudragaṇa "in order that the worship of the god Annadāni-Mallikārjuna should not fail as long as the Nanjarāyapaṭṭaṇa kings of the Changālva family continued" (Hs 36). But Piriyapaṭṭaṇa was taken by the Mysore king in 1644, Vīra-Rājaiya, the ruling prince, falling in its defence, after putting to death his wives and children on seeing that his situation was desperate. This was the end of the Changālvas.

4. KONGĀLVAS

The Kongālvas ruled a kingdom consisting of the Arkalgūd tāluq in the south of the Hassan District of Mysore and the adjoining Yēlusāvira country in the north of Coorg. It was more or less the Kongal-nāḍ Eight Thousand, of which the Ganga prince Eṟeyappa had been governor in about 880 (Hs 92). But the Kongālva State now in question was a creation of the Chōlas in about 1004, as recorded in Cg 46. It is there said that the great Chōla king Rājakēsarivarmma-Permmānaḍigal (Rājarāja), on hearing how Panchava-mahārāya had fought without ceasing in the battle of Panasoge (Yedatore tāluq) and annihilated the enemy (the Changālvas), resolved to bestow on him a crown and give him a nāḍ. Accordingly, when he appeared before the king, the latter bound on him a crown with the title Kshatriya-śikhāmani Kongālva, and gave him Mālavvi (now Mālambi, in Coorg). Of this Panchava-mahārāya we have an inscription at Balmuri (Sr 140), dated in 1012, in which he is described as a bee at the lotus feet of Rājarāja, and is said to have been invested by him with the rank of mahā-daṇḍanāyaka for Bengi-maṇḍala (the Eastern Chālukya territory) and Ganga-maṇḍala (the Ganga territory in Mysore). He then claims to have led an expedition throughout the western coast region, in the course of which he seized Tuluva (South Kanara), and Konkana (North Kanara), held Malaya (Malabar), and put to flight Chēramma (the king of Cochin or Travancore), after which he pushed aside Teluga and Raṭṭiga (countries to the north of Mysore), and desired to have even the little Belvola country (in Dharwar and Belgaum Districts).

Kongālva kings with Chōla prenomens continue down to 1115 (Cg 33), and disappear on the expulsion of the Chōlas by the Hoysalas at that time. They were Jains, and the titles ascribed (Ag 99) to Adaṭarāditya, who ruled from 1066 to 1100, are: entitled to the *pancha-mahā-śabda*, mahā-maṇḍalēśvara, chief lord of the city of Oreyūr (the early Chōla capital near Trichinopoly, now called Warriore), sun upon the eastern mountain — the Chōla-kula — with twisted top-knot, crest-jewel of the Sūryya-vamśa (or Solar race). Adaṭarāditya had a learned minister named Nakulāryya, who boasts of being able to write in four languages (Ag 99). Which these were is unfortunately not mentioned.

Two occasions are referred to, in Mj 43 and Ag 76, on which the Kongālvas came into collision with the Hoysalas In the former, the Kongālva king attacked Nṛipa-Kāma-Poysala in 1022, when the latter was apparently saved by his general Jōgayya. In the latter, Kongālva claims to have gained a victory at Manni over the base (*muṇḍa*) Poysala in 1026. As no farther advance of the Chōla arms is recorded, it is evident that the Hoysalas checked the Chōla career of conquest in Mysore in this direction.

The Kongālva name survived till 1390 (Cg 39), when some Jain priests repaired the basadis at Mullūr (in Coorg) and a Kongālva-Suguṇi-Dēvī made grants for them, which are still continued.

5. PUNNĀḌ RĀJAS

Punnāḍ was a very ancient kingdom, situated in the south of Mysore. It is the Punnāṭa mentioned in connection with the Jain migration from the North in the third century B.C. led by Bhadrabāhu, who at Śravaṇa-Beḷgoḷa (Hassan District), in anticipation of his death, directed the pilgrims to go on to Punnāṭa (as stated by Harishēna in the *Brihatkāthakōśa*, dated in 931[1]). It is also mentioned in the second century by Ptolemy as Pounnata, where (he says) is beryl. Its name occurs again in the fifth century in connection with the Ganga king Avinīta (Cg 1). It was a Six Thousand province, and had as its capital Kitthipura, now identified (Hg 56) with Kittūr on the Kabbani river in the Heggaḍadēvankōte tāluq. Avinīta's soṇ Durvvinīta, who reigned from 482 to 517, married the daughter of Skandavarmma, the Rāja of Punnāḍ, who chose him for herself, although from her birth she had been intended by her father, on the advice of his own guru, for the son of another (DB 68). Punnāḍ was after this annexed to the Ganga kingdom (Tm 23), but the name continues to appear for some time.

Only one inscription has been discovered of the Punnāṭa Rājas (*IA.* xii. 13; xviii. 366). Its date is not certain, but it gives the following succession of kings: Rāshṭravarmma; his son Nāgadatta; his son Bhujaga, who married the daughter of Singavarmma; their son Skandavarmma; and his son the Punnāṭa-Rāja Ravidatta. The latter makes a grant of villages to Brāhmans, from his victorious camp at Kitthipura.

There was also a small district called the Punnāḍ Seventy in the Devanhalli tāluq in the tenth century (Dv 41, 43), but whether it had any connection with the other is not apparent.

[1] See above, p. 10.

6. SINDAS

The Sindas gave their name to the Sindavāḍi province, which extended over parts of the Shimoga, Chitaldroog, Bellary, Dharwar, and Bijāpur Districts. The account of their origin is first related in Dg 43, and repeated in Hl 50 and 20. From the union of Śiva and Sindhu (the name of the river Indus) was born a son, to whom Bhava (Śiva) with affection gave the name Saindhava, and made the king of the serpents his guardian. Saying that unless his son drank tigress's milk he would not become brave, Śiva created a tigress, whose milk the child drank, and grew in the world. Moreover, Paramēśvara directed the goddess Mālatī to aid his son in war, and gave him a second name of Niḍudōl Sinda (the long-armed Sinda). Being told that Karahāṭa (in Satāra District) was his abode, he took possession of it, driving out the kings that were there. Among his titles are: mahā-maṇḍalēśvara, lord of Karahāṭa-pura, obtainer of a boon from the goddess Mālatī, distinguished by the blue flag (*nīla-dhvaja*), of the Phaṇirāja-vamśa (the race of the king of serpents), having the tiger and deer crest. The Sindas also had (Hl 98, 26) the titles Sinda-Gōvinda, and Pātāla-chakravartti.

The earliest reference to their country seems to be in the fifth century (Kd 162), under the name of the Sindh-uthayā-rāshṭra, an outlying portion. But in 750 the Sinda-vishaya itself is mentioned (Mg 36). The Sinda inscriptions in Mysore are principally found in the Dāvangere and Honnāli tāluqs. In 968 a Sinda appears under the Rāshṭrakūṭa king Akālavarsha (Hk 23). In 992 the Sindas had come under the Western Chālukyas (Dg 114), in 1180 were under the Kalachuryas (Hl 50), in 1189 again under the Western Chālukyas (Hl 46), in 1198 under the Hoysalas (Sk 315), and in 1215 under the Sēunas (Hl 44). Their chief city at this period was Bellagavartti or Belagavatti, now called Belagutti, in the Honnāli tāluq; but in 1164 the royal residence was at Hallavūr (Dg 43), which is on the Tungabhadrā (Hulloor in the Rāni-Bennūr tāluq in Dharwar), the city at which, soon after, the Hoysala king Ballāla II lived for a considerable time. A list of the nāḍs included in the Sinda kingdom is given in Hl 50, the principal being the Edavatte Seventy, Beḷlave Seventy, Muduvalla Thirty, and Narivalige Forty (Hl 26, 28).

Īśvara-Dēva I, ruling from 1166 to 1180, seems to have been of some importance. At his coronation, the sound of the drums and conchs roused up Uragēndra (the king of the serpents), who came there in haste, saying, "This is a glorification of my line; Oho! I must see this." Śiva also came, with Gangā and Pārvatī, and Ganēśa, to bless the king. With a signet-ring of the serpent jewel on his hand, with his powerful arms and body, his sword and beard, this Sinda king Īśvara appeared to his enemies like a terrible dragon ready to swallow them up. In 1196 and 1197 the Sindas were exposed to persistent attacks from the Hoysala forces of Umā-Dēvī, the queen of Ballāla II, and in 1245 and 1247 fought severe battles at Kūḍali and Nēmatti (Nyāmti) against the Sēuna general Śrīdhara, whom they drove off in confusion.

7. SĒNAVĀRAS

The Sēnavāras were a Jain family of whom inscriptions are found in the west of the Kadūr District. The first mention of a Sēnavāra is in about 690, in the time of the Āluva king Chitravāhana (Kp 37), and of the Western Chālukya king Vinayāditya (Sk 278). In about 1010 a Sēnavāra was ruling the Banavase province under Vikramāditya (Sb 381). But a connected account of the period when they were independent appears in Cm 95, 61, 94 and others, among which Cm 62 gives a date that seems to correspond with 1058. We thus obtain the names of Jīvitavāra, his son Jīmūtavāhana, and the latter's son Māra or Mārasimha. They were of the Khachara-vamśa, had the

SĒNAVĀRA STONE, KANATI.

Size of Original, 4 ft. 6 in. × 2 ft.

serpent flag (*phani-dhvaja*) and the lion crest, and were lords of Kūḍalūr-pura. Māra received homage from all the kings of the Vidyādhara-lōka, and was master of Hēmakūṭa-pura. Sūryya and Āditya, the sons of Sēnavāra, were special ministers of Vikramāditya's court in 1128 (Dg 90). The first was perhaps the father of the experienced general Sēnāpati, who claims (Dg 84) to have selected which of the Pāṇḍyas should sit on the throne, from Palatta downwards, and kept them in power, so that without him they were ciphers (*pūjya*).

8. PĀṆḌYAS

The Pāṇḍyas of Uchchangi were an interesting and important family. They were Yādavas, of the Lunar race, and ruled originally over Hayve, one of the Seven Konkanas, with their capital at Sisugali. The Pāṇḍya king in 1113 claims to be lord of Gōkarṇa-pura, and protector of the Konkaṇa-rāshṭra (Sk 99). On the conquest of the Seven Konkaṇas by the Western Chālukya prince Jayasimha, the Pāṇḍyas became identified with Uchchangi (a celebrated hill-fort on the northern border of Mysore, in the south-west of the Bellary District), which became the seat of government for the Nolambavāḍi Thirty-two Thousand (the Chitaldroog District). The origin of the family is traced in Dg 41 to Mangaya or Āditya-Dēva, from whom sprang Pāṇḍya, whose son was Chēdi-Rāja, so called from his subduing the Chēdi kings.[1] Though king over the whole circle of the earth, he was permanently partial (says Dg 39) to the Pāṇḍya country, and so became famous by the name of Pāṇḍya. The blows from his bracelets had resounded on the conch-shell on the top of Paurandara's head, and his fish-crest was set up on great rocks on the chief mountains.[2] His son was Palanta, who secured their kingdoms to both the Chālukya and Chōla kings. The general distinctive titles of the Pāṇḍyas are: mahā-

[1] Chēdi is Bandelkhand. The Kalachuryas were rulers of Chēdi.

[2] The fish-crest was the emblem of the Pāṇḍyas of Madura in the south.

maṇḍalēśvara, lord of Kānchī-pura,[1] champion in cutting on both sides (*parichchēdi-gaṇḍa*[2]), defeater of the designs of Rājiga-Chōla.[3]

Tribhuvanamalla-Pāṇḍya, whose name seems to have been Irukkavēla (Dg 39), was ruling the Nolambavāḍi province under the Chālukya king Tribhuvanamalla in (?) 1083 (Ci 33). In 1101 he was also in charge of the Ballakunde Three Hundred (Dg 151, 128). His residence was at Beltūr (Bettūr, close to Dāvangere on the north-east). He is said (Dg 139, 90) to be the rod in Tribhuvanamalla's right hand, and such was the emperor's confidence in him (says Dg 3) that he was considered sufficient by himself to break the pride of Chōla, harass Āndhra, upset Kalinga, frighten and attack the Anga, Vanga, and Magadha kings, conquer Mālava, and trample on Gurjjara. By his valour he brought the whole earth encompassed by the four oceans into subjection to king Vikrama. Dg 155 shows him in 1124 ruling the Sāntalige Thousand and various agrahāras in Banavāsi-naḍ, as well as the Nolambavāḍi province, and controlling the *nidhi-nidhāna-nikshēpa* (apparently mines or banks and underground treasures), the *sahasra-daṇḍa* (the thousand force) and other affairs. He is here called Vīra-Noḷamba-Pallava-Permmānaḍi-Dēva's younger brother. This was the Chālukya prince Jayasimha, who was the son of a Pallava mother. Whether Pāṇḍya was really related to him, or whether this is only a complimentary expression of their intimacy, is not clear. But it may be pointed out that his grandson is stated (Dg 41) to be ruling *kumāra-vrittiyinda*, ? by his right as a prince. Both of them had married sisters of Vikramāditya (Dg 41).

With Dg 2 we come to Rāya-Pāṇḍya, who continued to rule Nolambavāḍi and Sāntalige from Beltūr. Dg 77 describes him as a confounder of the Chōla king, destroyer of Nēpāla, a warrior to Kalinga, uprooter of the unsubmissive Singala,

[1] Apparently adopted in consequence of their defeat of the Chōlas.
[2] Perhaps a covert allusion to the defeat of the Chēdi kings.
[3] Rājendra-Chōla II, afterwards known as Kulōttunga-Chōla I.

Chyēndra, Singha, and Kaulūṭa kings. He had the sons Paṇḍita-Pāṇḍya, Vīra-Pāṇḍya, and Vijaya-Pāṇḍya or Kāma-Dēva. Paṇḍita-Pāṇḍya had for his preceptor the learned Madhusūdana (composer of Dg 41), but seems not to have come to the throne.

Vīra-Pāṇḍya ruled Nolambavāḍi from the Uchchangi fort. He it is who is said to be standing in the right of a prince, as remarked above. He subdued Male and gave it to the ornament of the Chālukyas (Dg 168). At the time of a solar eclipse in 1148 he made great gifts at the confluence of the Tungabhadrā and Haridrā (Dg 41). There is little doubt that the grants claiming to be issued by the emperor Janamējaya at this spot, in connection with the *sarpa-yāga* or serpent sacrifice, emanated either from this prince or perhaps from his brother Vījaya-Pāṇḍya who succeeded him, and that they were modelled on the similar grant by the Çhālukya prince Vīra-Noṇamba (Bn 142[1]).

Vijaya-Pāṇḍya comes before us in Dg 115. Down to 1184 he seems free from any overlord. This was the period when the Chālukya power was declining and the Kalachuryas were gaining the ascendancy. In token of his splendour, Dg 5 says that the points of his crown were formed of separate large sapphires, and his arms adorned with golden bracelets. He subdued in mere sport the Seven Konkaṇas, set up in the Kanaka mountain a pillar of victory with the fish-crest, had a treasury filled with pearls from the Tāmraparnni, and had a pleasure-house among the sandal trees on the slopes of the Malaya mountain. The Chōlas, it would appear, made desperate efforts to conquer Uchchangi, but after besieging it for twelve years abandoned the enterprise as hopeless. The Hoysala king Ballāla II, however, now made the attempt and easily captured it. Kāma-Dēva threw himself on the king's mercy and was restored to his throne. In Hk 4 and 56 we accordingly find the Pāṇḍya-nāḍ under the Hoysalas, who it says had thrashed the Pāṇḍya kings on the field of battle.

[1] See section on the Pāṇḍavas in vol. vii. Introd. p. 1.

9. SALUVAS

The Sāluvas (or Sālvas) were of the Lunar race and originally Jains, located at Sangītapura, the Sanskrit for Hāḍuvaḷḷi, situated in Taulava-dēśa or South Kanara (Sa 164). A Sāluva-Tikkama was the general of the Sēuna kings Mahadēva and Rāmachandra, who invaded the Hoysala kingdom in 1276 and 1280, and claims to have plundered Dōrasamudra.

The records supply us with the names Indra, his son Sangi-Rāja, and his sons Sāluvēndra and Indagarasa or Immaḍi-Sāluvēndra in 1488 and 1498 (Sa 164). Then we have the Sāluvas Malli-Rāya, Dēva-Rāya, and Krishna-Dēva, down to about 1530 (Nr 46). In about 1560 the residence of the kings seems to have been at Kshēmapura (Gerasoppe, after which the celebrated Gersoppa Falls are named). We have in Sa 55 the names Dēva-Rāya, Bhairava, Sālvamalla, and again Bhairava and Sālvamalla. They were ruling the Tulu, Konkana, Haive, and other countries.

In 1384 a Sāluva-Rāma-Dēva, who seems to have been governor of Talakāḍ, was killed in battle against the Ṭurukas at Kottakoṇḍa (Ck 15). Sāluva-Tippa-Rāja was married to Harimā, sister of the Vijayanagar king Dēva-Rāya II (Cd 29). And in 1431 we have Sāluva-Tippa-Rāja and his son Gōpa-Rāja, to whom Tēkal was given by order of that king (Mr 3). These Sāluvas are distinguished by the epithets *mēdinī-mīsara-gaṇḍa* (champion over the mustaches of the world), *kaṭhāri-sāluva* (dagger falcon). From this family (see My 33) sprang the short-lived dynasty, composed of Sāluva-Nṛisimha or Narasinga and his son Immaḍi-Nṛiśimha or Narasinga, which held the Vijayanagar throne from 1478 to 1496.[1] The former was commander of the Vijayanagar forces under the kings Mallikārjuṇa and Virūpāksha. But after successfully defending the empire against the Bahmani Sultān's invasion, he took advantage of his position to usurp the crown. He is

[1] Immaḍi-Narasinga's son Sāluva-Dēvappa-Nāyaka was governor of the Tippur district in 1493 (DB 42, 45), and made a grant at Channapatna in 1494 (Kg 26).

said to have been the most powerful chief in Karṇāṭa and Telingāna, and a Muhammadan historian (see vol. x, Introd. 36) represents Kānchī as being in the centre of his dominions.

Notwithstanding the late usurpation, Sāluvas continued in favour. For Sāluva-Timmarasa was a minister under Krishna-Rāya (Nj 195). And in 1513 we have his younger brother Sāluva-Gōvinda-Rāja, to whom that king gave the Terakanāmbi country (Gu 3), which had been taken away from the Ummattūr chiefs. In 1519, 1521, and 1523 he is called Krishna-Rāya's minister (TN 73, 42, Ch 99). From 1520 to 1527 we have kaṭhāri-sāluva Krishna-Rāya-Nāyaka as the chief minister of Krishna-Rāya, and described as his right hand (Hs 48, Hg 78, 40); and in Nr 46 of about 1530 he is called a king—Sāluva-Krishna-Dēva-ṇripati, and said to be the sister's son of Dēva-Rāya.

10. PADINĀLKUNĀḌ

When the Hoysala power was nearing its end, in the reign of Ballāla III, there was a great minister Perumāla-daṇṇāyaka, who founded and endowed a college at Mālingi, on the Kāvērī, opposite to Taḷakāḍ (TN 27). His son Mādhava-daṇṇāyaka was ruling Padinālkunāḍ (the Fourteen nāḍs[1]) in the south of Mysore, with the seat of his government at Terakanāmbi (Gundalpet tāluq). He was in power to 1318, and (Gu 58) set up the god Gōpinātha in Gōvarddhangiri (the Gopālswāmi hill in the south-west of Gundalpet tāluq). He was followed by his son Kētaya-daṇṇāyaka, ruling in 1321 (Gu 69), and by Singeya-daṇṇāyaka, ruling in 1338 (Hs 82). Among their titles are: death to the Kongas, subduer of Nīlagiri, skilled in turning back Pāṇḍya, and lord of Svastipura.

Descendants from these were the Nava Dannāyaks of tradi-

[1] There is a Pāḍinālknāḍ tāluq in Coorg, but that probably refers to four nāḍs (Nālknāḍ) as in Yeḍenālknāḍ. But Terakanāmbi-nāḍ is also said (Gu 11) to be called Kuḍugu-nāḍ, which is the name of Coorg.

tion, nine brothers, identified with Beṭṭadakōṭe, the fort on the Gōpālswāmi hill, the chief of whom was Perumāl-dannāyak. Four of them, headed by Bhīma-dannāyak, quarrelled with the other five, and gaining Nagarapura (Nanjangūd) and Ratnapuri (Heḍatale), set up a separate government. After a time they returned to attack Beṭṭadakōṭe, which after a siege of three years was taken by stratagem. Mancha-dannāyak, who conducted the defence, seeing the citadel taken, leaped from the hill on horseback and was killed. The site of this leap is still pointed out. The four victorious Dannāyaks, placing a junior member of the family in the government of Beṭṭadakōṭe, set forth on expeditions of conquest, in the course of which tradition says that they overran the country from Ḍavasi-beṭṭa (the southern point of Coorg) in the south, to Goa in the north, and from Satyamangala (on the Bhavāni in Coimbatore) in the east, to the Bisale Ghat (in the north-west of Coorg) on the west.

The later rulers of Kōṭe or Beṭṭadakōṭe belong to from the fifteenth to the seventeenth century, and the seat of their government was apparently at Hura, in the south-west of the Nanjangūd tāluq. Their distinctive titles were: *mahā-maṇḍalēśvara*, *Chēra-Chōla-Pāṇḍya-mūvara-rāyara gaṇḍa* (champion over the three kings Chēra, Chōla, and Pāṇḍya), *Nīlagiri-sādarak-oḍeyar*, *Nīlagiri-nāḍ-ālva*, or *Nīlagiri-uddharana* (subduer, ruler, or protector of Nilagiri). But Mādhava-nāyaka (1530-1548) is given supreme titles (Hs 41).

11. PADINĀḌ

There was also a principality called Padināḍ or Hadināḍ, the capital of which at the end of the sixteenth century was Yelandūr (Yl 1). A chief of Padināḍ is mentioned as early as 1058 (Ch 69). Hadināḍ is also named in 1196 (TN 31) as a province of the Hoysala kingdom. It is now represented by Hadināru in the Nanjangūd tāluq. The inscriptions place the modern rulers in the sixteenth and beginning of the seventeenth century. In 1586 the chiefs took the names of the Vijayanagar kings at Penugoṇḍa (Nj 141). Before 1650 the province had been annexed to Mysore by Kaṇṭhīrava-Narasa-Rāja (Ch 42). In 1807 Yelandūr was given as a *jāgīr* to the Dewān Pūrnayya in recognition of his eminent services, and is now held by his descendants.

12. UMMATTŪR WOḌEYARS

The Ummattūr Woḍeyars were an important line of rulers in the south of Mysore, and the chief rivals in that quarter of the Mysore house. Ummattūr is in the Chāmrājnagar tāluq, but the principal fortress of the chiefs was on the island of Śivasamudram,[1] at the Falls of the Kāvērī, where also was the temple of Sōmēśvara, their family god (Gu 11). Their distinctive titles were: *mahā-maṇḍalēśvara, javādi-kōlāhala* (exulting in musk), *pēsāli-Hanuma* (Hanumān in artifice), *arasanka-sūnegāra* (slaughterer in war with kings), *ghēnanka-chakrēśvara* (emperor in fight with the dagger), *gaja-bēnṭekāra* (hunter of elephants). They were of the Solar race, called themselves masters of the Hoysala-rājya, and ruled also over Terakanāmbi and the Nīlagiris, where they had a fort at Mālekōṭa, near Kalhatti, in which they took shelter when in trouble.

They appear in inscriptions in the fifteenth century. In 1491 they take the royal titles, and seem independent (Nj 118). In 1505 they have the titles Chikka-Rāya, Penu-goṇḍa-chakrēśvara, and lord over all rājas (Gu 67). But Ganga-Rāja now openly rebelled, while parts of the Bangalore District were called the Śivasamudram country. The Vija-yanagar monarch Krishna-Rāya had therefore to march against him, and captured his fort at Śivasamudram in 1510, thus reducing him to submission. Ummattūr itself was finally taken by the Mysore Rāja in 1613, and the line brought to an end. Śivasamudram fort was ruined and deserted under

[1] See note, p. 119.

tragic circumstances arising out of struggles with local chiefs. In 1814 the island was given as a *jāgīr* to Rāmaswāmi Mudaliyār, who had been native secretary to the Resident in Mysore, and he erected between 1830 and 1832 the bridges over the Kāvērī which connect it with Mysore on the one side and Coimbatore on the other. His descendants now own the place. In 1902 the first electric power installation in India was set up there by the Mysore State at the Kāvērī Falls on the Mysore side.

13. KELADI KINGS

The Keladi, Ikkēri, or Bednūr kings ruled in the Shimoga District and along the west coast from the beginning of the sixteenth century to 1763. Their territory included Āraga and Gutti (Chandragutti), both above the Ghats, in Mysore, and Bārakūr and Mangalūr, both below the Ghats, in South Kanara (Sg 11). Their capital was removed from Keladi (Sāgar tāluq) in about 1560 to Ikkēri (in the same tāluq), and in 1639 to Bednūr (now Nagar). Their State was the most considerable and wealthy of those conquered by Haidar Ali and annexed to Mysore. The kings were Lingāyits, and had the titles: *Yeḍava-Murāri* (said to be the names of two slaves belonging to the founder of the line, who, on condition that their memory was preserved, volunteered to be sacrificed for the establishment of his power, for which a human sacrifice was declared to be necessary), *Kōṭe-kōlāhala* (disturber of forts), *viśuddha-vaidikādvaita-siddhānta-pratishṭhāpaka* (establisher of the pure Vaidika Advaita doctrine), *Śiva-guru-bhakti-parāyana* (devoted to faith in Śiva and the guru). A genealogy of the line to 1667 is given in Tl 156 in Sanskrit. Most of their inscriptions record grants to Lingāyit *maṭhas* or remission of transit duties on articles carried on pack bullocks for the use of such *maṭhas*. The following is a table of the kings :—

- 1. Chauḍappa-Nāyaka, son of Hulibail Basappa, 1499-1513
  - 2. Sadāśiva-Nāyaka, 1513-45
    - 3. Sankaṇṇa-Nāyaka I, 1545-58
      - 5. Rāmarāja-Nāyaka, 1570-82
      - 6. Venkaṭappa-Nāyaka I, 1582-1629
        - Bhadrappa-Nāyaka
          - 7. Vīrabhadra-Nāyaka, 1629-45
        - 8. Śivappa-Nāyaka, 1645-60
          - 10. Bhadrappa-Nāyaka, 1661-63
          - 11. Sōmaśēkhara-Nāyaka I, 1663-71
            - 12. Chennammāji (widow of No. 11), 1671-97
              - (adopted) 13. Basappa-Nāyaka I, 1697-1714
                - 14. Sōmaśēkhara-Nāyaka II, 1714-39
                  - (adopted) 16. Chenna-Basappa-Nāyaka 1754-57
                - Vīrabhadra-Nāyaka
                  - 15. Basappa-Nāyaka II, 1739-54
                    - 17. Vīrammāji (widow of No. 15), 1757-63
                      - (adopted) 18. Sōmaśēkhara-Nāyaka III.
        - 9. Venkaṭappa-Nāyaka II, 1660-61
    - 4. Sankaṇṇa-Nāyaka II, 1558-70
      - Siddappa-Nāyaka

The first prominent king was Sadāśiva-Nāyak, who received his name from the Vijayanagar sovereign Sadāśiva-Rāya, in reward for his services against rebellious chiefs in Tuluva or South Kanara, and he was invested with the government of the provinces above mentioned.

After the fall of Vijayanagar, Venkaṭappa-Nāyak I assumed independence. He drove back the invasion of the Bijāpur forces commanded by Randulha-Khān, and extended his dominions on the north and east to Māsūr, Shimoga, Kadūr, and Bhuvanagiri (Kavaledurga), and on the west and south to the sea at Honore (North Kanara), by victory over the queen of Gersoppa, the pepper queen of the Portuguese, who was a feudatory of Bijāpur. At the same time he acquired territory down to the borders of Malabar, and established his power so firmly that he was able to add 50 per cent to the land assessment in great part of Kanara. His valour is said (Sh 2) to be like adamantine armour to the Karnāṭa country, and he is described as an elephant-goad to the rutting elephants the bounding Taulava kings, a sun to the darkness the Kirātas, a boundary mountain to stop the great ocean of Mlechchas ever seeking to overflow the South in victorious expeditions. In 1621 he re-established the *maṭha* at Śringēri (Sg 5), originally set up in the eighth century by Śankarāchārya (Sg 11), the abbot of which was instrumental in founding the Vijayanagar empire in 1336. By espousing the cause of the queen of Ola against the Bangār rāja, he came into collision with the Portuguese, who call him Venkapor, king of Canara. But their Viceroy at Goa, being anxious to secure the trade in pepper for Portugal against the English and Dutch, sent an embassy to him in 1623 to form an alliance.

Vīrabhadra-Nāyak averted a formidable invasion threatened by Bijāpur, which was to be assisted by the rājas of Sunda and Bilige, and the chiefs of Tarikere and Bānāvar. But the capital was removed to Bednūr, and Śivappa-Nāyak, who was in command of the army, subdued Bhairarasa of Kārakala, invaded Malayāla, and entered Coorg. Vīrabhadra is said (Sh 2) to be like a long right arm to the rājādhirāja Venkaṭādri (Venkaṭapati-Rāya II of Vijayanagar), and to have given protection to the southern kings alarmed by the great army of the Pātuśāha (the Ādil-Shāhi Sultān of Bijāpur).

Śivappa-Nāyak himself next ascended the throne, and was one of the most distinguished kings of the line. He greatly enlarged Bednūr and made it a central emporium of trade. He also introduced the land assessment called *shist*. His expeditions in Mysore extended over Balam or Manjarābād to Vastāra, Sakkarepaṭṭaṇa and Hassan. Father Leonardo Paes, then travelling in Kanara, says that he had amassed enormous treasure, that his possessions extended from the Tudry river to Kāsargōd or Nīlēśvar, and that he had a standing army of from forty to fifty thousand men. There were more than thirty thousand Christians among his subjects, originally natives of Goa and Salsette. In 1646 Śrī-Ranga-Rāya, the fugitive king of the Vijayanagar dynasty, fled to him for refuge, and Śivappa-Nāyak not only gave him the government of Bēlūr and Sakkarepaṭṭaṇa, but attacked Seringapatam on his behalf. In 1652 Śivappa rescued from the unlawful hands into which they had fallen the lands with which the Śringēri *maṭha* had formerly been endowed, and restored them to the *maṭha* (Sg 11, 13).

In the time of Bhadrappa-Nāyak the Bijāpur army is said to have taken Bednūr and besieged Bhuvanagiri, whither the king with his family had retired, but a peace was eventually concluded. In 1664 the Mahratta leader Śivāji made a sudden descent on the coast of Kanara, sacked Kundapūr and sailed back to Gōkarna, plundering all the adjacent tracts. Sōmaśēkhara-Nāyak was seized with sensual madness, which led to his assassination. But his widow succeeded in carrying on the government for a considerable time. Her army captured Basavāpaṭṇa and other places to the east, where she fortified Harikere and named it Channagiri after herself. She also gave shelter to Rāma-Rāja, the son of Śivāji, when he was hiding from the Mughals, until he could escape to his own country. Peace was made between Mysore and Bednūr in 1694, the former retaining the Bēlūr country. Basappa-Nāyak I was devoted to works of charity and the care of ascetics, vagrants, and infant children. As an atonement for the murder of Sōmaśēkhara, he imposed a small extra assessment, to be spent in feeding pilgrims.

Sōmaśēkhara-Nāyak II is said to have attacked Sīra and taken Ajjampur, Sante-Bennūr, and other places from the Mughals. In 1748 was fought the battle of Māyakoṇḍa against Chitaldroog, in which the enemy suffered a disastrous defeat, Medakēri-Nāyak, their chief, being slain. Besides this, an incident of some importance was connected with the event. Chanda-Sāhib, nominated by the French as the Navāb of the Carnatic in opposition to the English candidate, Muhammad-Ali, had just been released from the Mahrattas at Sattāra. Being on his way south, he took part in the battle on the side of Chitaldroog. But his son was killed, and he himself was taken prisoner. While being led in triumph to Bednūr, he induced his Musalmān guards to march off with him to the French instead. He took Arcot in 1750, but in 1752, when the French surrendered to the English at Trichinopoly, fled to the protection of the Tanjore general. This man treacherously put him to death and sent his head to the rival Navāb, who made it over to Nanjarāj, the Mysore commander. The latter despatched it to Seringapatam, where it was exposed on one of the gates for three days. In 1751 a treaty was concluded between Bednūr and the English factory at Tellichery.

An adopted son next came to the throne, but on remonstrating with his adoptive mother on her amours, which had become a public scandal, he was strangled, and Vīrammāji reigned in her own name. She was the last of her line. Haidar Ali, after a career of conquest over the eastern parts of Mysore, met at Chitaldroog with a pretender who professed to be the Bednūr prince supposed to have been murdered. Haidar resolved to make use of him, and invaded Bednūr in 1763 ostensibly to restore him. Making a feigned attack at the barriers, he entered by a secret path and captured the city. The Rāni, with her paramour and adopted son, fled to Ballālrāyandurga (Kadūr District), having set fire to the palace. The inhabitants deserted the place *en masse*, and in panic took shelter in the surrounding woods. The triumphant Haidar, extinguishing the flames and sealing up the houses, acquired a booty estimated at twelve millions sterling. The Rāni, her lover, and her adopted son were all seized and sent as prisoners to the hill-fort of Maddagiri (Tumkūr District), together with even the pretender. They were liberated by the Mahrattas when these captured Maddagiri in 1767. Virammāji died on the way to Poona, and Sōmaśēkhara ended his life there unmarried.

14. BĒLŪR AND MANJARĀBĀD

The Bēlūr family were descended from the Haḍapa (or bearer of the betel-bag) to the king of Vijayanagar. Era-Krishnappa-Nāyaka, who is generally represented as the head, seems (Hk 112) at first to have received a grant of Bāgūr (Hosdurga tāluq), but early in the sixteenth century was invested with the government of the Bēlūr country. The principal titles of these chiefs were: lord of Maṇināga-pura, Sindhu-Gōvinda, dhavalānka-Bhīma. In 1645 Bēlūr and parts dependent on it were overrun by the Bednūr forces under Śivappa-Nāyak, who bestowed them on the fugitive king of Vijayanagar, then arrived as a refugee at his court. By the treaty concluded between Mysore and Bednūr in 1694, six nāḍs of Balam (Manjarābād) were ceded to the Bēlūr chiefs, and the remaining Bēlūr territory was annexed to Mysore. In 1792 Krishnappa-Nāyak joined the Maḥrattas in their advance with Lord Cornwallis against Seringapatam, but on peace being made with Tīpu Sultān, fled to Coorg in fear. Tīpu, however, induced him to return, and gave him the government of Aigūr, the south of Manjarābād. On the fall of Seringapatam in 1799, Venkaṭādri-Nāyak attempted to gain independence and to recover the rest of Manjarābād. But he was captured after two years and executed.

15. CHITALDROOG

The Chitaldroog chieftains received their kingdom in Holalkere, Hiriyūr, and Chitaldroog, after the fall of Vijayanagar in 1565, from the representatives of that empire.

The chiefs were Bēḍas by caste, of the Kāmagēti-vamśa, and claim to be of the Vālmīki-gōtra. They were styled mahā-nāyakāchāryya, and had the distinctive prefix Kāmagēti-kastūri. They were mostly named Medakēri-Nāyak. In the latter part of the seventeenth century they were engaged in contests with the Sante-Bennūr and Harpanhalli chiefs, and extended their territory at the expense of the former. Frequent wars afterwards arose with Bednūr and with the Mahrattas, as well as with the Mughals. The alliance with Chanda-Sāhib, and the fate of the battle of Māyakoṇḍa in 1748 have already been related above. Chitaldroog made a prolonged defence against Haidar Ali, who succeeded at last in capturing it in 1779 mainly through the treachery of some Musalmān officers. To break up the Bēḍa population, whose blind devotion had enabled the place to hold out so long, Haidar transported 20,000 of the inhabitants to people the island of Seringapatam, and of all the boys of proper age he formed regular battalions of captive converts or Chēlas.

16. SANTE-BENNŪR

The Sante-Bennūr family appeared early in the seventeenth century. They were of the Puvvalānvaya, and adherents of Hanumanta, the servant of Rāmachandra (Tk 22). Their founder seems to have gained possession of the Dhumi hill. His son built the fort of Basavāpaṭṇa, and acquired a territory extending from Anantapur to Māyakoṇḍa, and from Harihar to Tarikere. Basavāpatna and Sante-Bennūr were taken by the Bijāpur forces in 1637, and the chiefs retired to Tarikere. But one is said (Tk 21) to have been a rod in the right hand of the Vijayanagar king Venkaṭapati-Dēva in 1649. Their territory was conquered by Haidar Ali in 1761. In the rebellion of 1830, the Tarikere chief suddenly left Mysore and joined the insurgents. His son continued to create disturbances till his capture two years after.

17. NIḌUGAL

The Niḍugal territory had rulers in the eighth and down to the thirteenth century who are styled Chōla-mahārājas. Their capital was Penjeṟu or Henjeṟu, in Tamil called Pperuncheru, now Hēmāvati, on the northern border of Sīra tāluq. Irungōla I was ruling in 1128 (Si 7), and in connection with him the kings are described as of the Solar race and Inavamśa, descendants from Ḳarikāla-Chōla. They were mahāmaṇḍalēśvaras, and had the titles—lord of Oreyūr (the ancient Chōla capital near Trichinopoly), Gōva (or guardian) of Rodda, champion who had taken the heads of sixty-four chieftains. Irungōla's kingdom was composed of the Rodda Three Hundred, the Sīre Three Hundred, the Harave Three Hundred, and the Sindavāḍi Thousand. The Hoysala king Vīshnuvarddhana is said (Ng 70) to have captured the powerful Irungōla's fort, and Nārasimha I is described as breaker of the pride of Irungōla. In 1218 Ballāla II was encamped at Niḍugal (Hn 61). In 1269 another Irungōla made a raid into the Ānebiddasari-nāḍ in the Tumkūr country (Tm 49), and in 1276 joined the Sēuna army in its invasion of Dōrasamudra (Bl 164, 165). In 1285 Nārasimha III marched against Niḍugal (Ak 151) and reduced it.

In the fourteenth and fifteenth centuries there was a line of Nāyakas ruling in Niḍugal. Among their titles were included (Pg 54) *kaṭhāri-rāya*, champion who took the head of Mēsa, *bhādra-maluka*, subduer of the Hoysaṇa army.

The Harati chiefs held the Niḍugal territory from 1640, when they were invested by the Vijayanagar king Venkaṭapati-Rāya II with the government of Doḍḍēri, Siroha, Tāvaregere, Hiriyūr, Ayamangala, and Niḍugal-durga. By tradition the founder is said to have come from the Bijāpur country. Hoṭṭeṇṇa-Nāyaka in 1559 is described (Cl 54) as brother of the Nāga virgins of Nāga-lōka, a Bēḍa without guile, of the 850 worthies of the 350 gōtras. They continued in power till the time of Tīpu Sultān, who annexed the place to Mysore.

18. VAIDUMBAS

The Vaidumbas seem to have been connected with Tumba in North Arcot. In about 900 a Vaidumba-mahārāja, described as Gaṇḍa-Trinētra, was ruling (Bg 62, Sp 85), with the Kiru-dore or little river as his boundary. What river is meant is not clear. The Chōla king Parāntaka defeated the Vaidumbas, and they subsequently came under the protection of the Pallava-Nolambas. Subordinate to Dilīpayya or Iriva-Ṅolamba was the Vaidumba king Vikramāditya Tiruvayya (Bp 4), for whom we have the date 951 (Ct 49). He restored the breached tank at Vijayādityamangala or Bētmangala. His son was Chandraśēkhara (Mb 198). The Kalinga Ganga king Kāmārnava VI had for his queen Vinaya-mahādēvi, a Vaidumba princess, who became the mother of Vajrahasta V, crowned in 1038. The Chōla king Vīrarājēndra claims now to have subdued the Vaidumbas. And after this we have (Ct 9) a succession of Vaidumba gāmuṇḍas, who received the title, and permission to use the insignia, together with the grant of a village in Mēlai-Mārājapāḍi or Western Mahārājavāḍi.

19. CHANNAPATNA

The Channapatna chiefs generally bore the name Rāna Jagadēva-Rāya, after the founder of the family in Mysore (Cp 182, Md 86). He was of the Telugu Banajiga caste and had possessions in Bāramahāl. His daughter was married to the Vijayanagar king. In 1577 he vigorously repelled an attack by the Musalmāns on Penugoṇḍa, and was rewarded with territory in Mysore yielding a revenue of nine lakhs of pagodas. He made Channapatna his capital, and his descendants held possession till 1630, when the place was taken by Mysore.

20. ĀVATI-NAḌ PRABHUS

The Āvati-nāḍ Prabhus were Gauḍas or farmers of the Morasu-wokkal tribe, who came from the east in the fifteenth century and settled in the Āvati village, with the Nandi-maṇḍala (CB 40) and the Dēvanapura (Dēvanhalli) kingdom (Dv 51) as their territory. Their immediate descendants became founders of the modern States in eastern Mysore which were subordinate to Vijayanagar. The leader of the Āvati Prabhus was named Baire-Gauḍa, and the inscriptions of the family date from 1428 (CB 40) to 1792 (Sd 95). In 1640 the Āvati Prabhu is said (Sd 31) to be a protector of the family of Venkaṭapati-Rāya II. In Dv 51 and later inscriptions the Prabhu describes himself as of the fourth gōtra, that is a Śūdra.

The Yelahanka-nāḍ Prabhu is mentioned even in 1367 (Ht 117), but the inscriptions of this Āvati branch run from 1599 (Kg 12) to 1713 (Ma 3). They generally had the name Kempe-Gauḍa, after the most celebrated of the line. He founded Baṅgalore in 1537, and his son of the same name gained possession of the Māgadi country (Ma 1) and Sāvandurga. Though at first describing himself as of the fourth gōtra (Ma 1), he is afterwards said to be of the Sadāśiva-gōtra (Ma 2). Bangalore, which had been taken by the Bijāpur forces and included in the *jāgīr* of Shahji, the father of Sivaji, was eventually sold to the Mysore Rāja in 1687. Māgadi and Sāvandurga were captured by Mysore in 1728, the chief being sent as a prisoner to Seringapatam, where he died.

Of the Dēvanhalli and Dod-Ballāpur branches of the Āvati line there are no inscriptions. But of the Chik-Ballāpur chiefs there is one (CB 54). Of the Holavanahalli or Korampur branch, which founded Koratagere (Mi 31), there are a few, dating from 1627 (Mi 32) to 1726 (Mi 30). Baire-Gauḍa was the general name of the chiefs.

More prominent were the Sugaṭūr-nāḍ Prabhus, who usually had the name Tamme-Gauḍa. Their territory included a great part of the Kolar District, and they founded Hoskōte (An 47). For his aid in defeating the Musalmān attack on Penugoṇḍa, the chief received the title of Chikka-Rāya, and his possessions were extended from Ānekal to Punganūr. The inscriptions of the Sugaṭūr Prabhus date from 1451 (Mb 241) to 1693 (Ht 105). When Kolar and Hoskōte were taken by the Bijāpur army, the chief retired to Ānekal, but was expelled when this place was taken by Haidar Ali.

III. FEATURES OF ADMINISTRATION

VARIOUS statements and references in our inscriptions afford some glimpse into the ideals and methods of administration in past times. Thus, an early Ganga king is said to have assumed the honours of the kingdom only for the sake of the good government of his subjects. In the twelfth century, a high official appointed to rule over the southern province is admonished to govern the country like a father, putting down the evil and upholding the good. This indeed was always recognised as the special function of sovereignty.[1] The Kadambas are uniformly represented (according to one version) as studying the requital of good and evil. In the case of the governor above referred to, it is said (Sk 119) that the happiness of his dependants he reckoned as his own happiness. And the results of his administration were general peace and contentment. " None were filled with conceit, none made themselves conspicuous by a display of splendour, none were in opposition, none calling out for more influence, none creating disturbances, none in suffering, no enraged enemies, none who received titles had their heads also turned by the eulogies of the bards." And as a tribute to such ability in exercising authority, it is added, that to apply the name master or king (*dore*) to men of straw (*pul-mānasar*) is like calling a stone a jewel. The invariable phrase used with regard to monarchs on the throne describes them as ruling *sukha-sankathā-vinōdadim*, in the enjoyment of peace and pleasant (or profitable) conversa-

[1] The usual phrase is: *dushṭa-nigraha śishṭa-pratipālana.*

tion, especially, it would appear, stories relating to benefactions for charity or religious merit.

The signs of prosperity in a country are thus enumerated in the seventeenth century: The lord of the gods sent good rains, the earth brought forth full fruit, all points of the compass were unclouded, the various orders were diligent in the performance of their respective rites, all the people were free from disease, the land was free from trouble, the women were devoted to their husbands, and all the world was prosperous (Sr 103). A thriving town is thus described in the thirteenth century: The Brāhmans were versed in the vēdas, the guards were brave, the traders wealthy, the fourth caste of unshaken speech, the women beautiful, the labourers submissive, the temples ornaments to the world, the tanks deep and wide, the woods full of fruit, the gardens full of flowers (Ak 77).

The advice of the priesthood was ever deemed of importance, and they often played a prominent part in political affairs. Megasthenes, in his account of India in the fourth century B.C., says of the Sarmanes (the Jain śramanas) who live in the woods, that they communicate with the kings, who consult them by messengers regarding the causes of things. Aśōka's edicts, which belong to the third century B.C., are evidence of his solicitude for all classes of his subjects, induced in part by Buddhist precept. In the second century A.D. the Jain āchārya Simhanandi made the Ganga kingdom, as it is expressed. In the eleventh century a Jain yati put the Poysalas or Hoysalas in possession of their kingdom. But Brāhmans had the foremost place in more modern times. In the twelfth century the policy of Vishnuvarddhana was radically affected by his conversion from Jainism to the Vaishnava faith through the reformer Rāmānuja. He is thus said to have given his own country to the Brāhmans and the gods, while he himself ruled over the foreign countries won by his sword. Mādhava or Vidyāranya, an abbot of the monastery at Śringēri established in the eighth century by the reformer Śankara, was instrumental in founding the Vijayanagar empire in the fourteenth century. In the seventeenth century the Mysore king Doḍḍa-Dēva-Rāja, it is said, divided his kingdom into four parts, of which he gave the first to the Brāhmans, the second to the gods, the third to charity, and reserved the fourth for his own use.

The heir to the throne was styled the Yuvarāja. But in order that they might gain acquaintance with the duties of administration, he and other princes of the royal house were often previously appointed as viceroys or governors of certain provinces. Thus Aśōka had been a viceroy at Ujjain in the time of his father. In his own time we have his edicts in Mysore issued by the Ayaputa (Āryaputra or prince) at Suvarnnagiri. Among the Gangas, Śrīpurusha ruled over various provinces in the east before coming to the throne. In like manner Eṟeyappa was a governor of Kongal-nāḍ and Pannāḍ in the west. The Chālukya prince Vikramāditya was, a viceroy at Balgāmi, and when he came to the throne, his half-brother Jayasimha was put in charge of the Banavase province. Chōla princes were appointed to govern the Vengi kingdom. The Vijayanagar princes held the position of viceroys at Muluvāyi (Múlbāgal) in the east, and at Āraga in the hill country in the west.

The king, in Hoysala times, and doubtless in others not specified, was attended by five ministers, the *pancha-pradhānar* (Cn 260, Ci 72). The prime minister was the *sarvvādhikāri*, *sarvva-pradhāna*, or *siraḥ-pradhāna*. He (in one case at least) was the tongue in the council, the other councillors being like statues (Dg 25). The functions allotted to the several ministers cannot be determined from the inscriptions. But under the Chāḷukyas there is mention in the eighth century of the great minister for peace and war (Kl 63). In the eleventh century he appears as the great Lāla Kannaḍa minister for peace and war (Sk 106), and in the twelfth as the senior Kannaḍa minister for peace and war (Sk 267). He apparently combined in himself the offices of secretary of state for foreign affairs and for war. Of the Hoysala kings, Vishnuvarddhana in 1125 is said (Cn 149) to have acquired Angara's sevenfold (*saptānga*) kingdom, and Ballāla II in 1183 is said (Bl 137) to have acquired Pāṇḍya's sevenfold (*saptānga*) kingdom; while the Vijayanagar king Bukka-Rāya in 1377 is said (Yd 46) to be ruling an empire perfect in its seven parts (*saptānga*). These are explained in the *Chandraprabha Purāṇa* as—the king, minister, ally, territory, fortress, treasury, and army. In Bl 128 the king is said to have acquired not only the *saptānga-rājya* but also the *chatur-upāya* or four expedients against an enemy (explained in the *Jaimini Bhārata* to be—sowing dissension, negotiation, bribery, and open attack), as well as the *panchānga-sanmantra* or fivefold wise counsels. These remind us of the *panchatantra*.

The policy of provincial governors in the twelfth century, under the Kalachuryas, was supervised by *karaṇams* or imperial censors, appointed no doubt independently by the supreme government, to whom, it is said, they were like the five senses. They were *dharmmādhyakshangal* and *rājādhyakshangal* (Sk 123), or scrutineers of morality and of judicial or political affairs. They were five in number (Sk 102), and their office, as here described, was to see that the Lakshmī or lady—the State—was free from adultery, which may be interpreted as meaning, that their duty was to check any disloyalty to the throne, and to maintain the purity of justice or morals and of charitable endowments.

The high officials generally bore the title *daṇḍanāyaka*, in more recent times shortened to *dannāyak*, denoting both military and civil rank. These were indeed frequently combined, as witness the designation of a general as *mahāpradhāna sarvvādhikāri senādhipati hiriya-hadavala* (Bp 9, Hn 69). They were also often styled *sāmantādhipati*, implying control over feudatory chiefs. But the express military title was *senādhipati*, or, in modern times in Mysore, *dalavāyi*. The life guards, as we might term them, in the time of the Hoysalas called themselves *Garuḍas*. The general

Chokimayya claims to be Biṭṭi-Dēva's or Vishnuvarddhana's Garuḍa (Hn 69, Bp 9[1]). The prince Lakshma was Ballāla-Dēva's Garuḍa (Bl 112), and he and his force of a thousand men, who had vowed to live and die with the king, committed suicide when the latter died. In like manner, a family of Nāyakas, vowed in succession as Garuḍas to the kings Ballāla, Nārasimha, and Sōmēśvara (Kp 9, 10), gave up their lives along with their wives, and their servants, male and female. In battle, when victory hung in the balance, it was customary for the commander to call out some noted champion to lead a forlorn hope and devote his life to gain the day. To be chosen for such an enterprise was always represented as a great honour, and the charge was confirmed with the presentation of betel leaf to the champion from the hand of his chief (Sa 84, 86). A grant of land was made for the family of the fallen man, which in some early cases is styled *bāl-galchu*, but is mostly called a *kalnāḍ*, though the term *sivane* is used in the west. Similar grants of rent-free land, called *koḍagi*, were made to men who fell in battle. In the interesting case of Ballāla-Dēva's Chōla queen, who was distressed on account of a man killed in the force sent to punish a village for an insult to her name, the grant is called a *rakta-koḍagi* (Cn 205). Such a grant was also called *nettara-koḍagi*, meaning the same. The weapons of the foot-soldiers were mostly bows and arrows. But the infantry of the Sēuna army are said to have carried thunderbolts (*aśani-sannāha*, Dg 25), which looks as if they had fire-arms of some sort. The cavalry in the same force wore breast-plates. The courage of warriors was stimulated by the belief that their deeds of valour were eagerly watched by the celestial nymphs, who, if they fell, would bear them immediately away from the battle-field in a triumphal procession to enjoy the delights of paradise. The verse usually quoted in this connection is to the following effect :—

[1] The *garuḍa* is the bird of Vishnu, a kite of striking aspect, having a fine rufous-coloured body, with a pure white head and neck. A chief under the Pāṇḍyas in 1123 calls himself Nolamba's garuḍa (Cd 34).

By the victor is gained Lakshmī[1] (or fortune), by the slain the celestial nymphs;
The body being destroyed in a moment, what fear of death in war?[2]

Another verse to the same effect says:—

By only these two men in the world is the disk of the sun burst through;
The *sannyāsi* absorbed in *yōga*, and he who is slain in the front of the battle.[3]

Of the secretariat there are a few notices. The private secretary (*rahasyādhikrita*) is mentioned so far back as the fifth century, under the Kadambas (Sk 29). But the most detailed account is in connection with the Chōlas, in the eleventh century (Kl 112, 111). Here is mentioned the royal secretary, who communicated the king's orders to the chief secretary, and he, on approval, transmitted them to the revenue officers to be carried out. These then assembled the revenue accountants, who made entries accordingly in their revenue registers. The nature of these may be inferred from the mention under the Hoysalas, in the twelfth century, that among his conquests Vishnuvarddhana wrote down the Banavase Twelve Thousand in his *kaḍita* (Bl 17). The *kaḍita* or *kaḍata,* which is still in use among native traders in the bazars, is made of cloth, folded in book form and covered with charcoal paste; it is written on like a slate, with a style or pencil of *balapam* or potstone, and though liable to erasure, forms a durable record.

As to the form of official orders,—our Edicts of Aśōka, of the third century B.C., are prefaced, in the ancient mode, with a greeting wishing good health to the officials addressed (Mk 21), followed by—"the king thus commands." In the second century A.D. and onwards for some time, the early

[1] The goddess of fortune and beauty.

[2] In the original—

jitēna labhyatē Lakshmīḥ mṛitēnāpi surānganā
kshaṇa-vidhvamsini kāyē kā chintā maraṇē raṇē.

[3] The original is—

dvāv imau purushau lōkē sūryya-maṇḍala-bhēdinau
parivrāḍ yōga-yuktaś cha raṇē chābhimukhē hataḥ.

grants are prefaced by the word *siddham*, (?) confirmed (Sk. 263). In mediæval times the inscriptions begin with invocations of deity, according to the creed of the donor. Then follow genealogies of the ruling sovereigns, with often long drawn out eulogies of their heroic deeds and conquests. The provincial governor is next introduced, with the phrase *tat-pāda-padmōpajīvi*, dweller (like a bee) at his lotus feet, and the same phrase is used of each subordinate with reference to his superior. The royal signature, where it is given, comes at the end. The style in the seventeenth century, as illustrated by the practice under the Keladi queen Channammāji (Sk 79), contains some up-to-date features. At the head are the words *nirūpa prati*, copy of order, followed by the date and the royal signature. At the end are the words *nirūpa band*, the order ends. The document was despatched by the hands of a court official, who was charged to see to its execution and that it was entered in the sēnabōva's *kaḍita*.

In revenue matters the measurement and assessment of the land were naturally of the first importance. The Sātakarnni grant of the second century is addressed to the *rajjukam* (Sk 263), which, as previously stated (p. 15 above), literally means holder of the rope, that is, a survey officer. The *rajjukas* were originally appointed long before, by Aśōka, but perhaps for other purposes. The *prāku-pramāna* or ancient measurement is referred to in 1513 (Nj 195). The instrument used for the purpose was generally a pole, of which different ones are mentioned. There was the *bhēruṇḍa* pole (Sk 120), taken perhaps from the Bhēruṇḍēśvara pillar; the *dāya* pole of 18½ feet, the distance between the central pillars of the Aghōrēśvara temple at Ikkēri; the pole of 18 spans, each of 12 fingers breadth (Mb 49); and so on. Poles of 36 steps and 48 steps are also referred to (Ak 12, 13), and an *ottōla* pole (Ci 64). The assessment is said, under the Chōlas in 1046 (Dv 75), to be one-sixth of the produce, and this was the recognised Hindu rate from the earliest times (see vol. ii, Introd. p. 4). But a quarter of a century later is described in more detail (Mb 49) as a fifth of the produce of forest tracts and of lands on which dry (unirrigated) crops are raised, and a third of the produce of lands below a tank on which paddy is grown. Tīpu Sultān, however, claimed three-fourths of the produce of irrigated land (My 54), at the same time asserting a title to the whole.

But from an early period all the great provinces and their subdivisions commonly had their revenue value attached to the name. Thus, while Kuntala and Raṭṭavāḍi were a Seven-and-a-half Lakh country, Gangavāḍi was a Ninety-six Thousand, Banavase a Twelve Thousand, Noḷambavāḍi or Noṇambavāḍi a Thirty-two Thousand, Toṇḍanāḍ a Forty-eight Thousand. Haidar Ali's territory is called a Three Crore kingdom (Si 98). Of smaller districts, Kongalnāḍ was an Eight Thousand, Punnāḍ a Six Thousand, Sāntalige a Thousand, Hānungal a Five Hundred, Belvola a Three Hundred, Bellave a Seventy, and so on. This system is still commemorated in the Yēlusāvira or Seven Thousand country, the north of Coorg. The figures apparently indicated *nishkas* (see Yd 53, 54), long obsolete, the value of which varied at different times and cannot now be precisely stated, but they are popularly supposed to be equivalent to *varahas* or pagodas.

Some idea of the burden of taxation may be gathered from certain inscriptions. Towards the close of the Hoysala period, in 1290, we find (TN 27) the following imposts levied on lands, whether occupied by houses or cultivated: land rent, plough tax, house tax, forced labour, accountant's fee, provender, unexpected visitor, army, double payment, change of district, threshing floor, tribute, coming of age, festivity, subscription, boundary marks, birth of a son, fodder for elephants, fodder for horses, sale within the village, favour of the palace, alarm, seizure, destruction, or injustice caused by the nāḍ or the magistrate, and whatever else may come. Under the Vijayanagar rule, in 1505, we have (Gu 67): land rent, fines, tribute, alms, gold, *hombali*, tolls on corn and grain, tax on Jangamas, tax on . . ., tax on meetings, duty on betel leaves, tax on Mādigas, duty on salt-pans, tax on Jīyars, customs dues, and all other taxes and imposts. See also Ml 95. Besides the revenue thus raised, taxes were imposed to provide for the festivals and offerings or other needs of temples (Gu 3, 8, 34, Sk 129). In 1491 a tax for this purpose was laid on looms, houses, oil-mills, grazing grounds, marriages, . . ., eggs, customs, imports, exports, cotton, et cetera (Nj 118). While in one case the funds for providing marriage pandals, and mirrors for dancing girls, were given up (Sk 295). In 1775 the Eighteen castes agreed to pay an addition to their land and other taxes, owing to the palace having taken for itself the funds previously provided (Yl 4). Remissions of taxes were sometimes granted, either generally or in specified parts of the country. In the sixteenth century, under Vijayanagar, the marriage tax was abolished, causing much rejoicing among all classes (Hk 111, Mi 64). Soon after, the tax on barbers, forced labour, *birāda*, customs, toll for watchmen, and other imposts were given up (Hk 110, Tp 126). Sometimes there was a vigorous protest against illegal taxation (see Sr 6, Mb 49).

The customs duties, or *sunka*, are spoken of as the *perjjunka* or *hejjunka*, those on wholesale articles in bulk, and the *kirukula*, those on miscellaneous petty retail articles. There was also the *vaḍḍa-rāvula*. An elaborate system existed for the levy of the duties, especially in the west, where the transport of grain and other commodities had to be carried on by means of pack bullocks. A list of forty-two *ṭhānas* or customhouses is given in Sa 123. The nature of the goods carried may be gathered from the account of those which were allowed free, within certain limits, for specified Lingāyit monasteries. For instance, Sh 28 was a permit for fifty bullocks to pass without paying toll. These might be laden with grain, areca-nut, pepper, fringed silk cloths, dried coco-nuts, grass, husked rice, rice in the husk, salt, tamarind, jaggory, oil, *ghī*, baskets, *vidala*, catechu, tobacco, cloths, et cetera; but silk, areca-nut, pepper, coco-nut kernels, and wood, were still liable to duty (Tl 83, 49). Another list will be found in Tl 72. The colour and age of the bullocks to be exempted were to be registered at the various *ṭhānas* concerned. The goods thus passed free were not to be sold outside, but to be stored in the monastery for the use of the priests and their disciples.

Of judicial procedure there is very little sign in the inscriptions. But a rough and ready justice was dispensed, and disputes were often decided by an ordeal. In 1020, under Chōla rule, a dog, which had run away on the death of its master, was appropriated by a local chief. As a penalty for this, the king's officer on the spot went into his residence, dragged out the dog, burnt the place, and seizing fifty golden images belonging to the offender, sent them to the king (Hs 10, 11). In 1057 a young chief who was a powerful wrestler had a bout with an opponent, who was thrown and died in the crush. The latter was apparently some connection of the king's. For his share in this affair, the survivor was marched off straight to Talakāḍ the capital, and there put to death (Hg 18). It may thence perhaps be inferred that death was the appointed penalty for murder. In 1417, when a Gauḍa, who had gone to visit the local governor, fell down dead in his presence, a sort of inquest was held on the body, and it was sent back to his home (Sk 37). This was under Vijayanagar rule. Under the Gangas, in 910, the destroyer of a tank or grove is said to incur the same guilt as one who has committed the five great sins (Sr 34). In 1450 we find the theft of gold and drunkenness classed with the most heinous crimes, such as the slaughter of cows, or the murder of guru, wife and Brāhmans (Cd 29). In 1654 a farmer having been put to death unjustly by a Muhammadan official, a *rakta-koḍagi*, or grant of rent-free land, was given to his son as compensation (Yl 29). In 1757 orders had been sent from the Bednūr court to arrest an offender who was defying the law, but the local official, on capturing him, beheaded him. For this he seems to have been deprived of some land he owned. He afterwards petitioned that the *pagadi* money for the time the land was put out of season should be given to him. This was refused, with an order that petitions of this kind from the country for payment of money must not be made (Sk 209, 210).

The king himself was the judge, especially in deciding important cases. Such was the dispute between the Jainas and the Vaishnavas in 1368, in the time of the Vijayanagar king Bukka-Rāya, who, after hearing the evidence of the leaders on both sides, took the hand of the Jainas, and placing it in the hand of the Vaishnavas, delivered a decree reconciling the two (SB 136). Sometimes the mediation of a guru acceptable to both sides was invited (Ht 105). But trial by orḍeal is mentioned in several cases. The earliest method consisted in the accused making oath in the presence of the god, holding at the same time the consecrated food. If guilty, it would choke him on partaking of it. Instances of this ordeal appear in 1241 and 1275 (Sb 387, Md 79). In the first the payment of some money was in question; the second was a boundary case. The ordeal of grasping a red-hot iron rod or bar in the presence of the god Hoysalēśvara is recorded in 1309.[1] A later form of ordeal was perhaps a severer test, and consisted of making oath as before, and then plunging the hand into boiling *ghī* (clarified butter). If no injury resulted, the defendant won his cause. Instances occur in 1580 and 1677 (Yl 2, Ag 2, 3). The first was a protest by the barbers and washermen against the potters paring the toe-nails and putting on an upper cloth (in wedding ceremonies). The other was regarding the rightful claimant for the office of syānabhāga or village accountant, and the decision was recognised and acted on by the court. But under the Mughal government we find in 1720 a regular magisterial process in the case of a Gauḍa whose village had been taken possession of by some one else during his absence abroad (Si 112).

The earliest reference to famine is in SB 1, where one of twelve years' duration is said to have been predicted by Bhadrabāhu. This was in the third century B.C., and in the

[1] *Mys. Arch. Rep.* for 1908.

north. The ill effects of the calamity on that occasion were avoided by wholesale migration to other parts of India, but this was a sectarian movement, and though Chandra Gupta took part in it, the action was not in his capacity as a sovereign. Of a famine equally prolonged there is mention in Grant Duff's *History of the Mahrattas* (i. 43). It began in 1396, and from its severity was specially distinguished by the name of Durgā Dēvī. But no steps taken by the State for the relief of famine are recorded in our inscriptions. On the other hand, Ch. 108 of 1540 says that at that time all grains sold at 7 *mana* (maunds) for 1 *hana* (fanam), and that men ate men (*manuśa manuśara tindaru*). Things were apparently left to take their own course.

Crimes of violence are occasionally mentioned, such as carrying off a dancing girl by force (Sk 300), or a guru's bondman (Sk 139). But by far the most numerous were cattle raids, especially in border districts. Though sometimes the work of organised bands of robbers, many were hostile demonstrations against an enemy. The cows of a village belonging to another ruler were driven off from the grazing-grounds in the intervening woodlands as an act of defiance. The cowherds often gave up their lives in defence of their charge. Or some village hero, fired with indignation, would sally forth with a few followers and recover the stolen cows, only to die of his wounds on his return. Such an exploit was reckoned as patriotic, and the man's family were provided for with a grant of rent-free land. In more daring cases the villages themselves were pillaged and the women molested. Memorial stones, rudely sculptured to represent the incidents of cattle raids and to record the grants made in connection with them, are found in all parts.

Of measures designed for the public good, we are told (Ak 82) in 1234 that the towns in the Poysala country were surrounded with gardens, that many tanks filled with lotus were formed in their vicinity, and that groves were planted from *yōjana* to *yōjana* (about nine miles) for travellers to rest in.

The college founded and endowed in 1290 by the Hoysala minister Perumāla at Māilangi (TN 27) deserves mention, though it was a private rather than a State institution. Provision was made in it for masters to teach Nāgara, Kannaḍa, Tiguḷa (Tamil), and Ārya (Mahratti). Then the Vijayanagar king Achyuta-Rāya established in 1539 a bank or fund, called Ānanda-nidhi, for the benefit of Brāhmans (Dg 24, Hk 123). It was apparently regarded as a great wonder, and the verses in praise of it have been found inscribed in no less than ten places. Perhaps this may be taken as a specimen of the old-time method of advertisement. Of the Mysore king (Doḍḍa)-Dēva-Rāja, it is said (Kg 37) that he made wells, ponds, and tanks, with *chatras* or inns from road to road, while temples of the gods he had made, was making, and would continue to make. He is also said (Yd 54) to have established *chatras* in every village for the distribution of food, as well as (Sr 14) at every *yōjana* on all the roads from Sakkarepattana (Kadūr District) in the west to Sēleya-pura (Salem) in the east, and from Chiknāyakanhalli (Tumkūr District) in the north to Dhārāpuram (Coimbatore District) in the south. In the Bednūr kingdom a veto was retained on the appointment of the heads of *maṭhas* or monasteries. To ensure the selection of qualified men, it was decreed that they must be in agreement with the court and the *mahattu* (the Lingāyit priesthood), not quarrelsome, hospitable, trustworthy, and having disciples (Tl 81).

The vital importance of providing a good supply of water, whether for irrigation or for the use of towns, was always recognised. Accordingly, we find the erection of dams to rivers, from which channels were led off, and the construction of wells and tanks or reservoirs mentioned in every period. A few instances may suffice.

One of the earliest recorded in the inscriptions was the formation of the tank at Tālgunda in the fourth century by the Kadamba king Kākustha (Sk 176). To the eighth century or before belongs the Vijayādityamangala or Bētmangala tank on the Pālār river, named after the Mahāvali or Bāṇa king who caused it to be made. It breached more than once, as it was restored in about 950 by the Vaidumba king (Bp 4), and again in 1155 by the Hoysala general Chōkimayya (Bp 9). Of the tenth century were the tanks made by the priest who ruled at Āvani in the Mulbāgal tāluq (Mb 65), and of the twelfth century those in the Tumkūr tāluq made by the liberal-minded Kaydala chief who, it is said (Tm 9), supported all the four creeds—those of Jina and Buddha, Śiva and Vishnu. In 1358 we have the account (Ml 21, 22) of a number of tanks made by a Bhaṭṭa or bhāṭ, who also planted lines of trees on the four sides, and performed the *upanayana* ceremony to the *pīpal* trees planted at the four corners. In 1653 was made the tank in Channagiri tāluq called Vali Surūr, by the Bijāpur governor Bari Mālik (Ci 43, 44). In connection with this is quoted the verse describing the merit acquired by all who assist in the formation of a tank. It runs thus: "The quail and the boar, the she-buffalo and the elephant, the teacher and the performer,—these six went to svarga." The explanation given is that a quail once scraped a hollow in the ground to nestle in; a boar came and made it larger; a buffalo and an elephant each in turn enlarged it still more; a holy man then pointed out that it could be made into a tank or pond, and the king to whom he gave this advice carried it out. For their shares in this work of merit they all went to *svarga* or paradise.[1]

A scheme for the water-supply of Penugoṇḍa, carried out in 1388, is described in Gd 6. The prince Bukka-Rāya, who was the governor, wanted all the subjects to be happy. For this purpose, water being the life of all living beings, he in open court directed the hydraulic engineer to bring the Henne river (the northern Pennār) to Penugoṇḍa. A channel was accordingly made from the river, at Kallūḍi, to the Siruvera tank, ten miles to the north.

[1] The merit of making a grant of land is thus expressed in Ck 42: "As many roots as the crops in the ground have, as many hairs as cover the cow, so many thousand years does the donor of land enjoy in paradise." See also Si 95.

As regards dams, with their channels for irrigation, an interesting account is given (Dg 23) of one erected at Harihara in 1410 on the Haridrā, near where it flows into the Tungabhadrā. It soon breached, but was restored in 1424 (Dg 29). The river is addressed as if sentient and responding to the wishes of the restorer. "When you said Stop!—at your command she stood still. When you called, she at once came on, flowing through the channel." In 1416 was restored a dam on the Pālār which had been breached from time immemorial and ruined down to the level of the ground (Mb 7). In 1460 was made a new dam in the Kāvērī (Sr 139), by the chief of Nāgamangala, the channel from which was extended to Harahu. The conditions on which the contract for making a channel in 1397 was given are stated in Bg 10, and included the present of a horse and bracelets to the contractor. But it was stipulated that these, as well as the funds advanced, were to be returned if water did not flow between certain specified points.

As regards municipal matters, we find (Sk 123, 119, 100) that Belgāmi included five *maṭhas*, three puras, and seven Brahmapuris, together with apparently three medical dispensaries (Sb 277). So also (Ml 109) Talakāḍ-Rājarājapura contained seven puras and five *maṭhas*. Agara, again, comprised three cities and eighteen *khampanas* (Tl 133, 197). In all important trading places there was usually a *paṭṭaṇa-swāmi* or town mayor, generally a prominent merchant. Some of the regulations laid down (unfortunately partly effaced) on the foundation of a town in 1331 were the following: "No fine was to be levied from a mother; brothers, elder and younger, were to share alike in property; if a female servant died, the body was to be carried forth and (? buried); if a wife died, the body was to be cremated" (Ml 114). On the rebuilding of Bāgūr in 1554, settlers were encouraged by freeing them from all taxation for one year from their arrival; after that they would be considered as permanent residents and be given full possession, all previous claims being cancelled (Hk 112).

Commerce on a large scale beyond the limits of the country was carried on by what may be styled merchant princes, who generally had the title *mahā-vaḍḍa-byavahāri* (Ml 56, Sk 247, Ak 108). In the last is an account of a family of Maleyāla merchants, experts in goods and conveyance. One of them was skilled in testing all manner of gems. "He was so liked both by the Hoysala emperor in the south and Ballaha himself in the north, that he was able to form an alliance between the two kings. The wants of the great Mālava king, of the Kaḷinga, Chōḷa, and Pāṇḍya rulers, he at once supplied. No Śetti was equal to him throughout the Hoysala kingdom—just, honoured, of kind speech, full of common sense, delighting in truth." But some great merchants were of Brāhman descent, such as those in Ak 22. One of these imported horses, elephants, and pearls in ships by sea and sold them to the kings. Another transported goods from the east to the west, and those that were suitable from the west to the east; also products from the north to the south, and those of the south to the north. The mercantile and trading classes are mostly included in the term vīra-Bananju-dharmma, at the head of which were the Five Hundred swāmis of Āryyāvale or Ayyāvale (Aihole in Kalādgi District—Arasikere is called the southern Ayyāvale in Ak 77). In inscriptions recording their agreements to pay certain dues on specified articles of merchandise, in order to provide for the support of local objects in which they were interested, they are described in long strings of somewhat amusing ironical or quasi-royal epithets (see Sk 118, Hg 17, Bl 117, DB 31, Hk 137). Their formal assembly was generally accompanied with setting up the diamond *vaisanige* or *baysanige*, as the symbol of their guild (Bl 75, Dg 59). A more sober account of them in 1181 (Sk 119) represents them as honoured residents of Ayyāvale and many other chief *grāmas*, *nagaras*, *khēḍas*, *kharvaḍas*, *madambas*, *dronāmukhas*, *puras*, and *pattanas* of Lāla, Gàula, Karṇṇāṭa, Bangāla, Kāśmīra, and other countries (the conventional number being fifty-six) at all points of the compass. With them are often associated, as here, the two sects of Nānā-Dēśis. The Panchālas or five guilds of artisans also describe themselves in a similar strain of ironical epithets, which are not without interest (Gu 34).

The Twelve Āyagār are mentioned in Śi 41, 112. They form the primitive village corporation, who are entitled to certain land rent-free, or to fixed fees or dues of grain and straw at harvest time. A reference to the Eighteen castes, which form the ancient Right and Left hand factions, appears so far back as in 459 (DB 67), which shows that they are much more ancient than generally supposed. In one case (Hk 104) they are spoken of as the seven-and-a-half and eleven-and-a-half. The sections included in them are called *phanas*, and comprise the agricultural, artisan, and trading communities. The Balagai or Right Hand[1] are headed by the Banajigas, with the Holeyas at the bottom; the Yeḍagai or Left Hand are headed by the Panchālas, with the Mādiga at the bottom.

Among the officials of rural districts, the nāl-gāvuṇḍa or nāḍ-gauḍa was one of the most important. There is an interesting account (Sk 219), dated 918, of the office being continued to the widow on the death of her husband. She was a Jain, and rejoicing in her beauty, was distinguished for the skill and ability of her management. Though a woman (it says), she well protected her charge, with pride in her own heroic bravery. But on being attacked by some bodily disease, she retired in favour of her daughter, and ended her life with the performance of the Jain vow of *sallēkhana*.

A number of inscriptions record the sale of villages to various applicants, especially in the hundred years from about 1670. The general valuation seems to have been based on ten years' rental (Tl 57, 85, An 90, Nl 51, Tp 112, Hn 132). But in a case four centuries earlier (Sk 282) the value was taken

[1] The great army of the Right Hand are mentioned in 1072 (Mb 49[a]).

at five times the annual rent, and a present of cloths was given besides to the headmen. Deductions were made in the purchase money for ruined condition (Tl 67), and for lands damaged by floods, but if trees had grown up on such damaged portions they were not to be cut down (Tl 71, 74).

An endless variety of details might be collected from the inscriptions to illustrate different features in administration, but the above may perhaps suffice to indicate some of the more salient points.

IV. MANNERS AND CUSTOMS

AMONG singular customs, those involving self-sacrifice of life may claim our notice. The Jain vow of *sallēkhana* (see *EC.* vol. ii.) involved suicide by gradual starvation, in cases of incurable disease, hopeless calamity, or the inevitable approach of death. It was the orthodox Jain mode of emancipation from the body when life could no longer be endured, and the instances of its performance are numerous, especially at Śravaṇa-Beḷgoḷa, from the earliest times. A more expeditious and pleasanter way of meeting death was that adopted in 1068 by the Chālukya king Sōmēśvara I (Sk 136), who, being prostrated with mortal fever, after performing *yōga* ceremonies, walked into the river Tungabhadrā up to his neck and drowned himself.

The practice of *sati*, or the burning of a widow with the dead body of her husband, was a recognised institution at all periods and with all creeds, but seems to have been more actively revived in the fourteenth century under the Vijayanagar empire. The memorials of *sati*, which was entered on with perfect readiness, as duty-bound in honour, are found in all parts. They are known as *māstikal*, that is *mahā-sati-kal*, and are generally sculptured with a pointed pillar or post, from which projects a woman's arm, bent upwards at the elbow. The hand is raised, with fingers erect, and a lime-fruit is placed between the thumb and forefinger. This is what is alluded to in Sh 61, 62, and Md 103, where women are said to have given arm and hand. No clear explanation has been obtained of the symbolism. Some of the stones are accompanied with elaborate inscriptions. Such is the stone of the fifth century to the memory of the Kadamba king Ravivarmma's wife (Sb 523). Another is the beautifully pathetic Belatūr stone of 1057 (Hg 18).

But other instances of self-sacrifice of life are fairly numerous. The earliest are connected with the Ganga kings. Thus, in about 865, we have (TN 91) Nītimargga's death-bed scene, and are told that his *mane-magattin* or *major domo* became *kīl-gunṭhe* under him, which may be interpreted as meaning—was buried under him, probably alive, in the same grave. Another *kīl-gunṭhe* sacrifice is recorded in 930 (Dg 119), at the death of the Ganga chief Chandiyammarasa. With the same object of attesting undying attachment and fidelity to a master, others entered the fire and were burnt to death. In about 912 we have (Ag 5, 27) two cases in which men committed themselves to the flames on the death of the Ganga king Rāchamalla. In 1130, a man who had taken a vow to die with the Kadamba king Tailapa, fulfilled his vow (Hl 47), but in what manner is not stated.

At the same time, vows of self-destruction were not confined to execution on the death of patrons. They were also entered into for the purpose of securing the accomplishment of some cherished desire. In these cases beheading seems to have been the usual method of despatch. In about 991, we are told (Sb 479) that a man vowed to give his head to a goddess at Hayve in order that the king Śāntivarmma might have a son. His wish having been obtained, he surrendered himself to the soldiers and was beheaded. In 1050 a servant had his head cut off in order to die with the king Pompala (Ct 31). But in 1123, a cowherd, when Bopparasa and his wife paid a visit to a temple in the rice-fields, perhaps with a view to offspring, vowed that he would give his head to swing on the pole before the god at Koṇḍasabhāvi if the king should obtain a son (Sk 246). In 1180 a chief gave his head in order that the army to which he belonged might be victorious in the war to which it was marching (Gd 41). In 1185 a man who had taken a vow that he would die with the queen, at her decease was reminded of it by her husband, and instantly gave himself up to be beheaded (Sk 249), for, as the inscription says, a word spoken with full resolve must not be broken. In 1215 a woman gave her head to the hook on the death of her chief's mother (Mk 12). From sculptured representations it appears that the process of these ghastly decapitations was as follows. The votary was seated close to an elastic rod or pole fixed in the ground behind. This was forcibly bent down over the head of the victim, and the hook at the end made fast to the top-knot of hair. On being severed from the body, the head flew up, carried with the rebound of the rod released from its tension.

In 1050 there was the curious case of the man who vowed to continually pull out the nail of his finger in order to prevent the giving of a fort to a particular person (Sk 152). But his vow was of no avail, and the grant was made. Whereupon he cut off the finger, and climbing to the top of the Bhēruṇḍa pillar, threw himself down on a row of spear-shaped stakes and was killed.[1]

The instances of the Garuḍa warriors under the Hoysala kings have already been mentioned above (p. 104). They were life guards, who took upon themselves a vow to live and die with the king, and at his decease committed suicide. This was done in a wholesale manner, the chiefs in Kp 9, 10 being joined in despatching themselves by their wives and servants, male and female. With the prince Lakshma, too (Bl 112), his whole battalion of a thousand men slaughtered themselves. In the former case the act is described as embracing Garuḍa (the kite which is the bird of Vishnu) on

[1] A parallel to such cases may be found in the present day if the following newspaper cutting be true. A St. Louis negro has bet his life, as announced by him in the following manner: "To all whom it may concern. Take notice that I, A—— P——, being sound in mind and body, do solemnly promise, with God for my witness, to put an end to my earthly existence by leaping into the Mississippi from the centre of Eads Bridge, within seven days after the Presidential election of 1904, if Theodore Roosevelt, the Republican candidate, be not elected."

the head of an elephant. One chief is said thus to have embraced Garuḍa six times, and another, to have confronted Garuḍa, shaken and embraced him. What took place is not clear, but it may be conjectured that they killed themselves when seated in state on an elephant, and the bodies remained to be devoured (as on Parsi towers of silence) by kites and vultures, which would be immediately attracted to the spot. The final acts attributed to the chiefs no doubt refer to their death struggles. In the case of the prince Lakshma, he is said to have mounted, with his wife, on the pillar which was to be their monument, and thus become united with Garuḍa.

References to the healing art may next be noticed. The earliest mention is a droll account in 1087, given (Nr 40) in connection with the army of Vikrama-Śāntara. While hurrying to the seat of war, the men, in order to appease the fire in their bellies, fed on carcases, and as the result were driven mad with indigestion. On applying to the army doctors, these said elephant was the remedy. So they swallowed elephant and were cured, whereupon the doctors laughed. More to the point is the statement (Sb 277) that in 1158 there were three medical dispensaries in Baḷḷigāve. And in 1162 the Kōḍiya maṭha there is described (Sk 102) as a place for the treatment of the diseases of destitute sick persons. In the thirteenth century there was a Vaidya named Dēvapilleyaṇṇa, who was physician to the mother of the minister of the Hoysala king Nārasimha III (Ak 8). Like Dhanvantari (the physician of the gods) was this Dēvarāja, and celebrated for his new system of medicine (Ak 9). In the fifteenth century, in the time of the Vijayanagar king Dēva-Rāya II, there was the famous and learned head of a line of physicians, known as Sālagrāma, whose name was Kēśava, the son of Aruṇāchalēśa-paṇḍita (Dv 81). In 1818, when an epidemic of small-pox and cholera had broken out and the people were dying around, it was stopped in the following supernatural manner (Kr 25). The goddess Mahākāli of Ujani became incarnate in a Śūdra virgin of the Gangaḍikāra tribe, named

Nanjamma, whose family descent is given. Wherever she went these diseases and other troubles, among Brāhmans, Kshattriyas, Vaiśyas, and Śūdras alike, were cured. And out of the gifts made to her a new temple of Mahākāli was erected at Kannambāḍi. Sixteen years afterwards she had a *ranga-maṇṭapa* built for it (Kr 24).

The accounts of the decorations and titles conferred on men who had distinguished themselves are of interest. The most dignified seems to have been the *paṭṭa* or golden band to be worn on the forehead. It was a symbol of royalty, but was also bestowed as a mark of royal favour, or for other purposes of distinction. Thus the Chōla king in 1005 decorated Panchama-mahārāya with a *paṭṭa* bearing the title Kshattriya-śikhāmaṇi Kongālva (Cg 46). The Chālukya king Tailapa-Dēva in 1096 bound a *paṭṭa* on the victorious general Ereyamma, with the title *Rājya-samuddharaṇam* inscribed in gold, and gave him also *keysere* (? bracelets) for his children (Sa 80). The rāja-guru and other priests in 1254 bound the *vibhūti-paṭṭa* on the Gaṇa-kumāri Chandavve (Ak 108). But a high distinction often mentioned in connection with prominent public men is the *gaṇḍa-peṇḍāra* (see Dg 36, 44, etc.). This was a golden anklet, apparently worn on the right leg. From Bl 112 of 1220, relating to the prince Lakshma, it seems to have been set with clusters of pearls. He also had another decoration, called *toḍar*, which was a golden chain or ankle-ring, embossed with medallions, and was worn on the left leg. It seems to have been regarded specially as a pledge of unswerving fidelity, and hence, when the prince received it, his wife also bound a *toḍar* on her left leg to signify that she would never desert him for another.

A singular custom, which was universal, was the ceremony of washing the feet of the guru or priest on making over the grant to a temple or for other objects. The transfer of the land or whatever was the subject of the benefaction is invariably described as accompanied with the performance of this act by the donor. But in one case, in 968, the guru's feet are said to have been not only washed but rubbed, ? dry (Hk 23).

The oriental custom of touching and remitting offerings, which is still practised in the case of *nazars* presented at darbārs, is mentioned in 1300, in connection with the dues payable by Brāhmans. According to the custom of the country, it is said (TN 98), the palace will touch and remit to the Brāhmans of Sōmanāthpura the former dues, whatever they may be. This was in the time of the Hoysala king Ballāla III.

Another incident mentioned in 1434 (Mr 1) was very likely typical of a custom. On the completion of a fort which the king had ordered to be built, he celebrated the occasion by having tigers captured and brought before the principal bastion, where he and his son hunted them, at the same time giving to the bastion its name as Rāja-gambhīra.

In Ci 64 is a reference to stichomancy, like the classical *Sortes*. One of the donees is described as a *salākāchārya*, a man who answers questions by putting a *salāka* or stick into a book (a palm-leaf book) at random and so finding a suitable passage. There are elaborate rules for the system, as for most Hindu mysteries.

Every one knows or has heard of the extraordinary feats of memory performed by certain natives of India. References to such accomplishments occur in some of the inscriptions. In 1103 is mentioned (Sk 98) Malli-dēva, known as the Niṭalāksha (Īśvara) among *āśu-kavī* (fast or extempore poets). Of him it is said that if two persons from different sides should come towards him writing it down from the end (that is, backwards) and reading it out, he would arrange the poem so read out, whatever the subject might be, as a new poem. He would also repeat four stories from hearing them related (simultaneously); and make calculations in any number of given figures. All this he was able to do by mental effort alone. In 1223 is mentioned (Cn 203) Viśvanātha, who could write letters with both hands (at once), and go through (at the same time) a hundred mnemonic feats these are known as *śatavadhāna*), so that the learned men who examined him nodded their heads (in approval). In 1079 there was the minister Nakulāryya, who was learned in writing four languages (Cn 99); but this is not exceptionally wonderful. In 1344 there was Sōma, who was a successful poet in eight languages (Mb 158, Gd 46).

V ART

WORKS of art are chiefly exemplified in engraving, sculpture, and architecture. The specimens of engraving are those to be found in inscriptions. The finest examples are the Kadamba inscription on the Tālgunda pillar, and the Ganga and Hoysala inscriptions on stone slabs and copper plates. Most of the Hoysala inscriptions, in particular, are beautifully incised on polished slabs of black hornblende, and the contents are so skilfully engrossed that no space is left where a single additional character could be introduced. Ornamental flourishes and elegant fancy letters are used where suitable, and the whole presents an attractive appearance. Under the Chālukyas in 1067 is mentioned (Cd 47) an artistic engraver (*rūvāri*) who could entwine the forms of elephants, lions, parrots, and other animals so as to make them appear from the letters. In 1159, under the Hoysalas, is mentioned (Ak 141) a sculptor who within the space of a single page (of a *ōle* or palmyra leaf) wrote the whole of the *Gō-grahana* in the highest style so as to please every one.

Sculpture and carving in stone attained to an elaboration perfectly marvellous. The colossal Jain image of Gomaṭa on a hill at Śravaṇa-Beḷgoḷa, erected in about 983 during the Ganga period, is one of the most remarkable monuments in India. It is a monolith, nude, and stands $57\frac{1}{2}$ feet high,[1] with no support above the thighs. "Nothing grander or more imposing exists out of Egypt," says Fergusson, the great authority on architecture.

[1] The sculptor has engraved his scale at the foot of the statue, and, curiously enough, it corresponds with the French metre. The use of this in the tenth century would form an interesting subject for inquiry.

The Hoysala crest of Sala stabbing the tiger, set up in front of the *vimāna* of temples erected by them, is a fine example of free standing sculpture. There is also some in the ruined Jain temples at Angadi. But the most intricate and astonishing carving is that employed in the decoration of the outer walls of the Hoysala temples, and in the ceilings of the small domes or cupolas of their interior. It is executed in a potstone of creamy colour, which can be polished till it resembles marble; soft when quarried, but hardening rapidly on exposure to the air. The carving has evidently been done when the surface had thus weathered. Fergusson's opinion may here also be quoted. "There are many buildings in India (he says) which are unsurpassed for delicacy of detail by any in the world, but the temples at Bēlūr and Halebīd surpass even these for freedom of handling and richness of fancy. . . . The amount of labour which each facet of this porch (Bēlūr) displays is such as I believe never was bestowed on any surface of equal extent in any building in the world." Of the minute elaboration of detail in the frieze of the Halebīd temple, he says, "it may probably be considered as one of the most marvellous exhibitions of human labour to be found even in the patient East. . . . No two facets of the temple are the same; every convolution of every scroll is different. No two canopies in the whole building are alike, and every part exhibits a joyous exuberance of fancy scorning every mechanical restraint."

In architecture the palm must be given to the ornate temples erected by the Hoysalas, or during the period of their ascendancy, in the style which has been named Chalukyan. Regarding these the same authority remarks as follows: "The artistic combination of horizontal with vertical lines, and the play of outline and of light and shade far surpass anything in Gothic art. The effects are just what mediæval architects were often aiming at, but which they never attained so perfectly as was done at Halebīd." Of the temples there, he says: "The great temple (the Hoysalēśvara), had it been completed, is one of the buildings on which the advocate of Hindu architecture would desire to take his stand. . . . And if carried out with the richness of detail exhibited in the Kēdārēśvara, would have made up a whole which it would be difficult to rival anywhere. . . . If it were possible to illustrate this little temple (the Kēdārēśvara) in anything like completeness, there is probably nothing in India which would convey a better idea of what its architects were capable of accomplishing. . . . By a curious coincidence it was contemporaneous with the English cathedrals of Lincoln, Salisbury, and Wells, or the great French churches at Amiens, Rheims, and Chartres, of course without any communication. But it is worthy of remark that the great architectural age in India should have been the thirteenth century, which witnessed such a wonderful development of a kindred style (meaning the Gothic) in Europe."

The following list of the principal temples of this style in Mysore, with the dates of their erection, may be useful for purposes of comparison :—

DATE	TEMPLE	PLACE	REFERENCE
1117	Chenna Kēśava	Bēlūr	Bl 58, 71
c. 1141	Hoysalēśvara	Halebīḍ	Bl 239
1171	Brahmēśvara	Kikkēri	Kr 53
1173	Būchēśvara	Kōravangala	Hn 71
1196	Amṛitēśvara	Amṛitapura	Tk 45
1219	Kēdārēśvara	Halebīd	Bl 115
1224	Harihárēśvara	Harihar	Dg 25
1234	Sōmēśvara	Hāranhalli	Ak 123
1235	Mallikārjuna	Basarālu	Md 121
1268	Kēśava	Sōmanāthpur	Dg 36, TN 97

Of course no single date can be given for the Hoysalēśvara, which was more like a national monument,—under construction for a long period, and never completed. It is a double temple, and Fergusson says was left unfinished, being interrupted by the Muhammadan conquest, after the works had been in progress for eighty-six years; but no authority is given for this statement. Of the positive dates obtained from inscriptions, the carving over the southern doorway is stated (Bl 239) to have been executed for the sculptor of Pratāpa-Nārasimha or

Temple at Sōmanāthpur

Nārasimha I. This indicates that the fabric of the building was then complete, say in 1141 or somewhat later. Of the votive offerings inscribed on the inner walls, the earliest appears to be Bl 105, in which the double temple, dedicated to Hoysalēśvara and Panchikēśvara, is fully recognised, and grants are made for the two gods by the *sēnabhōva* of the senior queen Kētala-Dēvī. Now, she was the queen of Ballāla II, and is mentioned in 1177 (Hn 54). The temple was thus begun after the one at Bēlūr, and the body of the building completed in the time of Nārasimha I. The sculpture of the exterior walls was no doubt carried on during the subsequent reign of Ballāla II, when decorative features were also added to the Bēlūr temple (Bl 72). There is a story, indeed, that the pierced medallions, like those at Bēlūr, which have evidently been removed from their brackets on the outer pillars, were taken away at the end of the eighteenth century by Count de Lally, the French ally of Haidar Ali, (or perhaps by the younger Lally), and that he sent a sum of money from France as compensation to the temple. The stoppage of work on the building was probably due to the Sēuna invasions in the reigns of Nārasimha II and Sōmēśvara, followed by the removal of the royal residence by the latter in about 1236 to Kannanūr, near Trichinopoly. But the beautiful and completed Sōmanāthpur temple was built after this, in the reign of Nārasimha III. It is a triple temple, and has often furnished a model for silver or gold caskets.

VI. LITERATURE

OF the notices of authors in the inscriptions, some are of the first importance, especially for the history of Karṇāṭa or Kannaḍa literature. The earliest relate to Ganga kings, among whom Mādhava II is invariably mentioned as having written a treatise on the *dattaka-sūtra* or law of adoption (see Mr 73, DB 68, etc.). This work may be assigned to the third century. In what language it was composed does not appear, but probably in Kannaḍa. Then Durvvinīta, another Ganga king, who began to reign at the end of the fifth century, is said (Tm 23) to have had as his preceptor the divine who was the author of the *Śabdāvatāra*, that is, the celebrated Jaina grammarian Pūjyapāda; and he is also said (Mi 110) to have walked according to the example of his guru. Moreover, Durvvinīta, in most of the Ganga inscriptions (see Gd 47, etc.), is said to have written a commentary on fifteen *sargas* of the *Kirātārjunīya*, which is a Sanskrit poem by Bhāravi. This commentary was no doubt in Kannaḍa, as we know that the Jains were the first cultivators of that language for literary purposes, and Nṛipatunga, in his *Kavirājamārgga*, names Durvvinīta as one of the early distinguished Kannaḍa authors.

In the works of the principal old Kannaḍa poets, Samantabhadra, Kaviparimēshṭhi, and Pūjyapāda, invariably in this order, are named at the beginning as the earliest and most illustrious trio among the authors who preceded them. From Jaina traditions it appears that Samantabhadra may be placed in the second century. Regarding him SB 54 supplies the following list of countries and places to which he travelled, and where he beat the drum,[1] as a challenge to any opponent who would meet him in public disputation. They were Pāṭaliputra (Patna, on the Ganges, the capital of the Mauryas or Guptas), Mālava, Sindhu, the Ṭhakka country (in the Punjāb), Kānchīpura (Conjeeveram, near Madras), Vaidiśa (Bhilsa, in Central India), Karahāṭaka (Kolhāpur, in the South Mahratta country or Karnāṭaka Prānth). Nr 46 refers to the Bhāshya composed by the great brati, in allusion to Samantabhadra's *Gandahasti-mahābhāshya*, a commentary on Umāsvāti's *Tattvārttha*.

Of Pūjyapāda, SB 40 says that his name was Dēvanandi; that on account of his great learning he was called Jinēndrabuddhi; and that from his two feet being worshipped by the deities he was known as Pūjyapāda. It adds that he was the author of the incomparable grammar—the *Jainēndra*; of the *Sarvvārtthasiddhi*, and of the *Samādhi-śataka*, and describes him as a critic in prosody. Nr 46 also mentions as works composed by him,—*Nyāyakumuda-chandrōdaya*, a Nyāsa on Śākaṭāyana's sūtras, the Nyāsa known as *Jainēndra*, the Nyāsa called *Śabdāvatāra* on the sūtras of Pāṇini, Vaidya-śāstra, and a *ṭīka* to the *Tattvārttha*. In Sk 124 Rāmasēna is said to be in grammar Pūjyapāda, in logic Akalanka, and in poetry Samantabhadra. In SB 47 Mēghachandra is said to be in logic Akalanka, and in all grammar Pūjyapāda. In SB 55 Jinachandra is said to be Pūjyapāda in the *Jainēndra*, in all logic Bhaṭṭākalanka, and in poetry Bhāravi. SB 105, again, compares Śrutamuni with Pūjyapāda in grammar, Dēva (Akalanka) in rhetoric and logic, Gautama and Koṇḍakunda in the two siddhānta, and Varddhamāna in spiritual philosophy.

To revert to SB 54. It mentions Vakragrīva as the author of *Navaśabdavāchya*; Vajranandi of *Navastōtra*; Sumati of *Sumati-śatakam*; Chintāmaṇi of the *Chintāmaṇi*; Śrīvarddhadēva of the *Chūḍāmaṇi*; and Śrīpāla as having expounded the *tattva*. But the most valuable of its statements is in connection with Śrīvarddha, for in relation to him a couplet is

[1] Fixed in a public part of the city for the purpose.

quoted in which Daṇḍi highly praised him as a poet. And as Daṇḍi belongs to the sixth century, this supplies us with a definite period for Śrīvarddha, the author of the *Chūḍāmaṇi*. Now, this work is mentioned in Bhaṭṭākalanka's great grammar, the *Karṇāṭaka-Śabdānuśāsanam*, as if the finest work in the Kannaḍa language, and it is described as a commentary on the *Tattvārttha-mahāśāstra*, containing 96,000 verses. It is also mentioned in TN 105, where it is called a poem, and the author is said to have been named Chūḍāmaṇi from his work, in which he had displayed all the ornaments of composition. In the *Rājāvali-kathe* he is styled the Tumbalūr-āchārya, and this place may be the Tombalūr, now commonly known as Dommalūr or Domlūr, immediately to the east of Bangalore; or, more likely, the Tumbala of TN 106-9.

It is evident that a work of such extent could neither have been produced nor required had there not already existed a considerable literature in Kannaḍa, together with a widespread cultivation of the language. And a eulogy by Daṇḍi indicates that Śrīvarddha flourished in or before the sixth century. But, both in SB 54 and TN 105, the mention of the *Chūḍāmaṇi* is preceded by that of the *Chintāmaṇi*, the author of which has the same name as his work. It is described as a lucid exposition of merit, wealth, love,[1] and salvation. That this was a Kannaḍa work is evidently implied, and one older than the *Chūḍāmaṇi*. But of neither, unfortunately, has any trace so far been found. On the other hand, there is a *Chintāmaṇi* in Tamil, which Dr. Caldwell describes as a Jain work by an unknown author, containing 15,000 lines, and little known on account of its difficult style. He adds, however, that it is without doubt the greatest epic poem in the Tamil language, and may be the oldest Tamil composition of any extent now extant.

Later Ganga kings are also credited with authorship. Thus,—Śrīpurusha, who reigned in the eighth century, is said (Nr 35) to have written a *Gaja-śāstra*, or work on elephants.

[1] *Dharmm-ārttha-kāma*, the three chief objects of human desire.

Specimen page of palm-leaf manuscript

His son Śivamāra-Saigotta, who had already mastered the difficult *Phanisuta-mata*, the yōga of Patanjali (Nl 60), next made a profound study of the system of elephant management as expounded by the great yati born from the mouth of the female elephant, that is, in the *Pālakāpyam* of Pālakāpya or Karēnubhu,—to which there is a commentary in Kannaḍa,—and then wrote the *Gajāshṭaka*, which, it is said (Nr 35), was so conspicuous for poetical genius that, if it could be imparted to a deaf mute, it would force him to speak. Būtugēndra, the younger brother of Rājamalla II, is also said (Nj 269) to have been like the son of Karēnu in knowledge of the great science of elephants.

Additional information regarding Jaina authors is contained in the following inscriptions.—SB 40, 42, and 43 mention Umāsvāti, also known as Gridhrapinchhāchārya, who had no equal in his time in discerning the *padārttha* or categories in logic. They also state that Guṇanandi was skilled in logic and grammar, and lord of the learning of poetry. SB 40 says that Śrutakīrtti wrote with great skill the *Rāghava-Pāṇḍavīya*, reading forwards or backwards. Bl 17 informs us that Śrīpāla, with a second name Vādībhasimha, wrote commentaries without number in prose, verse, and precept. Ak 141 and Kd 69 likewise refer to him. Nr 35 says that Anantavīryya wrote a *Vritti* to the *Akalanka-sūtras*, and Dayāpāla a *Prakriya* to the *Śabdānuśāsana*. Of Lōkāchārya, Ak 55 says that in the science of language he was a Kaumāra incarnate, being conversant with the branches that follow (or are studied) after grammar; and that in astrology he was well versed in the *Śrīkaraṇa*, *Laghumānasa*, and *Karaṇāratna*. In SB 42 we are told of Sampūrnnachandra that he was proficient in solar and lunar astronomy, and of Śrīdhara that he was skilled in mantras and medicine. TN 105 says that Indranandi was the author of *Pratishṭhā-kalpa* and *Jvālinī-kalpa*.

Brāhmans come into view in Sk 92 and 96 in describing the attainments of Vāmaśakti, the learned head of the Kōḍiya maṭha at Balligrāme. In grammar (they say) he was Pāṇini, in drama and music Bharata, in poetry Subandhu or Māgha, in siddhānta Lakulīśvara or Nakulīśvara.

Going back to Jain authors.—SB 105 states that Samantabhadra's disciple Śivakōṭi-sūri illustrated the *Tattvārttha-sūtra*, and that Śrutamuni composed new poems, and excelled in all advanced learning, especially in grammar. Nr 46 says that Vidyānanda's sayings were ever cherished in the mind like the great Bhāshya (of Samantabhadra), and his irreproachable reasoning was ever pleasing to the minds of poets, appearing like Bāna's prose-expressed poem (the *Kādambarī*). It farther says that Umāsvāti was author of the *Tattvārttha-sūtra*; Akalanka of a *Bhāshya* to Samantabhadra's *Dēvāgama-stōtra*; Vidyānanda illustrated the *Āpta-mīmāmsa*, and composed the *Ślōkavārttikālankāra*; Prabhāchandra wrote the *Mārttaṇḍa*; Nēmichandra was the author of *Trilōkasāra* and other works; and Vidyānanda made many commentaries, including the *Budhēśabhavana-vyākhyāna*.

Kālidāsa is praised in the *yamaka* verse Mk 39. Mb 42 mentions the Pōdiyam (mountain) where the three forms of Tamil (prose, poetry, and the drama) flourished. Ck 40 extols the attainments of a pandit named Mallikārjjuna, and describes him as highly versed in the five *pratishṭes*, namely, the *Māya*, *Bhūpāla*, *Yōga-pārāyana*, *Pratishṭe*, and *Pratishṭārṇṇava*, as well as in logic, grammar, and the *Vṛitti*, *Paji*, *Byōma-ṭīku*, and *Durgga-ṭīku* śāstras. Vaijaṇṇa appears as a poet in Bl 238. TN 23 refers to Patanjali's *Padastōma*, and to Rāmānuja as the author of the Bhāshya (the *Viśishṭādvaita-vēdānta-bhāshya*). In Dg 25 we are informed that the Hoysala general Pōlālva composed a *Hari-charite* in *shaṭpadi* verses. Sōma is said in Mb 158 and Gd 46 to have been a successful poet in eight languages, and to have acquired much wealth by his profession. Unfortunately we are not told what languages they were. In Sb 375 is an account of the Vijayanagar prince Mārapa, who, with his minister Mādhava, having collated the three vēdas and examined the text of the purāṇas, compiled the *Śaivāgama-stōtra*. The Vijayanagar king Harihara II is expressly stated in Kp 34 to have been a cultivator of Karṇāṭaka learning. Ādityāryya is said in Pg 69 to have been the author of *Bhāshya-bhūsha*. Sr 94 contains an account of the recitation of the Mahābhārata before the Mysore king by Alasingar-aiyangār.

Other notices of authorship may be drawn from the distinguished composers of various inscriptions. Thus, the fine and learned Kadamba record in Sk 176 was composed by the poet Kubja. The Chalukya inscriptions Sb 571 and Dg 66 were composed by the great minister for peace and war, Rāma-punyavallabha, and Kl 63 by the like minister, Anivārita-Dhananjaya-punyavallabha. The elaborate eulogy of Gomaṭa in SB 85 was composed by Sujanōttamsam, the poet Boppana, who has the distinctive title *Kannaḍa-kavi-bappa*. Ak 48 was composed by the ornate poet Śāntinātha, grandson of the southern Sōma, and known as *kavi-kula-tilakam*. Ak 118 was composed by Umēśadatta and corrected by the great poet Trivikrama. Ak 123 was composed by Sōmanātha, known as *su-kavi-kaṇṭhābharaṇa*. Sh 69 was written by the kavīśvara Brammadēva. The composer of Sk 281 was the learned Phanīśitu, son of Viśvanāthāryya.

There are several of the eloquent and elaborate Vijayanagar inscriptions composed by the court poet Sabhāpati (Sh 1, Hn 6, Gu 30, Pg 4, Cn 167, Pg 75, Hk 132, Md 55) and his descendants. Tm 1 is by his son Kaviśāsana Svayambhu; Ck 39 and Sh 83 by his grandson Krishnakavi Kāmakōṭi; and Mb 60 by his great-grandson Rāma, the son of Kāmakōṭi. Another accomplished author was the minister Tirumalārya, son of Alasingārya, who composed TN 23 and Ch 92. Then Sr 64 was composed by the poet Tirumaleyācharya, skilled in Karṇṇāṭa, Āndhra, and Sanskrit poetry, and in singing; constant reader of the *Rāmāyaṇa* and *Bhārata*.

The latest notice of authorship is in Ch 154, where Dēvachandra is said to have caused the genealogy of the fathers to be written. This probably refers to the compendium of Jaina traditions called the *Rājāvalī-kathe*, compiled for one of the Mysore queens.

VII. RELIGION

THE early inhabitants of the country were probably to a great extent, especially on the female side, Nāgas or serpent worshippers, that is, of the cobra, which is the Nāga. Effigies of the cobra are set up to this day at the entrance of every village or town for public adoration, and ceremonial offerings are made to the living cobra. In the Śātavāhana inscription at Banavāsi, of the first or second century, the king's daughter is named Nāgaśrī, and she makes the gift of a Nāga. The province corresponding with the Shikārpur tāluq, said (Sb 263) to have been ruled by the wise Chandra Gupta, was named Nāgakhaṇḍa or Nāgarakhaṇḍa. Some of the minor royal lines in the west claim Nāga descent. Thus, the Sēndrakas were of the Bhujagēndra-anvaya or lineage of the snake king (*IA.* vii. 106), and the Sindas were of the Phaṇirāja-vamśa (Hl 50, 20), which has the same meaning, while the Sēnavāras had the *phaṇi-dhvaja* or serpent flag (Cm 95). Jinadatta, the founder of the Śāntara line, is said to have married a Nāga virgin. The Chōla prince Rājādhirāja is said to have bravely gone down into a cavern, and by his radiant beauty won the hand of the noble daughter of the Nāga race. The professed Janamējaya grants (Sk 45, etc.), which really belong to the twelfth century, are records of donations made to Brāhmans for performing the *sarpa-yāga* or serpent sacrifice, perhaps indicative of a wholesale subjection or extinction of serpent worshippers or Nāgas. Of the Vijayanagar king Harihara II, it is said (Si 95) that his virtues were sung in pleasant stories by the Nāga maidens in Pātāla. Hottenna-

Nāga and Nāgini, from stone at Belgāmi

Nāyaka of Harati is described (Cl 54) as brother to the Nāga virgins of the Nāga-lōka.

Jainism prevailed in Mysore from before the third century B.C., when Bhadrabāhu, accompanied by Chandra Gupta, led a migration of Jains from the North to the South (SB 1), and it continued a popular faith during more than a thousand years of the Christian era. Aśōka, the grandson of Chandra Gupta, strove towards the close of his reign to propagate Buddhism (Mk 21), and in the fourth century A.D. a Bāna king is compared with Bōdhisattva in compassion for all living things in the world (Mb 157). Even so late as 1055 a Buddhist *vihāra* was erected in Belgāmi (Sk 170), and the Bauddha *sāvāsi* is mentioned in 1098 (Sk 106), while a great Bauddha town named Kalavati is mentioned even in 1533 (Tp 1). But Buddhists it would seem were never numerous. The spread of Jainism was greatly promoted in the second century A.D. by Samantabhadra (SB 54), and later by Akalanka, who defeated the Buddhists in public disputation at Kānchī in the eighth or ninth century (SB 54), in consequence of which they were banished to Ceylon. Jainism was the State creed in the time of the Gangas, of some of the Rāshṭrakūṭas and Kalachuryas, and of the early Hoysalas. Also of the minor states of Punnāṭa, of the Śāntaras, the early Changālvas and the Kongālvas, as testified by their inscriptions. But the Chōla conquests in 1004, the conversion of the Hoysala king in 1117, and the assassination of the Kalachurya king in 1167 were severe blows to its influence. In an endeavour to accommodate itself to the age, Jina is described in 1151 as the Universal Spirit who is Śiva, Dhātṛi (Brahmā), Sugata (Buddha), and Vishnu (Tm 9); and for a generation following we find (Ck 21, 13) chieftains who were supporters of all the four creeds,—Māhēśvara, Jaina, Vaishnava, and Bauddha.

Lists of the Jain hierarchy and the succession of Jain gurus are contained in the following inscriptions, arranged according to date: SB 1, Nr 35, Sh 64, SB 47, 43, 54, Dg 90, SB 40, 42, 105, Ng 76, Cn 149, Ak 1, TN 105,

SB 108, Nr 46. The first is of the (?) fifth century; the remainder are of the eleventh and twelfth centuries, except the last two, which are of the fifteenth and sixteenth centuries. The greatest detail for the early period is supplied in SB 105, which gives the names of the Tīrthankaras, the Ganadharas, the Kēvalis, the Śrutakēvalis, the Daśapūrvadharas, the Ēkādaśāngadharas, and Āchārāngas. It then continues, through Kuṇḍakunda, Umāsvāti or Griddhrapinchha, Balākapinchha, Samantabhadra, Śivakōṭi, Dēvanandi or Pūjyapāda, Akalanka, etc., to Arhadbali, who formed four divisions of the Sangha,—the Sēna, Nandi, (Tridivēśa or) Dēva, and Simha sanghas. The others contain some of this information, but not in a connected manner, and each one branches off at a certain point to give a succession relating to the immediate object of the inscription. There is none which is more interesting or which conveys more valuable information than SB 54, interspersed as it is with *chūrṇis* or quotations of the first importance in corroboration of the narrative. Its date is 1128, and its object is to record the death of Mallishēna-Maladhāri, who was a disciple of Ajitasēna, and who gained a great name in his day among the Jains. Nr 46 also contains much historical information relating to the sixteenth century in recounting the successes of the Jain orator Vādi-Vidyānanda.

According to Sk 186 there were no Brāhmans in the South in the time of Mukkaṇṇa Kadamba, the third century. Having sought diligently for them throughout the region and finding none, he went without delay to the North, and from the Ahichchatra agrahāra (said to be in the Bareilly District) procured a number of Brāhman families (see also Nj 269) whom he settled in the agrahāra of Sthānakundūr (Tālgunda), to the north of Belgāmi (Shikārpur tāluq). From his family sprang the royal Kadamba line, as related in the Tālgunda pillar inscription (Sk 176). On the other hand, it seems that there must have been *some* Brāhmans before, for the Śātavāhana grant of the first or second century on the Malavalli pillar (Sk 263) was made as a Brāhman endowment. But they may have left the country, as those above-mentioned from the north are said to have attempted to do. In the east, tradition attributes the introduction of Brāhmans to Mukunti Pallava, who is also of the third century. It is evident from the Tālgunda pillar inscription that Brāhman professors had gained a great reputation in Kānchī, the Pallava capital, when Mayūraśarmma, the founder of the Kadamba dynasty, went there at about that period in order to complete his studies.

The earliest form of the Brāhman faith was connected with the worship of Śiva, who was, it is asserted, doorkeeper to the Mahāvalis or Bāṇas (Sp 5, 6). But Vishnu, in his Vāmana or Dwarf incarnation, deprived Mahā Bali in two strides of all his possessions except Pātāla, which was left to him. And Krishna, who is another form of Vishnu, also found means, in a war against Bāṇa, to overcome Śiva who fought for the Bāṇas. It is difficult to separate the worship of Śiva and Vishnu in subsequent periods. They continued to be jointly recognised in all parts, and the united form Harihara, composed of Hari (Vishnu) and Hara (Siva), was a symbol of their general equality in religious estimation. Of Harihara, Dg 25 in 1224 says: "The celebrated Śiva acquired the form of Vishnu, and Vishnu acquired the great and famous form of Śiva, in order that the saying of the Vēda (that they were one: see Dg 36) might be fully established." Kēśava or Vishnu, again, is identified as follows in the fourteenth century (Bl 3) with the chief object of worship in all the sects: "He whom the Śaivas worship as Śiva, the Vēdāntins as Brahmā, the Bauddhas as Buddha, the Naiyāyikas as Kartta, the Jainas as Arha, the Mīmāmsakas as Karmma."

The worship of Śiva was from an early period specially associated with an ancient teacher named Lakulīśa, who apparently can be traced back as far as the first century (*JRAS*, 1907, p. 419). His name frequently recurs in our inscriptions (see Si 28, Sk 126, 107, 104, 108), and his creed and sect are referred to as the Lākulāgama (Ak 62), Lākulāmnāya, Lākula-samaya (Sk 107), etc. But there must have been a succession of gurus of the name. For Si 28 in 943 says that Lakulīśa, fearing lest his name and works of merit should be forgotten, became incarnate in the muninātha Chilluka. And Sk 126 records a grant made in 1036 to a Lakulīśvara; perhaps he was the same as the one mentioned in a grant of 1020 in Mēlpāḍi in North Arcot (*SII.* iii. 27). Sk 107, of about 1078, describes a Vāḷmīki-muni as being (?) a hand to Lakula. Sk 94 in 1094 praises Śrīkanṭha-paṇḍita as himself Lakulēśa, while Sk 98 in 1103 says that his son Sōmēśvara-paṇḍita caused the Lākula-siddhānta to blossom; and Sk 92 and 96, of 1168 and 1179, compare the *rājaguru* Vāmaśakti with Lakulīśvara or Nakulīśvara. But farther, Tp 12 of 1285 speaks of Lakula's new *samaya.* As hitherto generally known, Lakulīśvara was the founder, in about the eleventh century, of the Pāśupata sect, and this was at Kārōhana in the Lāṭa country, which Dr. Bühler identified with Kārvān in Barōda. The Lakula of our inscriptions belongs to the period between 1054 and 1156, and is generally mentioned in connection with the Kālāmukha sect, who are described as a branch of the Śakti-parshe in the Mūvara-kōneya-santati of the Parvvatāvali (Jl 10, Sk 107, 114, 316, Bl 117, Sk 104, 108). There is a list in Ck 35 of a succession of gurus of the Agastyēśvara maṭha at Śrīparvvata, all whose names end in *śakti.*

The Śaiva reformer Śankarāchārya opposed the Jains and revived Śiva worship in the eighth century, when also he founded the Śringēri maṭha in the Kadūr District (Sg 11). But in the middle of the twelfth century took place the Vīra Śaiva revival, a revolt against Brāhmanism, promoted by Basava, the minister of the Kalachurya king Bijjala, which resulted in the establishment of the Jangama, Śivāchāra, or Lingāyit faith, the popular religion to this day of the Kannaḍa-speaking peoples. Into this great numbers of Jains were merged, while Jain images and temples were converted to Linga use. Ck 21 mentions the Shōdaśar or Sixteen, a special class of Lingavantas. The Keladi kings, the Changālvas, the

Bhairarasu-Woḍeyars, the Coorg Rājas, and other smaller states, professed the Lingāyit creed, which was also adopted by the Mysore Rājas in conjunction with the Vaishnava faith of their origin.

The revival of Vishnu worship was due in great measure to the Vaishnava reformer Rāmānujāchārya, also called Emberumānār,[1] who, at the beginning of the twelfth century, took refuge from Chōla persecution in the Mysore country, where he converted from Jainism the Hoysala king Biṭṭi-Dēva, thenceforward called by the name Vishnuvarddhana. Rāmānuja established the Yatirāja maṭha at Mēlukōte (see Sr 64), and received a large tract of land on both banks of the Kāvērī near Seringapatam, named the Ashṭagrāma or eight townships. For the management of his affairs he appointed the Fifty-two. These were Śrīvaishnavas, and his first disciples.

Bitter animosity continued to exist against the Jains, and in 1368 (as already related above, p. 113) they complained in a body to the Vijayanagar king Bukka-Rāya of the persecutions to which they were subjected by the Vaishnavas. The king summoned before him the leading men of both sects, and after inquiring into the matters in dispute, decided that no difference could be allowed as regards their liberty to follow their respective ceremonials. He then took the hand of the Jains, and holding it in the hand of the Vaishnavas, decreed that the Jains were free to carry out their customary ritual, and that equal protection would be given to both sects (SB 136). This decree was to be set up at all Jain bastiṣ by the Vaishnavas, who were not to look upon the Jains as in a single respect different. And, from a fund which the Jains would annually raise among themselves, the Vaishnavas were to appoint twenty men as a body-guard for the Jain image of Gomaṭa at Śravaṇa-Beḷgoḷa, and were to repair such Jain temples as had been ruined. This was actually done at Kallēha (Kalya in Māgadi tāluq), as witness the copy of the decree set up there (Ma 18).

The Śringēri maṭha had assisted in the foundation of the

[1] His original name is said to have been Iḷaiyāḻvān.

Vijayanagar empire in the fourteenth century, and furnished the first minister to the kings, who in consequence liberally endowed it (Sg 1). From the Vīra-Śaivas, who had largely superseded the Jains in the west, the latter were exposed to violent opposition. For instance, Bl 128 states, in 1638, that an over-zealous Lingāyit official had stamped a linga on the pillars of the principal Jain basti at Halebīd. The Jain merchants remonstrated on this with the Śivāchāra high priests, and an agreement was come to that the Jain priests of the basti should first offer the usual Śaiva salutation of ashes and betel leaf, and then perform their worship and other ceremonies according to their own custom. This decree was engraved on stone by order of the minister of the Bēlūr kingdom. On the fall of Vijayanagar in 1565, the Śringēri maṭha fell for a time to ruin, but in the next century was restored, and its endowments were renewed by the Keladi kings (Sg 5, 11, 13), who also established and endowed Śivāchāra maṭhas all over the Shimoga District.

The Rājas of Mysore likewise established agrahāras for Brāhmans (see Kg 37, Yd 54, Sr 64, Yd 58), and erected or added to temples (see Bn 118, Ch 86, Nj 1). Of Doḍḍa-Dēva-Rāja it is said (Kg 37) that temples of the gods he had made, was making, and would continue to make. The Varāha (or Boar) which was lost in the Yavana invasion, Chikka-Dēva-Rāja brought from Śrīmushna (in South Arcot) and set up with devotion in Śrīrangapattana or Seringapatam (Ch 92). It is now in Mysore, having been removed there at the beginning of the nineteenth century.

Of Muhammadan records, Sk 324 is one of the principal. This informs us that in 1632 the Bijāpur Sultān, Muhammad Ādil Shāh, son of Ibrāhim Ādil Shāh, erected the fort on the hill at the Māsūr Maḍag tank as a sign of victory in the attempt to repel the wicked infidels and to establish the auspicious Islām. Si 66b is a memorial to Malik Rihān, Subahdar of Sīra, dated 1651. DB 31 contains an interesting inscription of the time of the Mughal emperor Aurangzeb

Ālamgīr, dated in 1691. Si 66a records the erection of the big mosque at Sīra in 1696. Ht 19 is a Mughal grant in the time of Dilāvar Khān, Navāb of Sīra, dated 1745.

There are some grants by Haidar Ali to Musalmān fakīrs in 1763 and 1767 (Cp 146, 16, 114). Of Tipu Sultan's inscriptions, one of the most characteristic is Sr 159 at the Elephant gate of the Seringapatam fort, the date of it being 1791. Those at the Gumbaz in Ganjam, the mausoleum of Haidar and Tipu, are of interest (Sr 23, 24, etc.). My 54 relates to the construction of a dam in the Kāvērī in 1797.

Of Christian records, an old inscription has been found at Ānekal, surmounted by a cross, and referring to the *Kumbara ane* or Potters' dam. Its date is uncertain. But Dominican friars are said to have built a church there in 1400. A stone or stones are also said to have existed at Kānkānhalli recording a grant to the "sannyāsis of Rome." Nr 46, of about 1530, in relating the successes of the Jain disputant Vidyānanda at various royal courts, says that he destroyed (*alidu*) the European faith (*Peringiya mata*) of the Viceroy (or Agent—*Käryya*) of Śrīranganagara or Seringapatam, who must, it would thus seem, have been a Roman Catholic Christian.

Of special religious ceremonies, one of the earliest mentioned is the *aśvamēdha* or horse-sacrifice, which was a royal rite symbolic of supreme power. The Kadamba kings claim to have performed many horse-sacrifices. Accordingly, the Brāhmans of Tānagundūr are said (Sk 178) to be residents of 144 villages acquired as donations for the 18 horse-sacrifices of king Mayūravarmma. The king Krishnavarmma (? fifth century) is expressly stated (Bl 121) to have performed the horse-sacrifice. The Chalukya king Pulikēśi I performed the horse-sacrifice in the sixth century (Kl 63, Gd 48, etc.). A much later instance is that of the Chōla king Rājādhirāja or Jayangonda-Chōla in the eleventh century, who is also said (Dv 75) to have performed the horse-sacrifice. Other sacrifices mentioned are the *vājapēya* (Cn 167), performed

P

in the sixteenth century for the Vijayanagar kings Nṛisimha and Krishna-Rāya; and the *agnishṭōma* (Mb 62) performed in the seventeenth century for the chief of Sugaṭūr. The Mysore king Kaṇṭhīrava-Narasa-Rāja is said (Ag 64) to have revived the performance of the *ēkādaśi-vrata*, like Ambarīsha and all the other kings. The Brāhmans of Sthānakundūr are described (Sk 176) as drinking *sōma* juice, and those of Kellangere are called (Ak 117) 200 ornaments of *sōma* drinkers.

An interesting term is that of *ghaṭika-sthāna*, which seems to indicate a place of public assembly for Brāhmans. It has been translated by Professor Pāthak as "religious centre"; and Professor Kielhorn has written an article suggesting that it was something like a Brahmapuri. The name occurs in Sk 176, where Mayūraśarmma, on going to the Pallava capital for completing his studies, is said to have frequented every *ghaṭika*. In Si 23 of 1167 the Noṇambēśvara temple is said to be the great *ghaṭika-sthāṇa* of the city of Henjeṛu. On the other hand, Sk 197 of 1182 describes *ghaṭika-sthānas* as supports to *dharmma* and mines for enjoyment (*bhōga*). Cn 178 of 1442 contains the statement that a *ghaṭika* was established in a certain place "in accordance with the saying (or directions) of Uttanka in the Sāma-vēda."

There are a few references to rarer religious sects. Thus, Hs 18 records a grant in about 450, by the Kadamba king Mrigēśavarmma, as made to an Ātharvaṇi Brāhman. The grant in Sk 281 was made to Kāśmīr Brāhmans. Then Gb 61 of 812 mentions the Yāpaniyas, a Jain unorthodox sect, who had the appearance of Digambaras, but followed the observances of the Śvētāmbaras (*EI.* iv. 338). And Hl 23 of 968 describes one of the places where the grant was made as a Lōkāyata city. The Lōkāyatas were an atheistical sect, followers of the doctrines of Chārvāka. Certain tenets and sectarian terms of the Lingāyits are set forth in Kg 49, in connection with the erection of a *maṭha* for the Tōṇṭada-svāmi. The essentials are detailed which constitute a primeval *bhakta*, and a primeval *jangama*.

Attention may be drawn to some notable donations. Bl 121, of about 420, describes a merchant as the donor of a thousand cows. Kg 33, of 1663, mentions a Brāhman who was known as the donor of a crore of virgins. Nl 88 records a grant for feeding 12,000 *oḍeyars* or Lingāyit priests in the Gangādhara temple at Śivaganga on a certain anniversary day. A singular statement is that in Sb 18, which speaks of the Vijayanagar king Dēva-Rāya II as having become after his death a *mahārājika* or demigod, reminding one of the apotheosis of the Roman emperors.

INDEX

THE END

Printed by R. & R. CLARK, LIMITED, *Edinburgh*